BURNED
IN
STONE

A sequel to
"THE LOST PHOTOGRAPHS"

BURNED
IN
STONE

RICHARD IRA CARROLL

Sojourn Publishing, LLC

Burned In Stone

Copyright © 2017 by Richard Ira Carroll. All rights reserved.

No part of this publication may be reproduced, stored in a retrieval system or transmitted in any way by any means, electronic, mechanical, photocopy, recording or otherwise without the prior permission of the author except as provided by USA copyright law.

This novel is a work of fiction. Names, descriptions, entities, and incidents included in the story are the products of the author's imagination. Any resemblance to actual persons, events, and entities is entirely coincidental.

The opinions expressed by the author are not necessarily those of Sojourn Publishing, LLC.

Front Cover Image: © 123rf
Published by: Sojourn Publishing, LLC
Printed in the United States of America

ISBN: 978-1-62747-070-4 Paperback
ISBN: 978-1-62747-074-2 Ebook

Website: RichardIraCarroll.com

PRAISE FOR "BURNED IN STONE"

A gripping well-paced story with strong historical research backing it up. The strong descriptions pull the reader into the scenes with sensory stimulation. The reader is kept engaged with the plot. Bounce per ounce, I enjoyed this book.
---Idony Lisele, Editor

I liked this novel very much for its slam-bang action and clever plot line. The author obviously did a lot of research on ancient antiquities and clearly knows what he is talking about.

The scenes in Israel, Thailand, the Mediterranean Sea, and Egypt's Sinai Peninsula are realistic and ring true.

There are some very tender scenes that contain heart-felt highly emotional writing with some nice tender touches of humor sprinkled here and there.
---Bill Worth, editor and author of "Outwitting Multiple Sclerosis:" How Forgiveness Helped Me Heal My Brain By Changing My Mind" and the novels "House of the Sun: A Metaphysical Novel of Maui" and "The Hidden Life of Jesus Christ: A Memoir."

This is a great action-packed novel that blurs the line between fiction and non-fiction by weaving traditional bible stories and historical facts into an adventurous plot that whisks the reader around the world. Matt Lane, the main character, is a rich and famous archaeologist looking for one of the most infamous and notorious biblical relics, the Ark of the Covenant. The plot moves quickly and is a nostalgic nod to the golden-age of classic mystery novels, which is refreshing. This novel gives the reader an interesting plot with well-developed main characters without the gore or gratuitous sex. As the character Lane gets closer to finding the Ark of the Covenant so does the danger, and

readers are taken on an exciting ride as Lane, his girlfriend Ann, his best friend Jim, and the mysterious girl Stephanie who gives Lane the map that beckons them all together on this spiritual mission. The meticulously researched facts about archaeology and the historical context of the ancient cities the characters visit gives this novel a tall-tale feeling where the reader can't distinguish between reality and fantasy. All in all, it is a wholesome, exciting and spiritual adventure that would spark anyone's interest who is a fan of the bible, historical theology, archaeology and traveling with a purpose.
---Tara Alatorre
2016 ANA Investigative Reporter of the year.

ACKNOWLEDGMENT

My wife, Yvonne, adds her magic touch to the stories I write. She makes each chapter more exciting and fun to read. Yvonne was an intricate piece in my quest to finish this novel. Together we pushed through the challenges of the publishing world to create another adventurous, romantic story for every reader to enjoy.

Thanks to my sister, Jackie Wolfe, and my friend, Dennis Stanley, for critiquing my rough draft of this book. I value their objective insight.

Special thanks to so many readers of my first novel, "The Lost Photographs", who encouraged me to write this sequel.

It was a special honor that my cousin, Tom Pettit, wanted to read my story and offered his suggestions before he left this world too soon. His positive outlook was inspirational.

PROLOGUE

Jerusalem
587 years Before Christ

In a panic, the old high priest struggled to climb the cold, uneven stone steps to the roof of the temple. His labored breath forced the sixty-eight year old man to pause, his shoulders drooping under the weight of his priestly robes. Continuing the steep climb, he reached the top. Exhausted but driven, he shoved the heavy door open and hurried to the parapet wall.

What he saw made him tremble in fear and anxiety. The hills west of the city were aglow with the light from a thousand camp fires. The smell of the heavy smoke drifting on the night air stung his nostrils.

The old man was taken aback. He turned his head away, not wanting to believe what he had just witnessed. Even though they had prepared for this day because of rumors of an imminent invasion, he never believed it would really happen.

Shouts of alarm and women crying brought his attention to the narrow cobblestone streets below. People were running in all directions in a panicked frenzy, fearing for their lives and the lives of their families.

He realized that soon every space in the temple would be filled to capacity with men, women, and children – families seeking refuge. Would the ruthless and barbaric Babylonian army respect this sanctuary? Or would blood soon run in the corridors and stain the walls of God's sacred temple?

Dropping his head in his hands, the old priest wept. Then, turning his face to the sky with rivulets of tears running down his checks, he cried out to God for help.

Finally regaining his composure, being careful not to fall, he made his way back down the precarious steps to the main floor of the temple. Those he had summoned earlier would be waiting for him.

David was just outside the high priest's office, a very worried look on his face. The priest had known this fine young man since he was just a little boy. He had watched him and his constant companions, Ben and Levi, grow from boys to husky young men. They were always together, either working or playing in the dusty streets of old Jerusalem. David was a few months older and the tallest of the three. He had strong muscular arms and thick black curly hair. Ben and Levi, who were twins, had lighter complexions and both had reddish-brown hair. They had always looked up to David – he was their leader.

It was cold and dim in the room just outside the office, the stone walls and floor adding to the gloom and chill. One torch on the wall behind the old man lightly illuminated the area with a flickering radiance.

"As you know, David, the Babylonian army has arrived," he said, his voice quivering. "There are thousands of men in their army to the west. Their scouts are already camped in the hills around the city. Tomorrow, or perhaps even yet tonight, the army will besiege Jerusalem. Our soldiers will never be able to hold them back.

"You know what you must do, David. You must hurry, and you must not fail! We believe there is only one gate where you can leave undetected. There are three carts this last time. They are fully loaded and waiting for you. Straw covers the gold they carry. Take it to Solomon's cavern and hide it with the rest of our treasure.

"You, Ben, Levi, and the family who guards the canyon are the only people alive who know where King Solomon's hidden cavern is located. You will lead four men, two in each of the other two carts. We took them from our prison – murderers who were sentenced to die – but you will need them to get the heavy treasure carried in and hidden quickly before anyone can see you at the cavern. Keep a close vigilance on these treacherous criminals. You three will have weapons. They will not. They have been told that if they cause no problems and obey your commands, they can keep the carts and the horses and be free men. They can never be free, David. When they leave the canyon, their lives will be taken."

David was shocked by the brutality of the men's sentence but understood there was no alternative. Once these men saw what the carts contained and knew where it was hidden, they could never be trusted. They would have to die.

"This has all been arranged. You don't have to worry about such matters. Be sure you are not followed out of the city. May the Lord protect you. You're like a son to me."

The old man was shaking as his gnarled hands hugged David. Then he said, "Now bring Ben and Levi to me please."

Turning, David quickly summoned his friends. Within minutes three wide-eyed young men knelt in front of the old priest as he outlined their assignment.

The old man blessed them. Then he whispered, "We have put our trust in you three. You have worked with us in Solomon's sacred temple since you were small boys. We know you would give up your lives before revealing the location of the great treasure of Israel. Go now, and God be with you."

It was midnight and the city was dark except for an occasional candle burning inside a dwelling as they started their perilous journey. The hooves of the six spirited horses were bound with a cushion of leather to prevent the clatter on the cobblestone streets as they slipped through the city. Not a word was spoken. David, Ben, and Levi were on the seat of the first cart while two identical carts followed close behind. Only the muffled clunk of wooden wheels resonated through the empty streets as the caravan eluded detection. Under the cover of darkness, they passed through the gate.

Levi excitedly pointed to the campfires of the Babylonian scouts on the hills just outside the city walls. The smell of the smoke was strong as it drifted across the road in front of them. David urged the nervous horses into a trot. Ben looked back to be sure the other two carts were keeping up. The young men sat rigid and motionless, clutching their weapons, each uttering a silent prayer. Never had they been faced with such peril. They could not fail in this mission!

At last all the campfires were in the distance far behind them.

At daybreak they were far south of the city. It appeared their escape was undetected. They moved off the sandy trail and removed the bindings from the horses' hooves.

By mid afternoon, they were on the plateau above the canyon lands. Finally they entered an Israeli encampment. The ruling members of this small village were trained soldiers and all members of the same family. They had lived here, father to son, since the days of King Solomon. Their sole purpose was surveillance of the area and preventing strangers from entering the canyon. David, Ben, and Levi were friends with the man in charge. They had been here many times before and had been given clearance by the holy man in Jerusalem. No one questioned the three loads of straw, but the soldiers were suspicious of the four unkempt men on the carts, making them nervous.

They stopped at the watering hole before reaching the lookout station at the entrance to the trail leading down into a very deep canyon. The air was stifling; beads of sweat covered their determined faces. The sun was scorching the rocks above the canyon, but small groves of trees along the canyon rim waved in the hot wind. David directed the men to water the horses and move them to the minute patches of grass before resting themselves.

On the plateau away from the edge of the canyon where the ancient family lived were fields of corn, wheat, flax and vegetables. Chickens darted about the dwellings scratching in the dirt, cackling over prized finds. Small herds of sheep and goats bleated as they grazed among the trees behind the small settlement.

The man in charge of the canyon patrol was named Eli. He liked the three young men on the first cart, and they looked up to him as though he were their older brother. A strong bond had formed between them, and Eli trusted them. He was thirty-six years old. He and all his brothers, sisters, and cousins were born in this settlement and had lived here all their lives. The men were trained soldiers. They had been trained by their fathers, older brothers, and uncles, and their fathers, older brothers and uncles before them as far back as the stories around the campfire at night could take them.

Eli and all the men on duty were dressed like soldiers in an army. Eli wore a leather tunic and helmet, both trimmed in bronze. Bracelets of bronze wrapped around each wrist and below his powerful biceps. He wore a thick leather belt with a bronze buckle. Leather straps extended from his sandals around his muscular calves to a leather band just below his knees. On his back was a quiver of arrows and a large bow.

Leaning his spear against the guard shack and pulling off his helmet, he walked quickly toward David, Ben, and Levi. "Shalom," he said as he enveloped all three in one big bear hug and led them to a small grove of cedar trees away from the four prisoners. He offered them cool water from a spring and bread and cheese to eat. In the center of the ancient trees were several stumps and large rocks where they sat in close proximity to each other. The smell of the cedar trees was comforting.

Eli's brothers on duty at the guard shack detained the other four men. The soldiers did not know these men who were on the other two carts, and they did not trust them. They did give them water and food, which was the tradition to welcome strangers.

In the groves of trees the birds were singing as though this was just another beautiful day. Not a cloud was in the clear blue sky. But it was not just another day. Today could be the last day on this earth for many, and the first day of years of cruel captivity for those who survived. The meeting was emotional for the four men as they spoke in low tones, telling Eli about the Babylonian army that was probably killing, raping, and pillaging Jerusalem as they spoke. Eli already knew about the invasion. The priest's messenger on a fast horse had been sent just before the carts had left Jerusalem. Eli now had a very unpleasant task to perform regarding the four men on the other two carts.

The young men shed tears for their families and for the old priest they dearly loved. They all declared their hatred for the Babylonians. David said they had watched the trail behind them and did not believe they had been followed, but with all the low hills between here and Jerusalem, he couldn't be sure. Eli told them that even if they were not followed, it would be only a matter of a few days before their settlement was discovered. He then thanked them for doing their duty for God and their country by hiding the last of the treasure. After a brief prayer and another emotional hug, they said their goodbyes. Eli told them to look back up to the lookout station from the canyon below. If they had been followed, his men would hold them off as long as they could and would signal them with the wave of a large flag.

With the horses now fed and watered, David started them moving. They passed the guard shack, but when they reached the starting point of the trail down into the canyon, the prisoners stopped their carts. They were afraid to go any farther. They refused to start down the steep treacherous trail. They were afraid the carts would slip over the edge, carrying them to their death on the rocks below. So Ben took the reins on one cart and Levi took the other one. It was a frightening ride, but they had done it many times before.

Finally, all three carts, seven men, and six powerful horses made it safely to the bottom. Sandstone walls towered above them as they continued a short distance single file down the canyon floor. Soon they stopped and the prisoners were instructed to unload the straw. They were astounded when they uncovered the chests of gold and other treasures each cart was carrying.

Then they moved to the opposite side of the canyon where David gave the order to stop. The pungent smell of sweat from the horses permeated the hot air. Ben and Levi immediately started digging a hole in the sand at the base of the rock cliffs, soon exposing the bottom of a massive flat stone leaning against the sandstone wall. It had a large round hole near the bottom that had been placed over a stone hub that protruded from the rock wall like the axle on one of the carts. This tall flat rock had been fashioned by stone masons long ago. The heavy piece of natural sandstone was like an upside down pendulum. When the sand was cleaned away from the base, the top of the stone could be moved right or left, parallel with the rock wall, as it pivoted on the hub. The four men who had never been here before were bewildered.

Levi pulled a wooden ladder from the cart and leaned it against the giant slab. The top of the irregular stone, about fifteen feet up from the canyon floor, ended with a jagged point. The backside had been ground away, allowing Levi to easily put the loop of the heavy braided-leather rope around the point.

Ben had unhitched the team from the cart and attached the end of the rope to their harness. He led the horses close and parallel to the wall, and the rope became taut. Straining, the horses started the stone moving. The sound of stone grinding on stone echoed across the canyon. As the top of the massive rock moved from left to right, a triangular shaped opening appeared at the bottom left corner. The triangle enlarged as the stone moved to its balance position at the top, revealing an entrance to a cavern.

Ben stopped the horses when the stone was at its top balance position. "Can we get the crates through the entrance?" he shouted to David.

"I can easily walk through," David answered as he ducked his head and entered the opening, "but no, these crates are too large. Open it all the way."

"Okay, but the horses are going to have a hard time pulling the stone back up to this position again when we close it. We could even break the rope."

"That's a chance we'll have to take. Hurry, Ben, pull it all the way open."

The stone was easy to move now. Just a few more inches at the top and the stone started its descent on its own, picking up speed as the top moved in an arc until it struck hard against the stop carved centuries before in the side of the mountain wall. The cavern entrance was now wide open.

At the entrance a plank was placed across the hole where the sand had been moved, and all the crates were moved inside the cavern. David watched the four men struggling with the heavy load while feasting their eyes on the treasure. These men were thugs, and they coveted the hidden treasure that would stagger the imagination of any man. David knew these men would plan to return and steal the treasure. That was unfortunate for them.

When all the carts were unloaded, they bid the prisoners farewell and watched them go, knowing the four men only had a few minutes to live. The archers from the encampment above were waiting for them where the canyon narrowed at the bottom.

Almost out of sight now, the carts were moving quickly away in the dark shadows of the rock-strewn canyon. The thundering of the horses' hooves running down the desert floor echoed up the cavernous canyon walls. The tops of the vertical walls across the canyon were still emblazoned with shades of gold, orange, and crimson. Soon even those colors would fade, and the whole canyon would be dark. The treasure was hidden safely, all except one chest.

"Pull the closure stone back up to the center," David said. "Levi, put the shovel near the stone so we can fill the hole with sand when the opening is closed. Are the tools ready to remove the footprints?"

"Yes, I've got them right here," Levi replied.

Ben, pulling his tunic up to his hips, clambered up on the wooden spokes of the tall cart wheel and jumped on the back of one of the horses. Levi was on the ladder reversing the heavy leather rope.

"We're ready, David," Levi shouted back to his friend. "Are you finished inside?"

"Almost," David replied, deep in thought as he turned his gaze away from the lookout station at the top of the canyon above them.

David picked up the last chest and carried it into the cavern. As he was putting it in place, he heard Ben yelling outside. He rushed back to the entrance.

"Look David! The lookout at the top of the pass . . . he's waving the warning flag!"

"The Babylonians must have seen us leave Jerusalem after all," Levi shouted. "They must have been following us!"

They stared in disbelief . . . Levi on the ladder . . . Ben trying to hold the excited horses. In the last rays of sunlight, the lookout was desperately waving the flag back and forth.

"They must be entering the encampment," David said. "The soldiers will try to hold them off, but they're probably greatly outnumbered. Soon they'll be coming down into this canyon. If they see us here or even see all these tracks, they'll search this spot until they find the treasure. We have to hurry!"

David raced through the entrance to the cavern one last time. "I'll bring the torch out. It's getting dark. We will need the torch to be sure we have erased all the tracks."

Deep in the cavern, David grabbed the torch from the slanted hole in the stone wall and headed back out. As he made his way through the labyrinth of wooden crates of gold and silver, he heard the grinding of the stone as Ben pulled it to the top balance position and then stopped. At the same time, he heard horses excitedly neighing and Ben and Levi yelling. Suddenly he heard the frightening sound of stone grinding on stone again. A shock of fear came over David as he realized the stone was closing. Like an angled guillotine, it started its scissor-action descent. David dropped the torch, leapt over two large crates, and ran as fast as he could down the long tunnel heading outside. Seeing the opening at the end of the tunnel closing, in one desperate move he plunged head first toward the opening at the lower right corner of the entrance. Sliding on the sand covered sandstone, he watched in horror as the stone rapidly closed off his escape. It was too late. David thrust out his hands to the moving stone, stopping his body just in time to prevent losing his arms. Instantly the area was dark except for the glow of the torch he had dropped back in the large cavern, the flames reflecting on the gold-laden chests and crates stacked around the room.

Under Ben's experienced handling, the horses had slowly pulled the heavy stone from its resting position to the top of the pivot point where Ben stopped and held them. They were waiting for David to finish inside. They had done this several times before, but this time something frightened the already excited horses. They lurched ahead, knocking Ben down and pulling the stone passed its pivot point. As gravity took over, there was no stopping it.

Ben and Levi stared in disbelief at the closure stone, it's craggy outside surface blending perfectly with the canyon wall. How could they have let this happen? A sick feeling came over both of them as they realized there was not enough time to move the horses, reopen the cavern, then close it again. They had to fill in the sand at the base of the closure stone to hide the pivot hub, hitch the horses to the cart, wipe out the hoof and foot prints in the sand, and flee down the canyon before the Babylonians saw them.

Richard Ira Carroll

David, staring at the sealed entrance, could barely hear his two best friends screaming as they filled in the sand at the base of the stone. "We're sorry, David. We'll come back. We promise. We'll come back."

But no one ever did.

CHAPTER ONE

The Rain Forest in Thailand

It was late afternoon and very hot. A myriad of sounds high in the rain forest canopy penetrated the calm of the jungle. Exotic birds squawked and soared across the open expanse. Monkeys swinging from branch to branch screeched a warning at her as if they knew she shouldn't be here, trying to persuade her to turn back. Large philodendron and bird of paradise leaves glistened in the thick moist air.

She was closer now. Standing on a log, she peeked through the leaves. She could see the murky watering hole, back water from the deep flowing river nearby. Wild animal tracks peppered the muddy perimeter. Finally she spied the elephants. She gasped at their enormous size and how close they were. Mud-caked "Lords of the Jungle" were cooling their huge bodies, some rolling in the mud, others lazily swinging their trunks back and forth.

The intruder was a scrawny little girl, scarcely seven years old. Her dark sun-tanned arms and legs poked out of her ill-fitting gingham romper. Beads of perspiration dampened fly-away strands from her chestnut pigtails forming a halo around her face. Her green eyes stared in wonder.

Fascinated, she continued creeping through the tall grass toward the shade of the trees. Now the only barrier between Stephanie and the herd was the trees around the watering hole. "Don't go near that herd of elephants," both her mother and father had repeatedly warned her. She knew she shouldn't be here, but curiosity prevailed. Crouching in the tree and bamboo area, she peeked through the dense foliage. Stephanie giggled with delight as she spotted the baby elephant. She was very close, maybe too close, but it was worth the risk.

The baby raised his trunk and turned to follow the human scent. Now he was looking right at her. Curious, he left his mother's side and sauntered around the water and up to Stephanie's hiding place at the edge of the trees. The elephant was so close Stephanie could see his long eye lashes as he blinked. She longed to reach out and touch him, but instead whispered, "Go back – go back to your mama."

Looking for her calf, the cow elephant spotted Stephanie. Her maternal instinct sensed danger, and trumpeting, she charged.

Terrified, Stephanie sprang from her knees and started to sprint back through the dense trees and bamboo. Glancing over her shoulder, she could see the huge elephant approaching the edge of the trees. Running even faster, she heard the terrifying trumpeting and the trashing of the dense foliage behind her. Frightened out of her wits, she was finally through the trees and into the tall grass. The grass and bushes tore at her arms and legs. She knew any second now the huge feet would stomp her into the ground!

Totally out of breath, Stephanie stumbled and fell. All was quiet. She no longer could hear any sounds behind her. Dare she look behind her again? Ever so slowly, she turned. The cow elephant had stopped at the edge of the grass. There she stood, taunting Stephanie, swinging her trunk back and forth. Pulling herself up from the dirt, the seven-year old dashed the rest of the way to the small bamboo hut.

She paused to catch her breath, hoping her mother hadn't been watching. Never would she do that again, and certainly she wouldn't tell her mother who would be extremely upset and would forbid her to leave the clearing around their hut again. But for now she was home, safe and sound.

She entered the hut, quickly walking past her mother in the kitchen and into her bedroom. With a sigh of relief, Stephanie vowed to be more careful.

In her room she used her pitcher of water to wash the blood from the scratches on her arms and legs and put on long pants and a long-sleeved blouse. She brushed the leaves and grass from her dark hair. Then acting like nothing had happened, she went to help her mother with supper.

Stephanie's mother, Amy, labored long hours to extract a home for the three of them from this unyielding jungle. Her husband had built the two-bedroom bamboo hut as a temporary dwelling, complete with an outhouse. There was no running water or electricity and only a bottled-gas refrigerator. Amy was petite, but strong, her hands rough and chapped. Her auburn hair with a few silver strands was pulled back from her face with tortoise-shell combs.

James, Stephanie's father, was tall and lanky, with well-defined muscles as a result of clearing the jungle for their farm. He dotted on his beautiful daughter –he was so proud of her. Often he would swing Stephanie up on his broad shoulders as he walked by the river.

Once when they were exploring by the rock cliff, he showed her a hidden cave where he kept a metal box with important papers. "Don't tell anyone about the cave," he admonished.

Stephanie was good at keeping secrets. She crossed her heart and swore she would never tell anyone about the cave or her daddy's special metal box.

After they finished eating, Stephanie climbed up on her father's lap as her mother cleared the table. She loved this time in the evening. The light from the coal oil lamp on the table lit her father's bearded face as he smoked his pipe and read a week's mail he had picked up in the local village earlier. She felt safe on his lap. Her mother smiled as she sliced the coconut cake James had purchased at the village market and poured two cups of coffee, and a glass of milk for Stephanie.

"Good news, Amy," her father exclaimed.

"What news is that?"

"The Thai family who has been interested in that parcel . . ."

"Yes?" Her mother's blue eyes danced with anticipation.

"They have agreed to my price. They have already put the down payment in escrow."

"Wonderful! Oh, we've waited so long for this," Amy said as she rushed over and gave her husband a big hug. "At last, we can afford to build a house in town and move out of this flimsy jungle hut. Five years is quite enough to live in these primitive conditions. It's not safe for Stephanie. Oh, I can't wait," she cried. "How soon can we move?"

"I don't mind living in the jungle," Stephanie pleaded. "I love it here. I play with the monkeys, and you said you loved the beautiful birds all around our hut." She didn't mention the elephants. "I don't want to leave."

"I know, sweetheart," her mother said. "But don't forget there are also a lot of dangerous animals around here – jungle cats, packs of wild dogs, and elephants. How many times have you come into our bedroom and jumped in bed with us because of the growling of some jungle cat? When you were little, I was afraid one of them would break through your bedroom wall and carry you off. This whole tiny house is all bamboo, no glass in the windows, just bamboo shutters. Under these mats, even the floor is bamboo. I want you safe and sound in a real house. And besides, I can't continue to home-school you. You need to be in a real school and make some friends."

Stephanie came over and sat on the bench next to her mother. Her mother stroked her hair.

"I want us all to be safe," she whispered to Stephanie, kissing her forehead and holding her tight. "Speaking of being safe, James, that herd of elephants is back, not far from here, and they're on this side of the river. They water at that wide spot by the tall trees. I heard them today, and Stephanie was playing outside."

Stephanie held her breath, but didn't say a word.

James put down his mail for a minute. "This side of the river?"

"Yes, this side," she said. "If they come this way, there's not much room between the cliffs on one side of us and the river on the other side. Those elephants could trample this little hut right into the dirt along with us."

"I don't think there's anything to worry about," James said. "They have always stayed downstream from us. They have never come up here."

"I know, but the sooner we are out of here, the better," her mother said.

Stephanie was thinking about how dangerous her mother said this place was. She remembered the night not long ago. She had been asleep. She woke up hearing a large animal just outside the bamboo wall of her bedroom. Peeking out the crack, she saw a large jungle cat looking right at her. Screaming, she ran to the other bedroom and woke her dad. He fired his gun, scaring it away. Still she loved living here – as long as her father was here to protect them.

Still reading his mail, her father said, "Look at this, Amy. This one is from my brother, George." Excitedly, he tore the envelope open. "It's been over two years since he has written."

"He's probably broke and wants you to loan him some more money," Amy replied sourly.

"*Dear James,*" he read.

"I know you and Amy will not believe me, but I have in my possession an ancient parchment. It almost pinpoints the location of the lost treasure of Israel. From my research, I feel certain the Ark of the Covenant is with this treasure. The map was drawn by a man who helped hide the treasure over 2,600 years ago. The parchment carbon dates to around 600 BC. The map leads to the canyon lands south of Jerusalem. It's very old and not in very good condition, but I've almost located where the hiding place is in one of the canyons. Unfortunately, I've depleted all my funds. I need about $10,000 to hire workers to help me search in the area until we find the treasure.

I'm coming home. When I arrive in Bangkok, I'll get my plane out of storage and fly out to our airstrip. I'll be there a few days after you receive this letter. Please be sure the strip is clear of brush and debris.

See you soon.
George
P. S. I'm bringing the parchment. I'm sure you will agree it is authentic."

James put the letter back in the envelope and looked at his wife in bewilderment, but she spoke before he could.

"Not a penny," she exclaimed. "You're not giving him one more red cent!"

"But I think he's really found something this time," James replied.

"Why can't he mortgage his airplane?"

"He did that the last time he was home."

Upset because they were arguing, Stephanie slid off her mother's lap. She knew her father was agitated as he trudged to the corner and picked up his flashlight.

"We will wait until we see the map," he declared. "Then we can decide whether to invest any more money with him or not."

"I've already decided," her mother said. "We're not giving him any more money! Please, James, I want the house you've been promising us."

"With the money we'll get from the sale of the land, we can afford to buy a house and still loan him the money. I'm going to put his letter in our metal box. I'll be back in a few minutes."

Turning and smiling at Stephanie, he said, "You better go to bed now, sweetheart. Daddy loves you." He gave Stephanie a big hug and kiss and went outside.

Stephanie went to bed. Soon she was dreaming about the baby elephant.

* * * * *

Loud noises penetrated the hut. Men were shouting. Something even shook the thin bamboo walls. She heard her mother scream! Then suddenly everything was quiet.

Stephanie was wide awake now. She lay in her bed shaking. Had she dreamed she heard her mother scream? Had she dreamed everything? It was too quiet. Where were the jungle sounds she was so used to hearing at night? It was never quiet like this. Swallowing hard and barely breathing, she slid out of bed. She tiptoed through the main room that served as both kitchen and family room toward the door to her parents' bedroom. Then she heard men's voices outside. Maybe her father was talking to someone. She felt her way to the shuttered window and pushed it open just a crack. Across the narrow porch, the moon was bright above the trees, but the jungle was covered with a heavy green fog. She had seen it before, and it frightened her. Her father had explained the fog came from the river, and the moon shining through the green leaves caused the fog to sometimes have a green tint. It was an eerie sight.

She didn't see anyone but as she closed the shutter, she heard the voices again. Two men were on the porch outside the front door. She listened. Neither voice was her father's. Then she heard someone growl, "Kill the kid! No bullets – use a club."

Paralyzed with fear and not knowing what to do, Stephanie froze. *Could that man be talking about me? There are no other kids, not for miles. Why would they want to kill me?*

Longing for the safety of her parents' arms, she moved again toward their bedroom, but the front door creaked and started to open. Someone was coming into the hut. Quickly she turned and felt her way back to her room. She didn't dare close her door, afraid they might hear it. Had they seen her?

A shadow moved across the kitchen toward her bedroom. A flashlight beam moved around her room. She held her breath and didn't move a muscle. Her heart was beating so hard she was afraid he would hear it. She was lying on her back, just as flat as she could and as close to the bamboo wall as she could get. The big old antique wardrobe she was lying on top of was just a little wider than she was tall.

The man's voice was loud. He spoke broken English with a heavy Thai accent. "I know you're in here. You better come out." Then he paused. "Come out right now! Your mother needs you." He chuckled as he pleaded, trying to entice Stephanie into revealing her hiding place.

She could hear him walking around her bed. Judging the direction of his flashlight beam, he was probably down on his knees looking under her bed. Slowly, he stood up and looked around the room. She saw a bright reflection on the ceiling. His flashlight must be shining on her mirror. He started toward the wardrobe. She shivered as she felt the big piece of furniture move when he yanked the door open. She heard him slide the hangers back. He was looking behind her clothes.

"I know you're here, little girl, and I'm going to find you. Why don't you just come out of your hiding place. I'm not going to hurt you."

Stephanie's body was trembling. Her teeth started to chatter. She clamped her mouth as tight as she could. She wanted to cry, but knew she didn't dare. *If he looks up here and finds me, he will hit me with the club. He'll kill me!*

Suddenly he shined his flashlight beam up to the top of the wardrobe. The yellow beam was bright on the wall just above her head.

"What are you doing? Can't you find her?"

"She not in here," he shouted back.

"Well, she can't be too far. Let's look under the hut. Maybe she ran into the jungle. If she's not there, I guess we'll have to forget about her. She won't survive anyway. Come on. Let's get back to the others."

As quickly as they left, Stephanie scrambled down, stepping and holding onto the bamboo cross bracing built into the wall. She had hidden up there before, playing hide and seek with her mother. Peering through the cracks, she saw their flashlights outside.

When she was sure they were gone, she slowly crept out of her room. It was so dark. She reached for the doorknob leading into her parents' bedroom. Just as she slowly turned the knob, she heard gunshots and then shouting. Instantly, she heard the elephants. They were panicked and trumpeting. The sounds were coming from some distance away, but they were getting louder. The herd was coming toward their hut.

Hoping her mother and father were okay and no other men were in the room, she opened the door. The lamp was not lit. The shutters were closed, and it was dark in the small bedroom. Sobbing, Stephanie ran to her mother's side of the bed, but she tripped over something and fell. She got up. Standing by the bed in the dark room, she cried, "Momma – wake up!"

No one stirred in the bed. She felt on the bed for her mother, but her mother wasn't there. She reached over to her father. He had his back to her. She tried to shake him as she cried, "Daddy, where's Mama?" Her father didn't reply.

Stephanie was terrified. She felt up on the dresser for her daddy's big flashlight but couldn't find it. Next she felt in the dark for the lamp and the matches on the night stand by her mother's side of the bed. As the flame in the lamp came to life, she saw her mother. She was lying face up at the foot of the bed. She had tripped over her mother's feet. Her mother's eyes were wide open, staring at the ceiling.

"Mama, what's wrong? You have to get up," Stephanie screamed. "Someone is scaring the elephants. They're coming down here."

The sounds of men yelling, guns going off, and panicked elephants running, were getting louder.

Her mother never moved. Stephanie held the lamp close to her face. She screamed when she saw the blood and the jagged gash in her mother's forehead. Blood had been flowing into her dark hair. Now it was starting to run down her forehead and her cheek.

Still screaming, Stephanie ran to the other side of the bed. "Daddy, daddy, something's wrong with Mama and the elephants are coming," she yelled at him, tears streaming down her cheeks.

He didn't say a word. She lifted the sheet covering his face, thinking for a second he was finally awake. The light from the lamp illuminated his face. His eyes were open, and he was looking right at her, but he didn't speak. Then she saw the dark red circle of blood under his head.

Stunned and in shock, Stephanie slowly backed away from the bed. She looked down at her hands and her nightgown. They were covered with warm, sticky, red blood. The coal-oil lamp she held was smeared with blood.

The loud noises were right outside the hut now. Men were carrying torches and shooting guns, driving the herd of elephants into the narrow area between the river and the high cliffs.

The terrified animals hit the front wall, crumpling the bamboo hut. The roof collapsed and James' and Amy's lifeless bodies were crushed under the feet of the thundering herd, as a traumatized little seven-year-old girl, covered in blood, somehow managed to crawl out of the debris and ran screaming into the jungle.

CHAPTER TWO

Mount Sinai, Egypt
Present Day

A hawk soared in the sun high above the granite domes that formed the top of Mount Sinai. It was hot at the base of the mountain where we sat with a multitude of anxious people. No one complained of the heat. Everyone was too excited as they waited for the wonderful event. The air smelled clean, with just a hint of sage from the bushes on the sandy desert floor that extended to the Red Sea far to the west.

This was the right place – a very sacred place. This was the mountain where the great prophet Moses conversed with God while the Israelites camped at the base, most likely at this very place. Moses had freed the thousands of Israelites from slavery at the hands of the cruel Egyptian slave masters. In their escape, Moses performed one the greatest miracles in the Bible. The Egyptian pharaoh sent his army with six hundred chariots to catch and bring back the slaves. The desperate Israelite families led by Moses found themselves on the banks of the Red Sea with no place else to go. They were trapped and would either die that day or be hauled back into slavery. At the last moment, Moses stood on a large rock facing the calm waters. He raised his staff above his head. Suddenly, God caused the sea to part. A channel was formed. Two giant walls of churning water were held back while the Israelites crossed to safety on the dry sea bed. When the soldiers pursued them, God released the waters and the entire Egyptian army, horses, and chariots were swallowed up and drowned. What an amazing miracle!

It was late afternoon when a few clouds began to form, but as the evening wore on and still nothing happened, a dreadful feeling began to engulf me. I tried to deny the feeling, but as the hours passed, I began to face the truth – perhaps I was wrong!

The night air was getting cooler. All alone now, the cleft of the rock wall where I had taken refuge twenty feet up from the desert floor shielded me from the light rain.

I, Dr. Matthew Lane, the incessant optimist, the strong-willed, never-to-be-defeated archaeologist, had never felt so betrayed by my own ego and stupidity. The entire day had come and gone. The event that I firmly believed would forever change the attitude of even the most staunch agnostic had failed to materialize.

I stared out into the darkness.

Midnight, the final hour, came and went. As the last few seconds of the day expired, those who had been with me quietly slipped back to their campsites. No one knew what to say, so most said nothing. Someone had draped a blanket over my shoulders. I pulled it a little tighter, hoping it would offer a bit of solace.

Flashes of lightning started to occur every few minutes. Each lightning strike lit the jagged vertical rock wall of Mount Sinai and a half mile of desert extending from the mountain.

Below me hundreds of tents flapped in the wind and campfires flickered in protest. Smaller campfires expelled white smoke as light rain tried to extinguish their flames. But the large bonfires were ablaze, warming those who had not yet gone to bed. Immediately below me at the base of the trail, I looked down on tractor-trailer rigs and white vans with folded antennas on the roof and TV logos on the door. They sat motionless in the light rain.

I had never felt so devastated in all of my thirty-two years! Now thousands of people around the world who had been laughing and scoffing at my prediction will say, "We told you so. We told you it wouldn't happen. It was too absurd. Only an idiot would believe it would actually happen no matter what kind of a vision or encounter you thought you had."

However, some did believe me. Most of the hundreds of people who were camped here in this rough terrain below believed me, especially the children. They shadowed my every move, the very young reaching out to me with their warm hands. Even the teens treated me with respect.

I've really let them down. I can't believe it didn't happen. My best friends had tried to warn me. They told me to never mention what I saw in that cavern. They said the 2,600 year old air in that sealed chamber had caused me to hallucinate. I refused to believe them. I knew what I saw and heard, and it was real. So real I had staked my whole career as a well-known archaeologist on it. I announced to the whole civilized world on public television what I saw and heard. I was so sure of it. I predicted that, at this exact latitude and longitude and on this very day, something unbelievable would happen. But it didn't. I was so sure, so positive. There was never a doubt in my mind.

I watched again as a long exaggerated flash of lightning lit up the area. It was 12:40 a.m. Feeling totally defeated, I leaned back against the stone wall and closed my eyes. Soon it was all coming back to me.

It all started when Ann and I flew to Bangkok, Thailand.

* * * * *

The rented silver Jeep Grand Cherokee moved effortlessly and perhaps a little too fast over the jungle road. It was mid-afternoon, and we wanted to arrive at the lodge before dark. Being out in the middle of the night in a jungle we were totally unfamiliar with would not be prudent.

The dense jungle of the Thailand rainforest was trying to reclaim the road, but we could see tire tracks in the soft red dirt so we knew the road was at least occasionally traveled. We had left the main highway over a half hour ago.

The afternoon sun filtered down through the high canopy of trees and vines. The narrow single-lane road began to wind like a snake around animal watering holes, large boulders, and vines that stretched across the road high above. We had rolled the windows down and opened the moon roof just to experience the exotic smells and sounds of the jungle. The road was a little precarious, but our adventure was exciting.

At one point, I had to hit the brakes hard causing our vehicle to skid to an abrupt stop in the soft dirt. Two massive elephants were standing in a small creek bed of running water in the middle of the road. Several more were at a watering hole where the creek formed an iridescent pool beside the road. A jaguar who had been getting a drink stared at us, then slowly slinked back into the dense foliage. The elephants in the road meandered over to the pool, paying little attention to us. We marveled at their enormous size as Ann took several pictures with her cell phone.

Putting the Jeep in low gear, four-wheel drive, I inched across the creek and up a fairly steep embankment to where the primitive road continued.

"Are you sure this is the road to the lodge?"

"According to this map they emailed us, it is. Maybe it's not going to be as nice as the picture in the brochure," Ann said.

"You may be right," I replied. "I don't think many people travel this road. Maybe there is another road to the lodge."

"I'm sure there is, but this is the only map we have. I know we didn't miss a turn."

I looked at my watch. It was 3:20 p.m. The clock on the dash of the car confirmed I had set it correctly when we left the airport in Bangkok.

Ann was studying the map. We had known each other a little over a year and a half and had been dating for only a short while when this opportunity presented itself. I could scarcely believe I had been blessed with the love of this talented woman. Her intelligence was only enhanced by her unsurpassed beauty – long auburn-brown hair, blemish-free complexion, and a perfectly proportioned body. She captured my heart at the first hello. Looking up, her twinkling brown eyes winked at me as she flashed an engaging smile my way.

The circumstances in which I first met Ann Tyler were unusual. I had just completed my presentation at Georgetown University in Washington, D.C. I had given the same lecture several times before, and the large auditorium was completely full of students enrolled in classes in archaeology. The lecture was on a subject I was very passionate about – "The possible existence of Noah's Ark buried in the ice cap on Mount Ararat."

That evening I was having dinner with some friends when the maitre d' ushered a beautiful young lady to our table. She apologized for interrupting, but wanted to meet me in private right then and there if possible. I was dumbfounded but she was strikingly attractive and very intriguing, so I escorted her to a quiet garden area of the upscale restaurant. She said she had attended my lecture that day and had come to the conclusion she could confide in me. I was speechless as Ann Tyler dangled the story of a secret her grandmother revealed to her when she was only twelve years old in her birth country of Russia. The plot thickened when she wouldn't reveal the secret that night.

The hook was set the following night when she revealed her secret to me. Ann knew the location of some very important photographs. They had been hidden under a brick floor in Russia more than a hundred years ago. What she told me that night started us on a joint adventure beyond all imagination. Now I find myself and Ann in Thailand tracking down a lead on another artifact.

As our vehicle followed a gradual curve, I again was unexpectedly forced to hit the brakes. In front of us a police car was parked crossways in the road.

Several rough-looking men dressed in police uniforms stood in front of the car, each holding a machine pistol. A large Caucasian in the middle had his hand out in front of him and shouted, "Stop," in English. The other men appeared to be Thai.

My mind kicked into "high alert" mode as I assessed the situation. Something did not feel right! Their car was old and had a dented front fender. I slid to a complete stop, still a few yards in front of the blockade. Quickly I shoved the gearshift in reverse and stomped on the accelerator. "These men are not the Thai police!" I shouted to Ann. "Look at those old uniforms. They don't even fit, and that car used to be a police car but it isn't anymore."

Out of the blue, an old rusty Chevy panel truck emerged around the curve behind us. I jammed on the brakes just as the van crashed into the rear of our car. The dense jungle on both sides prevented me from swerving around either vehicle. We couldn't go anywhere. We were trapped!

Three men in ragtag police uniforms ran up to us waving their machine pistols.

"I told you to stop!" the white man shouted as he came up to my driver's side window. "Get out of the car!"

Throwing open the door, he grabbed my arm and dragged me out, slamming me against the hood of the Jeep. No small man, I judged him to be more than six feet tall and maybe two hundred pounds. A brown ponytail hung down below his shoulders. He looked to be in his forties. There was a lot of gray in his hair, mustache, and goatee. I could tell he had spent time in a gym, but not recently. He was getting a paunch above his belt. He had a recent scar across his nose.

Ann bolted out of the car and scrambled to my side, grabbing my arm. She was terrified.

A small skinny Thai man they called Chi started dumping our luggage out in the back seat, searching the contents.

"What are you looking for?" I asked.

The burly man ignored my question. "Give me your passports," he said, shoving me in my chest.

"They're in the car," Ann responded with a touch of defiance.

"Then get them," he yelled, grabbing her arm and shoving her toward the passenger side.

Rubbing her bruised arm, Ann obediently retrieved her purse from the floor by her seat. Taking out both passports, she thrust them into his calloused hands.

"What do you want?" I asked.

No response. The man studied our passports, carefully comparing the photos to our faces.

"What you looking for?" I asked again trying not to raise his ire. "Maybe we can help you."

Chi, ransacking the car and luggage, stepped away from our car. Looking at the big guy who seemed to be in charge, he shook his head no and rattled off a string of Thai words. Obviously they had not found what they were looking for.

Ann and I were riveted in place by our rental car as the men in their shabby uniforms and the panel-truck driver walked back to their car. Passing a cigarette, they spoke to each other in muted tones in a language foreign to us, at times appearing to be arguing. The smoke drifting our way was the sweet, pungent odor of marijuana.

"Maybe they are going to let us go," Ann said hopefully.

"I doubt it, Ann."

"What could they possibly be looking for?"

"Remember the map we were going to bring? I think they might be looking for that."

"The map," Ann said. "Oh, you mean the one we're going to check out when we leave Thailand?"

"Yes. If it really could lead us to the Ark of the Covenant, that map would be worth a lot of money."

Several minutes ticked by.

"Matt, they've been discussing what to do with us for almost ten minutes."

"I know. Here they come. . . Don't make them angry."

"Oh God, please make them let us go," Ann prayed.

They had apparently agreed on something. The big guy said, "We're taking you in for questioning. If you cooperate, you'll be free in a couple of hours. If you resist, we will shoot you right now. It makes no difference to us. Tie their hands."

I put my hands in front of me and motioned for Ann to do the same. They tied our hands tight, making several wraps around each wrist, but only one piece of the rough, frayed, nylon rope secured one wrist to the other.

Hoods were pulled over our heads, and we were thrust onto the floor of the panel truck. I had to bend my knees to fit in the space. The hood, custom-built to cover a person's head, was repugnant from the smell of human sweat. It was made of heavy canvas and had a small hole in front of my mouth so I could breathe, but I couldn't see anything.

I tried to talk to Ann, but someone close to us said loudly, "No talking or I'll hurt the lady." I complied and we rode in silence.

The road seemed to be all dirt or gravel and very winding. The ride was bruising as we bounced across the uneven terrain. At times I felt we were going uphill – sometimes down. After what I judged to be about forty minutes to an hour, the van came to a standstill. We were pulled out of the back. They stood us up, and yanked our hoods off. Ann was gagging and gasping for air, but I was powerless to help her.

It took a few seconds to adjust our eyes to the light and steady our cramping legs. The sun was low in the sky. We were no longer on a road, just a path in a dense jungle. Ann was leaning against me for support.

"What are they going to do to us, Matt? Will they just shoot us here?" Ann whispered.

"I don't think so. They didn't take our money. This is more than just a robbery. From their conversation, I think the boss man is called Drake."

"I got that too, and the big Thai guy who looks like a sumo wrestler is called Tiny," Ann said.

The man in charge whom we had identified as Drake had disappeared, but the driver Nang, who now wielded a pistol, and Tiny forced us to walk on the path single file through the jungle. Nang led the way followed by Ann, then me, and Tiny with a machine pistol brought up the rear. Ann tried to say something to me, but she stumbled trying to match the quick pace set by Nang. As I lifted her to her feet, Tiny, with a rough push, warned her to shut up and walk or she'd be missing some toes! We had no alternative but to comply. I didn't want them to have any excuse to hurt Ann. I was so sorry I had gotten her into this. Somehow I had to rescue her.

The jungle was alive with sounds, mostly noisy birds, and sometimes punctuated with a grunting sound from a wild pig. The air was hot and humid. Sweat ran down my forehead stinging my eyes. I was amazed at the stamina Ann exhibited as we fought to survive.

The sun began to set, and it was getting a little dark when we came to a lake. We turned right and joined another path. The lake on our left was not always visible, but from time to time we got a glimpse of it through the jungle.

I watched for any chance to overpower these two men. I knew I was probably stronger than any of the men who abducted us. My best friend Jim and I have been active in martial arts for years. However, muscle is no match for bullets. If we were going to escape, we would have to wait for the right opportunity.

In the meantime, my concern for Ann was mounting. By these bullies' callous treatment of her, I knew they had no respect for women. Combine that with the drugs, and their actions would be unpredictable. I prayed for the best scenario, but prepared myself for the worst.

At the end of the lake was a clearing. An old aluminum boat with a small outboard motor was tied to a dock. In the middle of the area was a fire pit. A tangle of thick jungle surrounded the large lake.

Two of the Thai men we had seen at the roadblock were standing by the pit. They had changed out of the police uniforms. A few yards from the edge of the lake, a metal structure had been erected. I could see one window in the side facing the boat dock. The building looked like some kind of a shop or storage building. On the end close to us was a regular wooden door with a padlock and a rollup garage door next to that. The garage door was closed and locked. I caught a glimpse of our car parked under some trees behind the building.

They pushed us through the wooden door into the darkness, locking it behind us. Ann was close to collapsing from fatigue and anxiety. I put my arms over her head and held her tight.

"What do you think they want, Matt?"

"I think they want the map we don't have, and since we don't have the map, they might hold us and try to collect a ransom. Let's look around. Try to find something sharp to cut these ropes."

Our eyes slowly adjusted as we started searching the hot, dark room. "Over here, Matt. Will this work? "

It was a cement trowel. Using the edge of the trowel, we cut through the rope that bound one hand to the other.

"Leave the ropes tied around your wrist. Tuck the loose end under and don't let them know your hands are free," I instructed.

I moved down the center of the building. Ann followed. Most of the junk stored in the building was on the perimeter. Some rubber tires were leaning against one wall along with an old wooden cabinet that had some nuts, bolts and screws in glass jars. There were small stacks of lumber lined up parallel with the wall. The floor was just dirt.

On the other end was a stud wall with drywall on the opposite side. The room on the other side of the exposed wood studs might be an office, but there was no door leading to the part we were in. We heard a phone ring on the other side of the wall.

Ann leaned against the wall cupping her hands around her ears to hear better. I dumped some screws out of a quart Mason jar and put the jar against the drywall and my ear to the other end. Someone, probably Drake, was on a phone. He had it on speaker mode so we could hear most of the words on both ends of the conversation. They were speaking in English. Quietly, our heads almost together and our ears to the wall, we strained to hear.

"Did they have the map, Drake?"

"No, they didn't."

"Damn, are you sure?"

"Yes, I'm sure. Come up and search the car yourself."

"Wait! Wait! Wait a minute! Please tell me you didn't bring them to the lake. You didn't, did you?"

"Yes, we did. They didn't have a map, so we decided we could hold them for ransom. It's not like we haven't done that before. . . . Why are you so upset?"

"Why am I upset? Are you kidding me? Are you kidding me?" The voice on the other end was clearly agitated. "Don't you know who these people are?"

"How would I know who they are?"

"What world do you live in, you idiot? You don't recognize them?"

"No, I don't recognize them! Should I?"

"Any dummy would! . . . Wait a minute. Maybe you followed the wrong couple. You didn't get confused as you sometimes do and follow the wrong people, did you?"

"We followed the couple you pointed out at the airport. You said they would have some kind of a treasure map. The only map they had was a single sheet with a map of the old road they were on. It was supposed to lead them to a lodge. There's no lodge on that road."

"I know there is no lodge on that road, you fool! Who do you think sent them the brochure? . . . What do they look like?"

"He's a pretty big guy . . . looks like a quarterback for a pro football team . . . solid muscle, dark brown hair, blue-green eyes. Just a minute. . . . Okay, it says here on his passport his name is Matthew Lane. Looks like he's about thirty-two years old, maybe six foot two. He probably weighs a hundred eighty pounds."

"That's him. Let me guess . . . The girl's name is Ann Tyler."

"Let's see. . . . Yup, you're right. Her name is Ann Tyler. By the way, she is a real knockout. Is she maybe a movie star?"

"No, she's not a movie star."

"It looks like she's about twenty-nine. I'd guess her to be five ten and a hundred thirty-five pounds. She has brown hair and brown eyes. Like I said, a real looker! Me and the boys will have to have a closer look tonight," he said with a laugh . . . "Did we get the right people?"

Ann paled at the conversation, fearful of the fate awaiting her. Reaching out, I squeezed her hand trying to reassure her it would be okay. I could only hope I was right.

There was a long pause before the voice on the cell phone answered, "Yes, you got the right people."

"So who are they?"

"Their faces have been on TV for the last several months."

"Who are you talking about? Are they politicians or something? I don't recognize them as being anybody I ever saw before."

"Well, if you weren't stoned every night and bothered to watch the news, you would know who they are."

"Yah well, you're always stoned with us. So who are they anyway?"

"These two and a guy named Jim Morgan are the ones who found Noah's Ark."

"Noah's Ark?"

"Yes, they actually found Noah's Ark on Mount Ararat."

"Really! They are actually the ones who found it? I would have never recognized them. Man, this is even better. I heard the guy who discovered the Ark, this Matt guy, is rich – a multimillionaire! We can demand two million dollars ransom just for him."

"Shut up, moron, and listen to me! We're not touching this with a ten-foot-pole. Don't you understand? These people are known and respected worldwide. He has a doctorate in archaeology and teaches at Georgetown University in Washington, D.C. His father is a U.S. senator, for hell's sake! And the girl is also an archaeologist who is employed at the Smithsonian Museum as a linguist. If we tried to collect a ransom on these two, we would be dealing with the FBI. They'd have a hundred people over here, and we would be in prison within a week. There is no way we are going to try to get ransom money for these two."

"Well then, what do you propose we do with them?"

"That's your problem! You and your boys got us into this mess. When you didn't find the map, you should've just let them go like I told you. You should never have brought them to the lake. That was stupid . . . The dumbest thing you could have done! . . . Let me think."

A few seconds ticked by. The man in charge on the other end of the phone was obviously a calculating thug with no scruples. He more than likely controlled his henchmen by berating them and supplying them with drugs. Our situation was precarious at best.

"Okay! Here's the plan! Try not to screw this up. First, have Tiny go through all their luggage and check their car again carefully. I was informed that they have a map. It's on old parchment – possibly rolled up – maybe in a cardboard tube or something. It's very old and very valuable . . . I want it."

"Well, I know they don't have a map on them because we frisked the guy and the woman. The only map they had was that single-page road map."

"Wait! . . . Wait a minute. . . . . They wouldn't have brought the original parchment. It's probably just printed on plain white paper . . . They would have just brought a copy . . . Maybe that's why you didn't recognize it."

Ann and I then realized why Drake had his cell phone on speaker. He wasn't alone in the room. "Tiny, you heard him. Go search the car again."

A door opened and closed as Tiny apparently went out.

"Now listen, Drake, and listen good." The voice giving the orders was speaking lower now, but we could still hear. "Because you were stupid, you're going to have to kill these people. You can't just turn them loose."

"Why can't we turn them loose? We drove them around in the back of the panel truck, then marched them through the jungle to get them here. We could take them back to the road the same way. They wouldn't have any idea where they are or where they were. I don't think they could lead anyone back up here. There are lots of lakes in this area."

"You numbskull! It's a good thing you don't do the thinking for us. We would have been caught doing this ransom thing a long time ago. How many lakes have a large building with a shiny roof that could easily be spotted from the air? Would you like to start tearing down the metal building and burying the shiny tin? And when they locate the property, which they will, they will know who owns it. And when they drag the lake and find the bones of all the people you have murdered that the crocs didn't eat, who do you think they will be looking for? There is no way you can let them go. I'm not about to take that kind of a chance. I don't like it, but your dumb decision got us into this mess. Now you're going to have to kill them."

"Okay, so we have to kill them. No problem. We'll do it. It's second nature to us. You never worried about killing our hostages before. Why now?" Drake asked.

"Why now? We usually collect a lot of money for that. We get nothing for killing these two except one more chance to get the death penalty if anyone figures out what you guys do up there on the property I own. When it becomes apparent that these two have disappeared, people could be all over this area looking for them. So do what you have to do, but do it right. And don't mess it up. And no shots fired. If anyone should hear guns being fired around there, they may think there's poaching going on. That could bring the game warden up there. We don't need anybody poking around that lake. And one last thing. Don't let your men rape her."

"Why not? We always rape the women. She's going to die anyway."

"Hear what I say. Don't rape her!"

"Okay – okay. You're the boss."

Matt and Ann heard the door open and close in the office.

"Tiny's back. He said there is no map."

"Damn!" the other voice said. "Is he sure? Is he positive?"

"Yes, I am, boss," replied a deep rough voice. "I went through absolutely everything and I guarantee there is only the one single-page road map in that car. I went through all their luggage, under the seats, in the engine compartment, and under the spare tire. There is no map, no parchment, no cardboard tube, or anything like that."

"Damn it! I can't believe it. My contact in D.C. was positive they would have a map. I paid a lot of money for that information." A few seconds went by. No words were spoken. Finally, "Okay, you have no choice. There is no way out of this. Drake, you know what to do. Take them for a boat ride. Clean up everything that would hint that they were there. Did anyone see you on the road?"

"No. We didn't see a soul today."

"That's good that you didn't see anyone. I just hope no one saw you. Need I remind you the last guy you held for ransom got away, ran through the jungle, and almost to the road before you caught him. You could have landed us all in prison."

"But we did catch him, and we did collect the ransom, and he's no longer alive to lead anyone here now, is he?"

"Just do it right, and call me tonight when it's finished." The phone went dead.

"Well you heard him. Let's get ready. We'll do it about ten tonight," he told Tiny. "Tell Chi to drive their Jeep around to the deep end and run it off into the lake. Remember, windows up so the luggage doesn't float out of the car. Don't run it on top of one of the other cars we put in the lake. Don't take her jewelry. One of those Thai guys would probably try to sell it, and that would lead the police to us. Better bring her purse and any valuables to me. And, Tiny, you know if either one of these two should escape, we're in deep trouble. So watch out for that guy. He could be dangerous as a cobra."

"You got it, boss," Tiny said as the door banged shut.

Ann's shoulders sagged as she slipped to the floor in despair. I put my arm around her and drew her trembling body closer to me. I didn't know how I could prevent these savages from killing us, but I knew I'd give my life to save Ann's.

CHAPTER THREE

We groped our way back through the dark room and sat down on an old rear car seat beneath the only window. Vertical bars prevented any escape. The glass was caked with dust and dirt, but I could tell it was getting dark outside. Ann moved closer to me, and I put my arm around her.

A generator chugged as it started up and immediately a light just outside the door flickered and came on. Standing up, I saw another light come to life out on the boat dock. The fog now rolling in off the lake looked foreboding.

"Matt," Ann cried softly, "are they really going to kill us?"

"They are going to try, but they are not going to succeed."

"I don't want to die."

'We're not going to die, Ann! Someone may drown tonight, but it's not going to be either of us."

"But what can we do? How can we get out of this? We can't even escape from this building, and we're running out of time."

"I don't know yet. . . . What time is it? They took my watch."

"It's almost eight. Oh, God, Matt, we only have two hours to live!"

I stood up and walked around, searching for an escape. I didn't see any way out through the steel walls, and Drake was still in his office so we couldn't break through the drywall and out his door.

Ann came up behind me. I turned to face her. "They are going to tie a weight to our legs and push us out of the boat, aren't they?" Ann's voice quivered. "I'd rather be shot than drown. Have you ever stayed underwater too long in a swimming pool? You have to take a breath, and you haven't reached the surface yet. It's a horrible feeling!"

"Don't think about it."

"I can't stop thinking about it. I'm scared to death. What a terrible way to end our lives!"

"We're not dead yet. Somehow we'll find a way out of this. I know we will. I refuse to believe we are going to die tonight."

"I'm sorry. I guess I'm tired, hungry, thirsty, and really scared."

"Well, we may get some water to drink and a bath when we swim to the nearest shore after while."

"How can you joke, Matt?" she yelled. "We're about to die!"

"Sorry, Ann. . . . I know we are not going to die tonight. I know it. Just be sure you keep your hands together no matter what. If they see our hands are loose and retie them, especially if they tie them behind our backs . . . well, let's say the odds will change, and not in our favor. But if our hands are free, we have a chance. We just have to wait for the right opportunity."

"I hope you're right, Matt."

"I am right, Ann. We have a little advantage," I said. "Number one, we know they plan to kill us, but they don't know we know that. Number two, they don't know our hands are free. So no matter what happens, keep your wrists tight together and the loose ends of the rope tucked under. Don't let them even suspect our wrists are not tied."

"They have a much bigger advantage, I'm afraid," Ann replied. "They have the guns."

I could see the shadow of someone's feet in the light under the door. As the key turned in the padlock the door opened, and a small Thai man they called Sunan entered the room. He shined the bright flashlight beam directly into our eyes.

"You will soon be free," he said in broken English. "You must be thirsty . . . all this time with nothing to drink. The water here will make you sick and we have no bottled water, but here's some Coca-Cola for you. Sorry if you prefer Pepsi," he laughed.

He shined his light first on Ann, then me, and then on top of the fifty-five gallon drum near the door where he left two cans of Coke.

"The paperwork will be complete soon, and you can be on your way."

Then he left and locked the door.

We had not had anything to drink for hours, and it was very hot in the metal building. I picked up the already opened Cokes which were temptingly cold. Ann reached out for one, but I pulled it away.

"Don't drink it, Ann. My guess is that it's laced with a heavy sedative."

"Oh Matt, are you sure? I'm really thirsty."

"I know you're thirsty. So am I, but we don't dare drink it. Our only chance is to act like we're drugged, and wait. Be prepared for my signal. We're not going to die at the hands of these creeps. When they take us to the boat, look for anything you can grab onto if the boat should capsize . . . the place where the oars are attached, even the thick aluminum trim around the top of the boat . . . anything! When we get into the boat, try to end up letting me be closest to the bad guys. You're right. They will probably attach a heavy weight to our legs. If the boat tips over, be ready to grab onto something that would keep the weight from dragging you down."

About 9:30 the door opened. A bright flashlight played in the dark until the beam landed on me. I was lying in the dirt fifteen feet from Ann with my empty Coke can on its side next to me. Then the beam moved to Ann. I was right. They didn't act surprised at finding us asleep. Whoever was there left again.

I hadn't told Ann, but I was afraid of what these ruthless men might still try to do before they took us to the boat. Earlier, I had found an old tarp for her to lie on. It was better than her lying in the dirt. I put the tarp down close to the window so I could watch her in the dim light that came through. From my position, I could watch both Ann and the door. My eyes would appear to be closed, but I would see every move they made.

Ann finally fell asleep. She was exhausted from the long hike and the stress. I was fearful of our situation too, but tried to hide it as much as I could from Ann. Our hands were not tied and they didn't know that, but the odds were stacked high against us.

My mind began to drift back to who I was and how I came to be here. Drake was right. I guess I really am a multi-millionaire. I had never thought of myself that way. I didn't always have a lot of money.

I was raised in a middle-class neighborhood in Washington D.C. A lot of things changed in my life in a short period of time. I graduated from college with a degree in archaeology and landed a job with a university in D.C. I didn't make a lot of money, but I loved what I was doing.

Soon after my college graduation, my father was elected to the U.S. Senate. Tragically, within a year my grandfather passed away. It was a very sad time. I loved that old man, and he loved me. When he died he left both my father and me a sizable estate. My parents had just begun to enjoy being able to buy what they needed without having to finance it when my mother became ill and passed away. That was devastating to both my father and me. We had just drawn the plans for a new house when she died. She never got to live in it. So my father and I have this beautiful home in a suburb of Washington, but an element of maternal love is missing.

Just a short time ago, Ann and I and Jim Morgan, my best friend, received a great deal of notoriety when we discovered Noah's Ark buried deep in the glacier on Mount Ararat. And since Ann and I fell in love, our lives couldn't be happier. That is, until a few hours ago when we hit that roadblock.

Just then I heard the door knob turn, and I was rocked back to reality. Three men entered the room . . . Tiny, Chi, and Sunan. They were quiet and spoke in whispers.

"Did the Coke work?" Tiny asked.

"I think so," Sunan said.

"Don't take any chances. Go over and tie his legs."

"Where is he?"

"Over there," Tiny said as he focused his flashlight on me. "Just put that loop over his legs and hold on while we take care of business. Don't worry. You'll get your turn. If he wakes up, put the gun in his face. Don't shoot him unless you have no choice."

Sunan worked his way from the doorway around the room toward me. He had a machine pistol in one hand and a coiled rope in the other as he cautiously approached. Bending down behind me, he nudged me in the back with his pistol. I didn't move. Assured I was unconscious, he started to put the open loop over my legs. I clasped my legs and feet tight together. At the same time, I pressed them hard to the ground while pretending to be unconscious. Sunan couldn't get the rope under my feet without putting his gun down.

"Grab her legs. I've got her arms."

I heard Ann yelling, "Stop it! Let me go!"

Ann's cries were suddenly muffled. I could see Tiny holding her arms above her head with his left arm, and his right hand was over her mouth. Sunan, still by my legs, had his gun aimed at my chest. I was helpless.

Then Ann managed to get one leg loose and caught the side of Chi's head with her knee. Now he was mad!

Tiny released his right hand from her mouth for a second. Ann screamed, "Stop! Get off me!"

Grabbing a handful of hair and jerking Ann's head back, Tiny put the blade of his knife against her neck. "Shut up or I'll slit your throat!"

Ann whimpered.

"Now, damn it, hurry up before Drake comes in!"

Anger raged within me, but I had to keep my wits about me. Sunan's lustful eyes were glued on Ann, not me. He'd forgotten about tying my legs as he stared at Ann and the two men trying to rape her. In one fast move, I turned and kicked, striking the underside of the machine pistol, driving it into Sunan's face. His reflexes squeezed the trigger on the automatic weapon, firing a dozen shots in rapid succession. Bullets made a row of holes through the metal walls and roof over Chi's and Tiny's heads before he could get his finger off the trigger. Like a bat out of hell, Tiny and Chi released Ann and ducked for cover.

With blood spurting from his nose and cut lip, Sunan flew into a frenzy. He hit me with the barrel of his gun. Then he aimed the gun at me and started to squeeze the trigger.

Tiny yelled, "Stop! No more shooting!"

The door crashed against the frame as Drake burst into the room. "What the hell? I told you no shooting."

I staggered as I stood up and managed to cross the room to Ann's side. I could feel blood dripping from a cut on my temple. She was unsteady as I helped her to her feet. No one made a move to stop us. They just watched in silence. Through all of that, courageous Ann had still not revealed that her hands were free.

"I told you not to fire a weapon," Drake roared. "If anyone heard those shots, we're in trouble. There are people who live in the jungle on the other side of this lake. You'd better hope they don't come over here. Hurry up. Let's get this over with."

* * * * *

The yard light lit up the old dock. There was only one boat and a small frame structure on the dock which was probably used to store bait and gasoline.

A man they called Kai put a wrap of old rusty chain around my ankle and secured it tightly with a heavy padlock. Helplessly, I watched as he then did the same thing to Ann, putting the keys in his shirt pocket.

"Dear God, please help us," I prayed. "I can't let this happen."

It was hot and humid. Standing on the dock under the light, we could see sweaty-faced Kai and Chi grinning. They seemed to enjoy the mental and physical torture they were inflicting on us. Both were small Thai men, thirty to forty years old. Kai had some teeth missing and a jagged scar across his cheek. These men were no strangers to violence.

The water below the boat dock was dark and still. Bugs were swarming around the light above us, and the sounds of the jungle insects and frogs were at a high pitch.

Ann and I were each forced to drag a heavy concrete block attached to the chain around our ankle down to a lower platform where the boat was tied. Hampered by the weight of the block and chain Ann stumbled, but we managed to sit side by side where Kai indicated, facing the outboard motor. Chi lifted the concrete blocks into the bottom of the aluminum boat next to our feet. Quietly I shifted the block between my feet trying to make sure the chain was not tangled.

Ann was terrified. Her voice quivered as she shouted, "I hope you all die the same way. You're all disgusting pigs!"

The poor excuses for men roared in amusement.

Chi sat down on the bench at the rear of the boat, facing us. He sneered as he pulled the rope and started the outboard motor.

My head was spinning. I had to get us out of this. . . . But how? . . . I was hoping Chi would take us far enough from the dock so Drake couldn't see us anymore. Our hands were still free and they didn't know that, but they had the weapons. Chi was about four feet from me. . . . Was the chain long enough? . . . We were almost out of time now. Soon I would have to make one last effort.

Kai was sitting on the bow facing our backs with a machine pistol and a flashlight. Next to his feet on the flat aluminum seat was a long sword in a leather sheath. That is how we would be forced overboard. Sadistic as our captors were, they probably would make Ann go first so I would have to watch her drown.

The lights from the boat dock grew smaller as we motored away into the ominous darkness. Drake, Tiny, Nang, and Sunan were standing in the fog under the light watching us. Sunan had a bloody handkerchief up to his face. Lowering the handkerchief, he yelled a lot of angry Thai words at me and raised his fist in an obscene gesture.

As the old outboard took us further out, Chi seemed to be relaxed. He had his hand on the control arm of the motor, with a machine gun in his left hand aimed at my stomach.

We had gone about a half mile and could barely see the light from the boat dock through the fog. Chi slowed the engine to an idle. Taking his right hand off the throttle, he filled his palm with lake water and threw it on us and laughed. This erratic gesture made me think he was high on something.

"Better get used to the water. It's almost time for a swim," he said. Looking at Ann, he smiled. "You shouldn't have fought me so hard. I'm a good lover. You might have even enjoyed it."

Ann, ignoring him, scooted closer to me.

Chi continued, "Did you ever try to swim with your hands tied and a concrete block chained to your leg? . . . No?" he laughed. "I'll bet your lungs feel like they are on fire when you finally have to open your mouth and suck in the water. . . . There are a lot of crocodiles in this lake. Guess they'll have a good meal tonight. I'll take you where the crocs hang out. If you're lucky, one will bite you in two before you have to take that first breath."

Ann paled as she listened to his sadistic ramblings.

Increasing the speed of the old motor, Chi headed closer to shore. Fifty feet from the bank, he slowed down and turned parallel with the dark jungle at the edge of the water. I felt our odds might be getting a little better. We were now in shallower water, heading farther away from the boat dock. If Chi really was on some drugs, he wouldn't be as alert as he should be. I could see the reflection of the half moon on the water.

"Kai, shine your light over there by the bushes. Let's find us a nice size crocodile for the lady."

Chi was not paying attention to me. He was watching the shore looking for a big crocodile. Shadows concealed my movement as I slowly bent forward lowering both hands between my legs.

"You spot a big croc yet, Kai?"

I had been quietly pulling the slack out of the chain with my hands. I felt the block lift off the bottom of the boat. I pulled it over my shoes to muffle any sound. Placing my hands firmly on the concrete block, I said a quick prayer to myself and thought, *"It's now or never!"* In one quick lift and push motion, I threw the heavy block at Chi, hitting him right in the face. The blow broke his nose, knocking him unconscious. He slumped forward, and his gun clattered to the bottom of the boat. Quickly I bent down, groping for the gun in the dark. When it was in my hands, I turned and aimed it at Kai.

In the bow, Kai, taken totally by surprise, had been facing forward, his knees on the front seat, flashlight pointed ahead looking for a large crocodile. Caught off guard, he dropped his flashlight in the water. Spinning around he stood up, raising his machine pistol up just as I squeezed the trigger. Several rounds went off, most of them hitting Kai.

We were totally off-balance. The boat tipped to the starboard side, the same side Ann was sitting on, the same side Kai fell on. The boat capsized, propelling all four of us into the water. Both heavy concrete blocks slid out of the boat, dragging the chains toward the lake bottom.

Ann immediately grabbed the thick outer railing of the overturned boat with both hands. When her concrete block hit the end of its chain, it almost jerked her hands loose, but she held on tight.

I was pitched farther out. I grabbed for the side of the overturned boat, but my hands slipped past the edge. The block hit the end of its chain, jerking my ankle and plunging me straight to the bottom. When my feet hit the bottom, it was firm, not soft mud. The water was only about twelve feet deep. I could see the outline of the overturned boat still floating above me. My heart was pounding. I pulled the chain and got the concrete block in my left hand. My lungs were longing for a breath of air as I went into a crouch position. Then I jumped straight up toward the boat, using all the power I could muster, kicking with both legs and using my right arm to propel myself up to the surface. I grabbed the inside lip of the boat railing, but lost my grip on the concrete block. I held on with both hands while the block once again fell and jerked hard on the chain around my ankle. Immediately I grabbed the aluminum seat under the boat.

It was pitch black underneath with only a little moonlight on the surface. I caught a glimpse of Ann's hands still gripping the railing. Eagerly I sucked in a full breath of air that was trapped under the boat, but Ann's head was still underwater. Grabbing her wrist, I pulled her hand up to the seat I was holding onto. I didn't dare lose my grip. The weight would drag me to the bottom and I would never be able to swim up again. I reached down with my free hand and grabbed Ann by the belt and helped her raise her head above the water. She came up gasping for air.

"You okay?" I said.

"Yes . . . yes . . . think so." She was choking and coughing to expel the water that had entered her lungs.

We took a moment to recover from our close encounter of nearly drowning. Realizing we had little time to spare, I locked my left arm over the underside of the seat and raised my leg up as far as I could. Reaching down with my right hand, I grabbed the chain. Then using a combination of both legs and my right hand, I worked the block up a little at a time until I could grab it with my hand. I finally got it, setting it on the underside of the aluminum seat.

I helped Ann lift her block as high as she could with her leg using the same procedure. We finally got her block positioned on the underside of the seat also.

Kai had gone to the bottom, but I could see the shadow of Chi. He was hanging onto the back of the boat. I knew he had to have been badly hurt when the concrete block hit him in the head, but the cold water must have revived him.

"I've got to be sure we're still headed for the shore, Ann. Keep one arm over the seat and be extremely careful not to let those blocks fall off."

I could tell she was shivering from shock and cold, but she nodded she understood.

Slipping out from under the boat, I looked around. We were heading toward the tree-lined bank all right, but now I heard men shouting back at the dock. They had heard the gunfire. Soon they would be running around the lake, right where we were heading. Our only hope was to get to shore before they arrived and hide in the jungle. I ducked under and quickly instructed Ann to start paddling. We were able to slowly maneuver the overturned boat toward shore. Soon our feet touched the bottom. The shouting was still quite a ways off.

Suddenly there was a lot of thrashing in the water and a blood-curdling scream not far behind us. A deathly silence followed. Chi had finally found the croc he was searching for.

We found a place where we could get through the foliage and up to the shore. After I helped Ann get up the bank, I found a large rock. A few heavy blows broke the concrete blocks, releasing the weight, but not the chain. The sound of the rock breaking the block would bring Drake and his men. Back along the edge of the lake, I could already see their flashlights through the trees. We had to get away from here and fast!

"Pull the end of the chain under your belt. The links aren't heavy, but until we can get the padlocks open or cut the chain, we have to try to keep it from rattling."

I put my arms around Ann for a minute. Trembling and trying to catch her breath, she was traumatized from our ordeal over the last several hours, but we couldn't let Drake and his men catch us . . . Not now!

"That chain may start to wear into your ankle. Let me know if it gets too bad."

"Okay."

A little moonlight was shining through the trees, but we still couldn't see many of the obstacles in front of us.

"Can you keep going, Ann?"

"We have to, Matt! Just let me catch my breath," she said as she sucked in the night air.

"Follow close behind me. Straight out from the lake, we should find the path we were on yesterday . . . the one that is parallel with the lake . . . the one that led us to the camp. Only we'll go back the other way."

"I can't stop the noise of the chain and the squeak of my wet shoes," she whispered.

"Don't worry about it. Just keep going." I felt Ann grab the back of my belt. "I don't think they can hear us."

A few yards out from the lake, we found the trail we were on yesterday. "We can move faster now," I said as we turned right and joined the path. "We've got to get away from here. When they find the boat, they will know where we entered this path."

The jungle was eerie at night with light from the moon filtering down through the trees. Soon we heard Drake's voice on the trail behind us. "There's the boat. They are probably still close to it. We'll check it out. Sunan, you go on ahead. Stay on the path. Look for signs. They can't be far away.

Scrutinizing the path, I stopped and picked up a piece of wood about three feet long. Then I led Ann off the trail about five yards into the jungle. "Get down and stay right here."

"Where are you going?"

"I'll be back."

Back tracking on the trail a short distance, I hid in the camouflage provided by the density of the jungle. Armed with my piece of wood, I waited in ambush. A light filtering through the vegetation drew closer.

Just as he was even with my position, I stepped out and swung as hard as I could. The sound resonated like the crack of a bat connecting with a baseball as I hit Sunan in the back of the head. It happened so fast he never saw me, and he never knew what hit him.

Rushing back to Ann, I reached out, grasped her arm, and pulled her to her feet. "Come hold the light while I drag Sunan off the trail."

She let out her breath. Apparently relieved, she complied and stumbled along behind me as we retraced our steps. There on the trail laying face down was Sunan's crumpled body. Ann gagged at the sight and turned her head away.

"Just hold the light in front of me so I can see where I'm dragging him. Hurry!"

I dragged Sunan's body into the jungle. In robot-like compliance, Ann held the light while I cleaned up the trail.

Then we heard voices. . . It was Drake, Tiny, and Nang back on the trail. We crouched down by Sanun's body. The three men ran right past us as Drake was calling for Sunan.

"One down, three to go," I whispered, "but with this gun and flashlight, our odds just got better. I'm sorry I had to kill him, Ann, but I had no choice. It was him or us."

"I know. . . How are we going to get out of here, Matt?" she whispered, her voice shaking.

"One step at a time, Ann. Is your watch still working?"

She held it under the beam of my flashlight.

"No, look. The secondhand isn't moving. It stopped at 10:25."

"Well I'm guessing it's probably closer to 11:15. We have about six hours before daylight. We'll rest for a while. Then we'll look for a way out."

We pushed further into the jungle. Using the flashlight sparingly to avoid detection, I bent down some elephant-ear leaves close to a tree, and we flopped down on them. Our clothes were wet, and the night air was cool. Holding each other tightly, the temperature of our bodies staved off the night chill, and our shared love blanketed the dangerous situation we were in. We had to survive!

Ann whispered, "I can't believe what we've been through. If it wasn't for you, Matt, I'd have been brutally raped by three horrible men, and we'd both be dead, drowned in the lake with crocodiles eating our bodies. You didn't let that happen. You stopped all those men with machine guns from killing us. You're the only reason we're still alive!"

"Well," I responded, "I'd like to take all the credit and be like Superman in your eyes, but I think somebody upstairs helped us . . . We're not out of it yet. Now we've got to get out of this jungle and back to civilization without being caught."

"You are Superman in my eyes, Matt. You've always been. Sometimes you're so amazing I can't believe you're real. I'm sticking with you like glue. If there is any way for us to get out of this jungle, I'm sure you'll find it."

We were both exhausted, but holding each other, we finally warmed up. Still afraid, but fairly comfortable, we lay there listening to the night sounds of the jungle.

Ann fell asleep. I catnapped for about a half hour, my arms still around her. I watched her face in the dim light of the moon as she slept, trying to figure out what to do next. I felt her stir. She opened her eyes and smiled at me.

"We've never been this close before," she said, "except for dancing a couple of times. If it were under any conditions except the one we are in, it would be wonderful."

"You mean just because our clothes are damp and we are being hunted at night in the Thailand rainforest by three killers, the conditions aren't right?"

"Something like that," she quietly replied.

"It will be light in a few hours. The jungle is too dense to walk through. Let's get back on the path around the lake. Stay behind me. We'll have to keep the chains as quiet as we can. We may run head-on into Drake and his men as they backtrack."

"I know. I'll be quiet."

We tried to slip some leaves between the chain and our ankles, which I knew would soon be raw and bleeding, but they didn't stay there very long. Each step was excruciating, but Ann never complained.

We continued walking for several hours before the path started going downhill. I kept the machine pistol I had taken from Sunan slung over my shoulder. The moon was bright enough to see the path without the flashlight except when the tree canopy was too thick.

"The terrain is getting rougher. Grab hold of me if you start to slip. We must've missed the intersecting path, the one that went back to the van. We were never on this part of the trail. I don't think the lake is on our right anymore. We must be past the end of the lake. Listen . . ."

Through the jungle to the right where the lake had been, we could hear the roar of a waterfall.

"I think there's a canyon where the lake ends. There must be a river feeding the lake where we were being held, and this is where the water comes out on the other end. Be careful. It's getting even steeper."

We trudged on, pushing through the jungle foliage, which scraped our skin. Suddenly I stopped. "Look. There's a hill in front of us. The path curves to the right at the base of it. I think we're heading toward the river. "

The moon had disappeared, but morning light was making it easier to see. We stopped to rest for a while. I could see cuts and scratches on Ann's arms and legs. I bent down to look at the chain around her ankle. It looked bad. She couldn't continue much longer.

"You have a cut on your temple, Matt. That's where Sunan hit you with his gun, isn't it? And look at that swelling on your shin. Does that hurt?"

"Not much," I said.

"You kicked Sunan's gun, didn't you? That's how you got that bruise. I couldn't see what you did, but I knew you risked being shot to save me. All I can say is thank you. It hardly seems enough."

"You don't have to thank me, Ann. We are in this together . . . Can you walk a bit farther?"

Ann nodded and slowly limped down the path. We hadn't gone far before I stopped again. The roar from a waterfall was getting louder.

"Be careful," I said as I cautiously continued on the curving, narrow jungle trail.

"You be careful, Matt," Ann said behind me.

After a few more steps on the path through the dense jungle, I abruptly stopped at the edge of a cliff. The sound was deafening. Right before our eyes the river plunged to a pool a hundred feet below. We were mesmerized at the sight.

Cupping my hands, I leaned closer to Ann so she could hear me. "There used to be a bridge here. It was just a few feet in front of the falls. Look. Part of the old supports are still on the other side of the canyon. It's a long way straight down."

Cautiously, holding onto my arm, Ann peered over the edge to the pool below. "Oh my Lord," she said as she jerked back a few feet. "It really is a long way down. We've got to go back. We can't go right or left. There's nothing but jungle, and it's too steep and dense to even try to walk through."

"You're right, Ann. We have to go back."

"Where do you suppose they went, Matt? This trail is a dead end. Thank God we haven't seen them."

"I think they took the path we missed, the one from the lake back to the road. Probably the one we'll have to find and take to get out of here."

We started back up the trail. The sun was just peeking through the trees. I froze in my tracks. Ann almost ran into me.

"I heard something on the trail in front of us," I whispered.

Quickly we turned and headed back toward the waterfall and the edge of the cliff. Terrified, Ann looked at me. "I can't jump, Matt. It's too far down. I'm a girl, remember? I'm no Butch Cassidy or Sundance Kid, and this isn't a movie. I can't jump. I won't jump!"

I peered over the edge again. "We might survive if that pool down there is deep enough but I agree, it's a long way down."

"Drake, is that you?" someone called out. He was close, probably where the path turned toward the waterfall. "Drake, Tiny . . . where are you guys?"

We both moved back from the edge. The jungle was thick on both sides of the trail. We quietly pushed back into the vines and leaves. We had no choice. I was closest to the narrow path. I had my gun ready. We stood motionless in the dense foliage, Ann a little behind me. I had the safety off ready to fire, but Nang didn't come. Then we heard him going back away from us.

"What's he doing?" Ann whispered.

"Probably waiting for Drake and Tiny."

"I'm glad he didn't come down here," Ann whispered. "Maybe he's gone back."

"I hope so. A shot would bring Drake and Tiny down here for sure."

Without warning and catching us totally off guard, Nang walked right past us with a pistol ready in his hand. His eyes were glued on the narrow trail. Cautiously he leaned over the edge to see the pool below. Even with the roar of the falls, Nang heard the bushes move and my chain make the slightest sound as I pulled some slack from under my belt. Abruptly he turned to face me just as my foot hit him in the midsection, sending him two feet out over empty space. A surprised and terrified look on his face, he dropped his gun. It fell to the pool below. His hands were flailing as he desperately reached for the rock face. Looking me straight in the eye, his mouth was trying to say something. Then he disappeared. He was screaming all the way down, but the sound of the waterfall was louder than his scream.

I looked over the edge. His body was floating face down. In a few seconds I turned to Ann, still at the edge of the path. "Good thing we didn't jump. The pool is not deep enough."

I came to her. She was shaking. "I'm sorry, Matt. You must think I'm a real sissy, but I'm not used to all this kill-or-be-killed stuff. I'm glad you didn't have to shoot him, and I know he had it coming but I still hate to see people die."

"So do I, Ann, but better them than us. Two down and two to go. "

We located a place upstream in the river where we could get a drink of water.

"I'm really getting hungry. I'm sure you are too, but we have to keep going. How's your ankle?" I said, kneeling down to look at it. "Oh Ann, I'm so sorry. It's bleeding all around under the chain. I know it's got to hurt." I tried to think of what I could do for her. "I could probably beat the links with a couple of rocks until they broke, but that would just shorten the chain. It wouldn't get it off your ankle."

Ann knelt down with me. "Your ankle is bleeding too, Matt, and hitting rocks together would bring Drake and Tiny right to us. We're just lucky we didn't lose our shoes in the lake. Let's keep going. I'm okay."

We couldn't find the path we had taken yesterday that led us to the lake. The path we finally did come across took us in an entirely different direction. The jungle was amazing but frightening, with the scenery changing often. The paths were only animal trails. Most of the area was covered with hanging vines that would thrill Tarzan. Jungle birds watched from a high perch as we hurried through, trying to be aware of what was ahead of us and behind us. From time to time the protective canopy would disappear and the sun would shine directly on the path. We were on constant alert knowing we could run into Drake or Tiny or a jungle animal or a poisonous snake at any time.

Hungry and exhausted, we walked for hours. It was dark when we finally encountered a road and caught a ride in an old pickup into a fairly large suburb of Bangkok. It was simply called "The Village."

The old Thai farmer who picked us up didn't speak much English and kept looking at the chains on our ankles. Much to our surprise the old man knew where the lodge we had been heading for was located, but he drove right past it, taking us instead to the local Thai police office.

We had escaped from the clutches of Drake and Tiny . . . at least for the time being!

CHAPTER FOUR

"How are you feeling, Ann?" I asked. We had just been seated for dinner in the small dining room off the reception area of the lodge. The area we were in wasn't crowded, but we still spoke softly.

"I was so exhausted when I got to my room last night I just crashed. I slept right through breakfast. A bowl of soup for lunch, a hot shower, and several hours of sleep, and I feel human again."

"I was worried about you."

"No, really I'm fine, Matt. I've even checked out the lodge. It's wonderful. It has a great pool, a shop with a few clothes, and my room is very nice. Thank you very much."

"You're welcome," I said gazing at her by the light of the candle. "I see some scratches on your arm, but otherwise you look like you survived our ordeal."

"It was much more than an ordeal, Matt. We almost died out there," Ann said with a serious look.

"But we didn't."

"No, we didn't." Then she looked at my face and smiled. "Your rough stubble was pretty sexy in the jungle, but back in civilization, it's nice to see you clean-shaven."

"How's your ankle?"

"It's sore and swollen. I talked to a nurse. She gave me some antibiotic ointment and told me to put ice on it. If it gets worse, I'll go see a doctor. It felt a lot better when they cut the chain off at the police station. How about your ankle and your bruised shin? And let me see the cut on your temple."

I leaned over. "My ankle was never as bad as yours. My shin bone looks like it was painted blue," I laughed.

"Well, at least that cut on your temple looks a lot better. It's hard to see because it's mostly in your hairline."

"I'm okay. A little sore, but okay." Changing the subject, I added, "You look stunning. That native dress looks great on you."

"Oh, this old thing?" We both laughed. "Thank you again. I found myself literally without anything clean to wear. In fact, I looked so bad when I checked in, everyone in the lobby was staring at me. My purse was in the car, so I had no money and no credit card. I had to charge a few necessities to my room. I promise I'll repay you as soon as my wire transfer comes through."

"That's okay, Ann. Consider it a gift. As soon as we get to a city, I plan to take you on a real shopping spree, my treat."

Ann started to protest, but I insisted.

The waiter brought us plates with a variety of Thai delicacies. After our ordeal, we were famished and ate heartily, enjoying the cuisine. We were both just glad we were still alive.

"Just so you know," I remarked in a low voice, "I didn't tell the Thai police everything. I left out a few things. I didn't tell them that those men tried to rape you."

"Good, Matt. I wasn't raped, thanks to you, and I'd rather forget the whole thing. I don't want to have to describe it all on national television."

"That's what I thought," I said.

"If they catch them and there's a trial, you can bet I'll tell everything."

"I doubt they'll ever be caught," I said. "By now Drake and Tiny have probably burned, buried, or torn down everything around that lake from the metal building to the boat dock. I doubt we could find it now. The Thai police want us to ride in their airplane and search by air as soon as they can get a plane. I told them we'd be glad to help in any way we could."

"What else did you leave out, Matt?"

"Well, I described them all and gave them the names we heard. I pretty much told them everything that happened except that four of them are already deceased. I told them there was a struggle in the boat, it turned over, and we were somehow able to get to the shore and hide.

I said at one point they ran right past us. The next day we found an old animal trail and got out. I'd rather not tell them I killed someone. I could be locked up and held on murder charges while they investigate. I doubt that would happen, but we are guests in their country. If they point-blank ask me if I killed anyone I won't lie, but I'm not going to invite that line of questioning."

"I think you're right, Matt. I think you did the right thing. I was really surprised the police offered to bring me here and helped me check in. And get this, the men at the front desk said they never emailed us a map of how to get here from the Bangkok airport."

"Interesting," I said. "The cover letter had all the lodge info at the top and looked very official."

"Yes, it did . . . How long were you at the police station after I left, Matt?"

"A long time. They interrogated me for hours, rehashing the sequence of events. Finally they were convinced our story was legitimate. They brought me a sandwich and some coffee while I answered questions and filled out paperwork for temporary passports. Meanwhile, they called the car rental agency in Bangkok and explained what happened to our car. The rental company agreed to bring down another car for us in the morning."

"Oh, good."

"After they brought me here and the concierge assured me you had arrived and were given a room, I collapsed from exhaustion. When I woke up, I had a hot shower and a shave and put on some clean clothes. I feel like a new man."

"You look nice."

Ann reached across the small table and took both of my hands in hers. "Thank you again for getting us through that unbelievably horrible experience, Matt."

"We did it together with a lot of help from someone more powerful than we are. Praying in your mind must work because I prayed a lot!"

"So did I, Matt. So did I!"

"Do the police have any idea who they were?"

"I don't think they have a clue who they were, and the whole police force seemed a bit lackadaisical. They lack the training to handle much more than petty crimes and minor disturbances. I did look through their mug shots and gave them a comprehensive report. Of course, I could only describe the person who had them follow us and condemned us to die as a voice I overheard on a cell-phone speaker through a wall and a glass jar. The officer in charge was nonchalant as he explained that several people have been abducted in the last year. They only learn about it after the ransom is paid, and the victims are never heard from again."

We skipped dessert and ordered cappuccino instead. As the sun set, I reminded myself of what a rarity Ann was. She had put our horrific experience behind her and was chatting about our future ventures.

"I think a change of scenery is just what the doctor would order. Are you up to driving back to Bangkok for shopping, Ann?"

"Oh yes! We need to replace almost everything we had in our luggage."

"I know a wonderful shop where we can order shirts, pants, and dresses custom-made. You pick the fabric, they make it, and they will have it ready the next day. We'll also need some new luggage to put those clothes in."

"Don't forget we need to buy new watches, Matt. They took yours and mine doesn't work anymore."

"Yes, I know. We'll be busy for a couple of days, but I think we can squeeze in some fun time too."

"What about the table from Noah's Ark?"

"We're still expected at the Green residence at seven tomorrow evening. John Green lives in this area. We could drive to Bangkok the next day and stay for a few days."

"Sounds like fun. I love shopping," Ann giggled with anticipation, "especially in a city like Bangkok, and I'm so excited to finally get to see the table that was taken out of the Ark. I hope it's authentic! . . . Oh, but what about your measurements of the table legs? Were they in the car?"

"No, they were in my wallet. Luckily I didn't lose that in the lake. I can't believe they didn't take my cash and credit cards. Everything in it that wasn't sealed in plastic was wet, but I can still read the measurements from leg to leg. If the table is really from the Ark, and they don't raise the price, I have been authorized to purchase it."

"Let's keep our fingers crossed. That would be wonderful."

"I'll walk you to your room. By the way, where is your room, Ann?"

"Right next to yours."

"Great! That's convenient. I can easily keep an eye on you."

We both laughed. Little did Ann suspect, I was serious. I was still very concerned about her safety. We finished dinner, and I walked her to her door.

"I'm really tired," Ann said.

"So am I. Breakfast at eight?"

"Yes, I'll knock on your door."

"Good night, Ann. I love you. You mean the world to me, and I want to keep you safe from now on." Gently I pulled her into my arms and kissed her tenderly. "I'll see you in the morning."

"Good night, Matt," Ann whispered as she brushed my lips with a light kiss. "I'm really looking forward to Bangkok."

"Me too. I've never been crazy about shopping, but I'll enjoy watching you, and I'm really anxious to see that old table."

* * * * *

Ann couldn't sleep. She was thinking about Matt. She was mesmerized at what a dynamic and handsome individual he was . . . tall, lean, strong, dark brown hair, evidence of a heavy beard even when he was clean shaven. When he looked at her, his blue-green eyes seem to penetrate right into her soul. He smiles often . . . a great smile. He makes me laugh and is always concerned about other people.

She witnessed first-hand on Mount Ararat that Matt had a special personality. He was a natural-born leader. The tough Turkish men on the mountain liked and respected him. He seemed to adapt to any situation.

Ann never felt so safe with anyone before. She doubted anyone else could have saved their lives on Mount Ararat. And Matt never doubted they could escape from their kidnappers at the lake. He was always a pillar of strength.

They were on top of Mount Ararat the first time Matt said he loved her. She was thrilled when he said it. She had loved him for a long time, but didn't know how he felt about her. Ann got emotional every time she thought about it.

But then, life is never perfect. This exciting new relationship could later cause unwanted pain and heartaches. Ann knew they both loved the adventure of traveling all over the world, studying and discovering different artifacts. Marriage, settling down to raise a family, is not what Ann wanted . . . at least not now. Her career had always taken precedence in her life, and she enjoyed her current position at the Smithsonian. A recent promotion gave her the opportunity to oversee larger projects and spend time at major archaeological digs.

Ann was struggling with her emotions. Would she be forced to make a choice between love or career? How did Matt feel?

CHAPTER FIVE

The replacement Grand Cherokee was delivered right on time, so we decided to check out the village before our appointment at the Green family residence. That appointment was the reason we had flown to Thailand in the first place. After we discovered Noah's Ark, a man named John Green who lived here in this village claimed he had in his family collection an artifact that had been removed from Noah's Ark in the early 1900's . . . a large table from the family's quarters on the Ark. He said it should be displayed with the Ark, and he was willing to sell it. We flew over specifically to check it out, and it was also a good excuse for Ann and I to get to know each other a little better.

The village was about fifty miles from Bangkok and not far off the main highway. The brochure we received in the mail had us leave the main highway twenty to thirty miles before we arrived here. If we had stayed on the main road, we would have easily found the village and the lodge where we had reservations.

Following the resort concierge's advice, we were on our self-driving tour of the village. Many Europeans come here on holiday as evidenced by some upscale hotels and resorts sprinkled around the area. We found a quaint walking bridge over a stream and a small waterfall that exemplified the beauty and charm of the small village. Main Street was only a few blocks long.

Not far from the downtown area, we saw vacation rental houses. Apparently a lot of retired people live in and around the village. In one of the nicer areas, there were very expensive homes. Some were gated communities with manicured lawns and flower gardens at the entrance. In fact, the Green family we were to meet lived in one of these communities.

The streets in the busy downtown area were filled with small noisy motorcycles. For most of the Thai families, this was their only means of transportation. We would see entire families, sometimes as many as four on one bike – two adults and two children – nonchalantly zipping in and out of traffic.

We parked on a side road and walked to the open-air markets, which were bustling with activity. Animated gestures and the din of bartering filled the air with melodic sounds. This was a souvenir hunter's paradise, and Ann scooped up several bargains.

Down the block we came upon a fish market. Weaving in and out of the aisles laden with a variety of unfamiliar species, at one point we had to sidestep several live octopus slithering along the floor. Leaving the odious smells behind, we moved down the street and found the welcomed fragrant flower bazaar. Ann gushed with appreciation for the artistic arrangements and felt compelled to purchase one of the largest for her room. Laughing, arms loaded with purchases, we returned to the car. After dropping off our treasures, we ate an early dinner at the resort restaurant.

On our way to the Green residence, we drove up a knoll overlooking the village and parked there for a few minutes. The streets in the main part of town were paved, but outside was a network of gravel roads much like a spider's web leading to rural areas for miles in all directions. The jungle extended as far as we could see except for areas that had been cleared for the village, roads, or crops. In the distance was a rock-faced mountain. A slide of tailings indicated remnants of a mine.

Secretly, I was scanning the area trying to find where we had been held captive, but the dense rain forest yielded no clues. I couldn't see anything but green forest for miles and miles.

Even though our first couple of days in Thailand had been very traumatic, now that we felt safe again we agreed it was still an exciting place for a few days' vacation. I put my arm around Ann and kissed her.

"This is really fun, Matt," she said. "Let's enjoy every minute of our time here."

I intended to do just that.

We arrived at the Green residence just before seven. It was getting dark and looked like it could start raining at any moment. I parked the Grand Cherokee in the circular drive. The house reminded me of my home in the suburbs of Washington, D.C. Manicured grounds outlined the sprawling two-story colonial home.

The butler greeted us and ushered us into the massive entry. Soon a large man, whom I judged to be in his seventies, entered. With a broad smile, he extended his hand.

"Doctor Lane . . . Miss Tyler. It's an honor to meet you both. I'm John Green."

As we shook hands, a young woman entered the room. John introduced her as his niece, Stephanie.

We had barely gotten through the introductions when we heard tires squealing in the drive. John seemed rather agitated. "That would be . . . my son, Jack. Apparently he has decided to join us."

The large entry door burst open. A nice-looking, meticulously dressed man, probably close to six feet tall, medium build, black hair, a little premature graying at the temples, entered the room. Jack was probably about my age, maybe a few years older.

"Sorry to just drop in like this, pop," he said, slurring his words. It was quite evident he had been drinking. "Introduce me to your friends."

We both shook hands with Jack as John introduced us as the leaders of the team that found the long-lost Ark of Noah.

Jack just nodded. "I thought you were the ones. I saw your pictures on television." Ignoring me, Jack smiled and took Ann's hand and held it . . . maybe a little too long.

"Please excuse my son's lack of manners, Dr. Lane," John said, obviously embarrassed.

"No problem," I replied.

Stephanie looked embarrassed and disgusted at Jack's behavior. She appeared shy, maybe uncomfortable to be here. She seemed to withdraw from her cousin Jack. Her long reddish-auburn hair was in a ponytail. The light blue sweatshirt she wore over her designer jeans concealed some of her shape, but her face was beautiful. All she needed was a smile. She was almost as tall as Ann . . . had green eyes and a clear, fair complexion.

John ushered us into a large comfortable living room. After we were seated and offered a refreshing drink, John initiated the conversation. He appeared to be a forceful man, but maybe milder now in his older years. He had thick gray hair and was a little overweight. "We feel so fortunate to have the two of you in our home. I was surprised and alarmed to see your pictures in the news today. Are you both okay?"

Ann and I looked at each other in surprise.

Ann said, a little apprehensively, "We didn't know we were in the news today. I guess we haven't seen the news."

"Yes," Jack said. "They showed some clips of the two of you that were taken earlier when you first discovered the Ark. The newscast said you came to Thailand for business and some sightseeing but had been abducted and held for ransom. It sounded like a terrible ordeal. The news reported that you had escaped and spent a terrifying night in the jungle." After a liquor-induced hiccup, a strange sneer-like smile formed around Jack's mouth as he paused waiting for one of us to reply.

We told them the same story that we had told the Thai police, leaving out the fact that I had killed four of them.

"That's terrible," Stephanie shyly responded. "Were you hurt or anything?"

"Do they know who did it?" Jack interrupted before we could answer Stephanie.

"They didn't know who abducted us as of yesterday," I replied.

"Luckily neither of us were badly injured," Ann said. "Just a few cuts and bruises."

"Oh look at your ankle. Was that from the chain? The news said you were chained," Stephanie asked showing concern.

"Yes," Ann replied.

"Maybe you should see a doctor. It looks swollen."

"Yes, I plan to go tomorrow. I think it looks worse this evening."

"I think it does too," I added. "We'll definitely see a doctor tomorrow."

Ann, not anxious to divulge any more details of our abduction, said, "Mr. Green, pardon me, but we are really anxious to see the table from the Ark."

"Of course you are, Ann, and please call me John." He started to get up from the couch. "But I must say after what you told me about your ordeal, I think you can be very glad that you two are still alive. Some areas have just recently become very dangerous. According to the news, there apparently is a ruthless renegade group preying on tourists. They have held several people for ransom. I've heard the family is contacted and warned not to call the police, or they will kill the hostage. Then they collect the ransom and kill the hostage anyway. It would be my guess they were going to try to hold you for ransom. If you had not escaped, they might have killed you."

I agreed. I didn't mention they were looking for a copy of an ancient parchment map that we had originally planned to have with us.

"Do you think you could find the location where you were being held?" Jack asked.

"I'm not sure. We may be able to retrace back from where we were picked up and find the general area. Then maybe we could find it from a plane," I replied.

"Are the police investigating?" Jack asked. "I mean, they have to catch these guys!"

"The police want us to take a plane ride out over the jungle to see if we can find where we were held."

"When are you going to do that?"

"They mentioned requisitioning a four-seat aircraft, but they said that might take a while. If Ann doesn't have a problem with her ankle, I may rent a plane myself and try to find where we were."

"Oh, do you fly?"

"Yes," I replied.

"How would you even know where to start looking?" Jack asked.

"I know it would be a long shot, but I'll try to find a certain waterfall at the end of a lake."

"I hate to disappoint you, Lane," he said sarcastically, "but this whole region is full of waterfalls flowing out of lakes. I wish you luck, but I think you would be wasting your time."

"Nothing ventured; nothing gained." Jack was getting under my skin.

A crack of thunder followed by a flickering of the lights shook the room as trees and bushes by the large windows were being whipped by the wind. Soon heavy rain pelted the landscape.

John crossed the room and looked out. "We're getting quite a storm," he said, "but that's not unusual for this time of the year. Well, now for the reason you came to see us . . . the table we have always believed came from Noah's Ark. Come, let's go take a look."

Excitedly, John led us to the next room which was full of archaeological treasures. The room itself was a small museum.

"This is our family collection," John said proudly. "It was all legally purchased, one piece at a time for over one-hundred and fifty years. It's all in my trust. It will go to Jack and Stephanie when I pass on."

We were amazed at how wonderfully displayed each piece was, much of it in illuminated glass enclosures. Our attention was drawn to the center of the room where a beautiful chandelier lit up a large marble base with a glass enclosure. Inside was an old heavy wooden table with six legs. An embossed sign stated, **"Table from Noah's Ark."**

Ann and I circled the display, closely surveying the artifact.

"The table has been in my family for as long as I can remember," remarked John. "I'm sure it is from the Ark. It's always been vacuum-sealed in this case to preserve it, and we keep a dark cover draped over the case. I removed it just before you arrived. I was told my great-grandfather bought it from an antique dealer in Russia in about nineteen-twenty."

Ann handed me the tape measure she had in her purse. With John holding one end of the tape, we carefully measured the spacing between the legs and compared them to the measurements on the card in my wallet. They didn't match exactly because of some warping, and we could only compare from outside the glass case, but there was little doubt in my mind that it really was the missing artifact from the Ark, probably removed by the Russian army in 1917. The color and the texture appeared to be the same as the six stubs that protruded from the rough timber of the Ark floor.

"So, Dr. Lane, do you believe this table really was removed from the living quarters of Noah's Ark?" John asked.

"From what I am seeing here, and these rough measurements, yes, I do," I replied. "Of course, it will have to be completely examined and analyzed by the experts in the lab. If you do indeed wish to relinquish the artifact for the price we agreed on, that would be wonderful."

"As you can imagine, Dr. Lane, we hate to part with it. It has been the centerpiece of our little museum for a long time, but we realize it should be displayed with the Ark. Therefore, we agree to the terms of the sale and the price."

Shaking John's hand, I said, "Thank you, all of you. I will see that a plaque is displayed next to the artifact when the exhibit is complete. The plaque will show it came from the Green family's private collection. I'll make arrangements to have it packaged and shipped as soon as you have received payment."

"Why were the legs cut off?" Stephanie asked, looking at me.

"Yes," John added, "I'd like to know that myself."

"Noah embedded the six vertical legs between the heavy floor timbers, then put the table top on. I'm sure he wanted something very stable the family could hold onto during a storm when the Ark was being tossed about. Whoever took the table from the Ark sawed the legs off down close to the floor to remove it. The table is very heavy. Pack animals would have been needed to get it off the mountain. That's why I believe the Russian army took the table when they took the photographs."

"That sounds like a logical conclusion," John remarked. "Come and sit back down. I was so surprised and pleased when I was informed the both of you, the ones who actually discovered Noah's Ark, were coming to see the table."

I glanced at Stephanie. She seemed fascinated by the conversation.

John said, "If you don't mind, I'd really like to know how you determined where to conduct your search for the Ark on such a large expanse of ice on Mount Ararat."

"I'll let Ann tell that story," I replied as the butler refreshed our drinks. "Without Ann, we would never have found it."

Ann smiled. "I'm afraid it is a very long story. Okay if I just give you a synopsis?"

"Yes, yes, that will be fine," John replied.

Jack seemed bored, but Stephanie was excited, leaning forward in anticipation.

"Well," Ann began, "I know you are familiar with the story about soldiers from the Russian army being sent to climb Mount Ararat in nineteen-sixteen. They were sent by the Czar of Russia to locate the Ark that had been spotted by a Russian aviator as he flew over Mount Ararat."

"Yes, of course, we're very familiar with the story." John nodded in agreement.

"I remember the story. It's a true story," Stephanie said. "The Russian soldiers actually found the Ark protruding from the ice. That summer had been unusually hot. A large portion of the glacier melted that year. They said the Ark was full of cages where the animals had been kept. They measured it, made drawings, and took photographs, but all the photographs, drawings and wood samples were lost in the Russian Revolution."

"That's right," Ann said. "You can find that story just by asking your phone about Russian soldiers finding Noah's Ark in nineteen-sixteen. The story has been in library books for years and also on the Internet. When my grandmother was a young girl in Russia, she discovered some of the photographs of Noah's Ark taken by that expedition. When I was twelve, she told me where they were hidden in Russia, but we couldn't go search for them. When I grew up, I became an archaeologist. I met Matthew, I mean Dr. Lane," she said smiling at me. "We went to Russia and found those photographs. When we were on Mount Ararat, we identified an outcropping of rocks that looked exactly like the rocks behind the Ark in one of the photographs." That's how we knew where to start looking. I'll let Matt tell the rest."

"Well, like Ann said, it is a long, and I might add, exciting story. It wasn't as easy as one might imagine, finding the Ark buried in the ice. With the help of the Turkish government, we built a complex of domed buildings on the glacier. Using some specifically designed tools to melt the ice, we finally uncovered the Ark. I'm sure you have heard the rest of the story."

I added, "One of the most gratifying things for me in our finding Noah's Ark was what the scientists discovered when they examined the animals' stalls. They confirmed what I had always taught in my class when I was teaching at the university. All the animals came to the Ark not long after they were weaned from their mothers. I always believed that was the only way the Ark story could have actually happened. Noah and his family didn't have to feed twelve-thousand-pound elephants, full-grown rhinoceros, or tall giraffes as they are always depicted in paintings. Small animals take up a lot less space and eat a lot less."

"Oh, I'd love to tell your story in a book, Dr. Lane," Stephanie exclaimed.

Blushing, she continued rather timidly. "I want to be a writer. I've taken classes in journalism. Has anyone ever written the whole story you two actually experienced?"

"Well, no. People have written newspaper articles so the story is known. But no one has written a book about our adventures."

"How long will the two of you be in Thailand?" Stephanie asked Ann.

"I'm afraid we'll only be here a few more days. I wish it were longer. I think it would be exciting to have our story told in a book."

Suddenly Jack, who appeared lethargic at times, blurted out, "My dad's brother was an archaeologist, wasn't he, dad?"

"Oh yes, my brother George. Yes, he spent years in the holy land searching for some lost Israelite treasure. He came back here every few years begging for money to continue his search. I never gave him any money, but my brother James, Stephanie's father, did. I always thought it was a big waste of time and money."

"Did he ever find anything?" Ann asked.

"No," John said. "He died trying, I guess. He just never came back from one of his trips."

"I was just a boy when Uncle George was back here visiting one time," Jack added, interested now. "I remember overhearing him tell Stephanie's dad that he had a lead on a map of some kind. He said he was sure it would lead him to the lost Israelite treasure. He was trying to get Uncle James to loan him money to buy the map. Has anyone ever found the Israelite treasure?" Jack asked.

"No one is really sure it actually exists," I replied.

"Oh, it exists all right," Jack said. "I've read a lot about it. The Ark of the Covenant is supposed to be buried with it." Jack was animated now. "I'd like to find it. The Ark of the Covenant is covered in pure gold. It would be worth a fortune. I know some people who would pay millions for it."

"Sell it? Sell the Ark of the Covenant? Why would you even think about selling such a treasure?" Demure Stephanie surprised us all with her outburst.

"Of course you wouldn't sell it, Jack," John added, "not the Ark of the Covenant. That belongs to the world, not in someone's private collection."

Jack, embarrassed at being chastised, glared at Stephanie. Then, attempting to reverse his comments, he said, "I was just kidding. Of course I would show it to the world. I might sell off some of the treasure. Just kidding again. But you have to admit, it would be tempting."

Ann and I smiled to cover our disdain at Jack's calloused attitude.

"Yes, I guess it would be tempting all right," I said. "Well, it looks like the storm is easing up. We should probably try to get to the resort before it starts again."

We thanked John for the opportunity to see and purchase the table and bid the family goodbye. The butler let us out, holding an umbrella over Ann all the way to the car.

It was quite dark as we drove back to the village. The streets were wet, covered with leaves that had blown onto the roadway. Many of the street lights were out. Soon we were in my room having coffee.

"Well, our mission has been accomplished," I said. "We have the table. I can't wait to see what the scientists in the lab think."

"Oh, it's wonderful, Matt," Ann said as she gave me a big hug.

We talked about the table for a while. Later I changed the subject.

"What do you think, Ann? If Jack found the treasure, do you think he would really try to sell it to the highest bidder?"

"I think he was just kidding, Matt."

"What about the Ark of the Covenant? He seemed pretty excited about all the gold the box is decorated with."

"I know he had to be kidding about selling the Ark of the Covenant. Who would sell that? It should be displayed for everyone to see. I'm sure he wasn't serious, Matt."

"Well, maybe it was just that he was sky-high on drugs and booze," I said.

"Well, he was drunk all right, but what makes you think he was also on drugs?"

"I saw him wipe white powder from under his nose as he came through the door."

"Really?" Ann said. "I didn't notice."

"Well, I saw it. And he was serious about selling the Ark until he realized we all were staring at him, and Stephanie chastised him. He acted really strange. Not only strange, but it was very apparent he couldn't take his eyes off you."

"Who me? I didn't notice," Ann grinned. "Why, Dr. Lane, are you jealous?"

But before I could answer, she said. "Talk about strange. I thought Stephanie acted strange. I really couldn't figure her out. Sometimes very withdrawn, and sometimes very bold. I was surprised she got so angry with Jack."

"I was surprised myself. I wonder what she is like when she's not at home with her uncle and cousin?"

"Why, Matt?" Ann said in mock surprise, feigning a little jealousy. "Did you find her attractive?"

"No! . . . Well, even you have to admit she is attractive. But no! I was just curious. I'm only interested in one girl, and she is sitting next to me right now."

"You better say that," she said, arching her eyebrows. "By the way, can we still do some sightseeing after we get our shopping done?"

"Absolutely. I'm looking forward to it . . . right after we get you to see a doctor."

"Do I have to, Matt? Maybe it will be better in the morning."

"If it's not a lot better, we're taking you to see a doctor. No arguments."

"Okay, if you say so, Dr. Lane. But first, doctor, how about kissing your patient good night?" she teased.

I wasted no time.

"Breakfast at eight?" she asked, as she headed for her room next door.

"I'll knock on your door."

"Don't be late," she said teasing as she gave me a hug and another warm kiss. "Good night."

I noticed Ann limping a lot as she left.

* * * * *

This is rather strange, I mused as I got ready for bed. The lost Ark of the Covenant to me is the most coveted of all the biblical artifacts. I have fantasized my whole adult life about being on the team that finally found it.

During all those years I have never heard of an ancient map that would supposedly lead to the lost treasure of Israel and the Ark of the Covenant . . . at least not one I considered authentic. Now if what Jack heard Stephanie's father say many years ago is true, maybe two maps exist. It seems unusual that the family who had the table from Noah's Ark would also have a family member who was searching for the same thing I am . . . the Ark of the Covenant. Then again, maybe that's not so strange. John's brother, George, was an active archaeologist, just like I am. What may be strange is that the men who abducted Ann and me are trying to get their hands on the map Dr. Ira Jensen, the curator of the university museum, discovered and purchased. I wonder what happened to George Green and the map he had a lead on. Did the lead turn out to be nothing? Did George really die in Israel?

I couldn't sleep. I lay there remembering.

Ann and I had originally planned to take a copy of an ancient parchment map with us on our trip. We were going to enjoy a few days of sightseeing and then meet with John Green to see if the old table he owned was actually from Noah's Ark. From Thailand we were to fly to Israel and see if the old map could lead us to the ancient lost Israeli treasure.

Things changed. We didn't bring the map with us. Ira, the man I and Jim Morgan work for, said he was beginning to believe his map might not be authentic. He needed more time to study it. Ann and I were looking for any excuse to spend time together, and we already had our plane tickets, so we came on ahead without the map.

Ira was sure he would know within a few days if the map was real. At that time a copy would be brought to Israel by my best friend, Jim Morgan. Ann and I would meet Jim, and our next adventure would begin. Somehow, someone knew we would be carrying that valuable ancient map. They just didn't know that at the last minute Ira changed our plans and we didn't bring it.

I tried several times to call Ira. He was still in an area where he didn't have a cell phone signal. I needed to warn him that he might have a spy on his payroll!

CHAPTER SIX

The light blue water in the pool was crystal clear. It was a beautiful morning. We smiled at each other as we listened to the laughter of children playing in their own shallow pool.

"Sounds like the little kids are having a good time," Ann said, as she limped from our table to a lounge chair. "I loved breakfast by the pool. It was scrumptious."

I sat down on the edge of her lounge chair and started applying some suntan lotion to her shoulders. "Scrumptious? My breakfast was fabulous, that's even better than scrumptious." That made Ann laugh. Looking at her ankle, I asked, "How's the ankle this morning? I hate to say this, but it doesn't look like it's getting much better."

"My ankle is going to be just fine. I'm doing everything the doctor told me to do. He said it would take a few days. I just have to use the crutches around here and stay off it as much as possible, and I can't get in the water. What a bummer. I'd love to take a swim right now."

"I don't think so. You're also supposed be lying down and keeping it elevated."

"Oh, I will soon, but not right now. Bangkok was so much fun, so magical. Matt, those neat little tuk-tuks would take you anywhere you wanted to go. And what a city to shop in. . . . by the way, how do you like your new watch?"

"I like it."

"I love mine. Thank you for buying it for me. You didn't need to. I could have bought my own watch."

"I wanted to buy it for you. I like buying you things," I said, taking her hand.

"I could get used to all this attention, you know," she said with a flirtatious grin.

"The same goes for me," I said. "I'm glad you enjoyed the shopping. The highlight for me was the bridge on the River Kwai."

"Oh yes. I'm so glad we went through the cemetery and the memorial to all those soldiers who died building that railroad. Thank you for staying another day and taking me to all those places."

"You're welcome, but we probably should have waited until your ankle got better."

"Well, do I look like I'm sick?" she asked as she posed in her new bathing suit, covering her swollen ankle and some scratches on her leg with a towel.

"No, you look sexy and gorgeous."

"Thank you. I had to fish for that compliment, but I'll take it."

"I'm sorry. I was busy thinking."

"Thinking about what?"

"About how I'm going to hold onto such a beauty as you. All the men around this pool keep glancing at you. If I were to leave for a few minutes, I'd probably have to fight to get my seat back."

"Oh really? I hadn't noticed," she teased. "Besides I'm the one who should worry. No one I see around here can compete with your physique. But I see some pretty girls who would love to be right where I'm sitting."

I hadn't been kidding about a lot of men wanting to meet Ann. With her long dark hair, big brown eyes, and drop-dead, stunning figure, she was exciting to look at. Her new cream-colored two-piece bathing suit highlighted her dark complexion.

Ann never returned anyone's admiring gaze, but I felt a pang of jealousy each time some good-looking guy glanced at her. I moved closer and kissed her.

"Wow," she said. "That was nice, but a little unusual for you. You're usually not that affectionate in public."

"Just claiming my territory," I said, grinning as I released her. "Just in case any of these guys are hoping I'm your brother."

Ann laughed out loud.

A waiter approached with a phone and plugged it into a phone jack. "This call is for you, Dr. Lane."

* * * * *

"Dr. Lane, I'm so glad you haven't left the country yet. This is Stephanie Green."

"Hi, Stephanie. No, I think we will be here for at least another week while Ann's ankle heals. What can I do for you?"

"Will you and Ann be at the lodge this afternoon?" she asked. "I need to ask a big favor."

"Yes, we'll be here. Would you like to join us for an early dinner?"

"Could I just come to your room about five instead?" was the stammering reply.

Promptly at five Stephanie arrived at my door. She nervously looked both ways down the hall before she entered.

Stephanie was dressed much like the first day we met her, hair in a ponytail and designer jeans. This time her sweatshirt was dark blue. With so much red in her hair, I expected a few freckles, but there were none.

Ann had come over earlier from her room.

When Stephanie saw Ann's ankle, she was very concerned. Ann assured her she was getting better.

"What can we do for you, Stephanie?"

"Well," she hesitated, "I don't want to get you involved in my personal problems, but I am desperate. First, I probably need to tell you a little bit about my family. Everyone always wants to know how we came to be living in Thailand. Foreigners can't buy land in Thailand, you know."

"Yes, I know they can't buy land. How did the Green family become land owners in Thailand?"

"Let me start at the beginning. I was seven years old when I came to live with my aunt and uncle, John and Marie. Uncle John has always been overly strict with me. Before that I lived with my mother and father, James and Amy, on some land a few miles from here. My Aunt Marie . . . she's dead now . . . told me my grandparents were very wealthy. They apparently owned a big ranch and oil wells somewhere in the United States . . . Texas, I think. They came here as tourists and ended up becoming partners with some Thai people who were trying to develop a tin mine. The Thai family needed money to buy the land. The government owned the land and needed money. Through some political maneuvering, a deal was struck. The Thai family could buy the land, and they could have a foreign partner. The government also wanted the mine developed for the tax money. So my grandfather became one of the few foreigners allowed to buy land in this area, and there were no restrictions on how much he could buy as long as he had a Thai partner. As the mine became more and more prosperous and land was cheap, he bought a lot of it. Later he bought out his Thai partners in the mine, and the government didn't complain. He became very wealthy, and the Thai government made a lot of money. This was in the 1940's and early 1950's.

"When he died . . . before I was born . . . all the land was divided between his three sons. Uncle John was the oldest, so he got the mine. My father, James, and my uncle, George, both got undeveloped jungle, but also received a nice sum of money every year from their share in the mine.

"Unfortunately, some time in the nineties the tin played out, and they had to close the mine. We moved to a bamboo hut on the land my father owned. The hut was on a bank next to a large river. There was a tall rock cliff on one side of our hut. I remember my father telling me we also owned a lot of land up on the plateau above the cliff. I think my father farmed the land up there.

"What happened to your parents?" I asked her.

"When I was seven, my mother and father were murdered."

"Murdered?"

"Uncle John doesn't believe me, but I know they were murdered. One of the men came in my room. Someone I couldn't see told him to kill me. But I hid on top of a clothes bureau. After the men left, I went into my parents' room. I remember trying to wake them up. Their pillows and bed sheets were red with blood. My mother had a gash in her head. Then a herd of elephants were stampeded through the bamboo hut. I remember all the details now. For years I was so traumatized by what happened that night that they say I didn't even talk for over a year."

Stephanie was crying now. Stopping for a minute, she apologized, dried her eyes, and then continued.

"Someone found me after several days and nights alone in the jungle and brought me to live with my aunt and uncle. Shortly after I came to live with them, my aunt died. As I grew older, the memory of that night slowly returned. Once when I was about ten, I tried to tell my uncle that I remembered seeing my mother and father lying in their bedroom, covered in blood before the elephants ran through the hut. I also heard men shooting guns and driving the elephants toward our hut before it was destroyed. But he scolded me and told me they died in an accident. He said the elephants probably stampeded because of a bad lightning and thunderstorm, and I was never to talk about it again. I don't know how I escaped being killed. Just a few months ago, a vague memory of me being in a cave surfaced. I was cold, and it rained and rained. I remember there was a cave in a vine-covered rock cliff not far from our bamboo hut. My father used to keep a storage box on a rock shelf in that cave. I've never told anyone about the cave or my father's metal box. I remember hiding in that cave while it rained."

Ann and I were listening intently.

"As I got older, I began to think maybe I might legally own the land that my father had accumulated. I got up the nerve to ask Uncle John about that when I turned twenty-one."

"What did he say?" I asked.

"He said he was sorry he had to tell me, but my father had borrowed a lot of money from him and couldn't pay it back, so Uncle John owned the land now. He showed me a paper with my dad's signature where he had borrowed fifty-thousand dollars with the land as collateral. End of discussion!

"I didn't dare challenge him further. However, I remember a cake and a celebration. I'm sure the celebration was because my dad had paid off a big loan and actually owned the land. I've been thinking a lot about that. Maybe my father paid off the note he owed Uncle John."

Stephanie paused while we tried to absorb the incomprehensible tale of her childhood memories.

"But now comes the big favor." Her pleading eyes were glued to mine. "I hate to ask."

"Ask away," I said, knowing I was caught up in the tale of intrigue. I couldn't refuse any request. At this juncture, Stephanie was a waif-like child in a woman's body.

"I need someone to take me out there. I need to see where it all happened. I need to see if there really is a cave. If I can find the cave, maybe I can find my father's metal box. If I wasn't dreaming all this, I'll find it up high on a rock shelf in that cave."

"Haven't you ever been back?" I asked.

"No, never. I've wanted to go, but my uncle said it's better to let those old memories die. When I was a teenager, I tried again to tell my Uncle John, but he didn't want to listen or believe it. He told me I was watching too many TV shows and imagining things. He said my parents' bodies were examined before they were buried, and the coroner found no knife or gunshot wounds. They were just crushed by a herd of elephants. It was just a terrible accident, he said."

"Didn't you ever drive out there yourself and try to find the cave?"

"No, I don't drive. My cousin Jack convinced my uncle not to teach me. He insists that it's too dangerous for women to drive in this country . . . one more way of controlling me. I had almost convinced Uncle John to let me try to get a job at a local store so I could at least learn to take care of myself, but Jack talked him out of it. He said it would be degrading to the family. I don't know exactly where we used to live, but I think if you would drive me out in that area, I could find it. I remember a special mailbox built like a boat where you turn off the main road that leads to our property. It wasn't our mailbox. It was a long way from our place, but if it's still there, I think I can find the road to our land. Uncle John is going out of town for two weeks. And Jack has his own apartment. I don't see him very often. John is leaving in the morning. I was hoping maybe the three of us could drive there tomorrow? I could call you when he's gone, and maybe you could pick me up on the corner so the servants don't see me leave. I'm sorry, I know I am being very presumptuous. This is such an imposition on your time, but I have no one to turn to!" Tears had flooded Stephanie's eyes as she shared her horrific experience with us.

"Of course, Matt can take you out there, Stephanie. I won't be able to go. I'm supposed to be keeping my foot elevated, but Matt will take you," Ann said.

"Are you sure?"

"Yes, of course," I said. "I'd be glad to drive you out there. Can I drive you home tonight?"

"No, thank you," she insisted. "If they find out I was here or I've asked you to help me, they will be very upset. I just need to go out and see for myself where it happened. And I am hoping I can find my dad's old metal box."

* * * * *

Before I fell asleep, the horror of Stephanie's story reverberated through my mind. I wished Ann was well enough to go with us. Tomorrow could be interesting. I wondered if there was anything left out there to find.

CHAPTER SEVEN

I pulled up to the corner a block from the entrance to the Green residence. Waiting there for me was Stephanie. She was prepared for our day's excursion into the jungle and had on sturdy hiking boots. Her khaki shirt and shorts complemented the reddish-auburn ponytail protruding from her baseball cap. As she opened the passenger door and slid into the seat, she smiled. She was very attractive even in the ball cap, and the smile was a great improvement.

"You'll have to excuse me, Dr. Lane. I'm just so excited," she said turning toward me. "I've been dreaming about this day since I was a young girl. I guess I'm scared and anxious at the same time."

"I'm sure you are, Stephanie. By the way, just call me Matt."

"Okay, Matt."

We drove for almost an hour, first on a busy four-lane highway, then on a two-lane paved road, and now on a gravel road. Only an occasional modest house dotted the countryside.

Stephanie had brought a map of the general area, but I could see she was confused and getting discouraged.

"I'm sorry this is taking so long, Dr. Lane . . . I mean Matt. I think we are in the right neighborhood where I used to see the boat-shaped mailbox, but I just can't find it."

"We've plenty of time, Stephanie. I'm sure if it's still there, we'll find it. I see a small neighborhood gas station just ahead. Let's get a Coke or something and take a short break. We can ask the owner if he knows where there is a boat-shaped mailbox."

Twenty minutes later we were turning off the main road by the old boat-shaped mailbox. A customer in the gas station had told us where it was.

With uplifted spirits, Stephanie directed me. "Turn here. . . . No . . . Sorry . . . Wrong turn. I think it's the next turn."

A half hour later and ten miles from the last residence, we were on a two-track road deep in the jungle. We came to a barbed-wire fence directly in front of us. Beyond the fence was a large field with a new crop.

"It looks like sugar cane," I said.

"Look," Stephanie pointed. "There's a gate into the field down there to the right."

She got out and walked to the gate and then came running back.

"This is it, Matt. The sign on the gate says, 'Green Family Farms Incorporated – Keep Out.'" Excited, Stephanie jumped back in the vehicle. "Turn left."

There wasn't much of a road, only dense jungle on the left and the fenced crop on the right. We drove for almost a mile along an overgrown dirt roadbed that hadn't seen a vehicle for years. Abruptly, the fence stopped at the edge of a cliff. Below the cliff to the right was a beautiful valley. A wide, slow-moving river curved in a half circle, running roughly parallel to the vertical cliff face, with jungle beyond. I could see an area between the river and the cliffs that had long ago been cleared of all trees and vegetation. The jungle was now trying to reclaim the virgin soil.

"There it is!" Stephanie exclaimed breathlessly. "In that clearing between the river and the rock cliff."

I shifted the Grand Cherokee into low four-wheel drive and headed down the old road, sliding in the loose gravel and bouncing over deep ruts formed after years of eroding rainwater. Slowly, I eased the car down the treacherous trail.

"There hasn't been anyone down here for a long time," I said. "I don't think it can even be called a road anymore."

"My dad had an old Willys' Jeep. Otherwise we couldn't have gotten out after a rain."

Finally we got to the bottom. The lush valley was wide and long with jungle-covered mountains on each side. This area was not fenced, but there was an old dried-out fence post with a wooden sign hanging at an angle. I stopped the Jeep, and Stephanie jumped out and ran to it. The letters were badly faded. She shouted, "It says 'James and Amy Green.'"

I could see Stephanie starting to cry as she tried to straighten the old sagging sign nailed to the post. She walked back to me, drying her tears.

"This is one beautiful area," I said.

"Yes, it is a large plot of land."

Grass and bushes were knee-high. The rock cliff was covered with vines. It was probably two hundred feet up to the plateau above where the crop was growing on the Green family farm.

Suddenly Stephanie saw something she recognized and started running across the open area toward the base of the rock wall. Grabbing a machete from the back seat, I followed her.

"There it is," she pointed. "Just this side of that rock wall is where our hut was."

The morning had been sunny and beautiful, almost too hot. But now the sky was starting to turn cloudy and dark as a storm approached.

"We'll have to hurry. I think it's going to rain."

"Oh no," Stephanie said. "I need to spend some time here. I need to heal some old wounds."

As we approached the area, we saw what used to be a kitchen stove lying in the weeds. Stephanie immediately remembered the stove. Then we found part of the original bamboo floor. It was covered with a tangle of vines and shreds of old dried-up bamboo stalks. Some of the posts that held the floor of the hut up were still standing, one end embedded in the ground. Parts of the bamboo walls were lying on the ground, and grass was pushing up through the bleached yellow poles. Stephanie reverently walked the area, pointing out where each of the rooms had been. A melancholic pause crept into her mood as she recalled where her parents' bedroom had been.

Off in the brush, I saw a broken, wooden headboard. Not wanting to contribute to Stephanie's heartache, I didn't draw her attention to it, in case it was from her parents' bed.

Stephanie spotted her old wardrobe closet laying on its back in the grass, both the doors gone and nothing in it but dirt and weeds. She sat down and started to cry again as she picked up a rusted flashlight, the corroded batteries protruding out the open end, the glass lens discolored and broken. I put my arm around her shoulder.

"This was my dad's flashlight," she sobbed, "and that old overstuffed chair is where he always sat."

After a few minutes, attempting to distract her from those sad memories, I asked, "Where is the cave, Stephanie?"

Wiping away the tears with her shirttail, she laid the flashlight on a rock and walked toward the vertical rock cliff. It was so covered with vegetation we could barely see the reddish-brown rock wall. She followed the wall a few yards and said, "It was in this area somewhere."

It had grown darker now, and the wind was getting stronger, swirling leaves and dust all around us. I began hacking through the thick tangle of vines searching for the cave. For the best part of a half hour, we continued to spread the vertical roots and vines apart. Then miraculously, there it was . . . a natural opening in the rock.

The entrance was about four feet wide at the bottom, tapering to a point at the top about seven feet up. I pushed and tore the vines enough for us to squeeze through the opening. The interior was very dark. I turned on the small LED flashlight I had in my pocket. The rock roof varied between twelve and fifteen feet in height, while the cave was about twelve feet wide and twenty feet deep. The irregular rough floor was part rock and part dirt.

"Up there, Matt," Stephanie said excitedly, pointing to a natural rock ledge about eight feet above the floor. "Just as I remembered."

I turned my light to the area Stephanie indicated. Under the rock shelf was a large boulder.

I stepped up on the boulder. Pulling myself up, I shined my light into the space. An explosion of wind and feathers, punctuated with a loud screech, startled me. Instinctively I ducked and slipped off the rock as Stephanie screamed, and I collapsed on top of her on the cave floor. The bird squawked and flew around until it finally escaped out through an opening in the vines. A bit chagrined by my less than machismo response, I pulled Stephanie to her feet and stammered a quick apology before climbing back up on the boulder.

Cautiously, I examined the area on top of the ledge. Under a pile of leaves and bird feathers, I spotted an old metal box. Lifting it down, I placed it on the boulder.

Now it was raining outside and we could hear thunder. Flashes of lightning lit up the entrance through the vines.

"It's the rainy season, Matt," Stephanie said. "Hopefully it will stop in a few minutes." She knew I was concerned about getting back up on the high road.

The box had an opening for a key, but it wasn't locked, and wasn't hard to open.

On top was an old, yellowed letter. The postmark was from Israel. It was addressed to James Green at a post office box. The return address was from George Green in Jerusalem.

Under the letter were five abstracts showing James had owned several parcels of land. I figured it probably included the land we were on and the land being farmed on top.

The next envelope was from a bank in Bangkok. It was a copy of the loan for $50,000. Stephanie was right. John Green had loaned her father, James, $50,000 to be paid back with interest. The bottom of the document was stamped, **Paid In Full**. It was signed, dated, and notarized by someone at the bank.

Also in the box was a will, drawn up by a law firm in Bangkok.

I studied the document.

"Well it looks like you own quite a lot of property, Stephanie."

"I do?" she asked in amazement.

"The will looks perfectly legal to me," I said. "The abstracts for the land are all in your father's name, and you are named as the beneficiary in his will."

"But what about the loan? Uncle John said he owns the land because my father never paid back the fifty-thousand dollars he owed."

"Unless there was another loan, and there are no papers showing another loan, your father paid your uncle back the entire fifty-thousand dollars."

"That's wonderful." Stephanie clapped her hands in glee. Then she hesitated. "But that means Uncle John has been lying to me all this time."

"It kind of sounds like it. We'll have time to check it out before he gets back."

"Oh, will you help me, Matt?"

"Of course I will, Stephanie."

"I'd really appreciate that," she said smiling at me.

At the bottom of the box was an old bank book. It was a register for a savings account. The bank was the same one that had notarized the paid in full document. There was $12,212 in the account.

"If your uncle hasn't drawn the money out of the account, I would say you just got your ticket out of his house."

"Oh Matt, this is so unbelievable!" Jubilantly, she put her arms around me and gave me a big hug. Tears of joy filled her eyes. "I'm so happy," she said. "I'll never be able to thank you for what you've done."

We read the letter from her uncle George.

After reading the old letter, I looked at Stephanie. "Do you know if your uncle ever arrived?"

"I have no idea. My parents were murdered the night they received this letter. I remember them arguing about the letter. Uncle John thinks he died in Israel. I don't think anyone knew Uncle George was coming home."

It had stopped raining. As we exited the cave, Stephanie had one last look around. She said, "See that dense jungle area down there on this side of the river . . . just beyond the grassy area?"

My eyes followed her gaze.

"I was chased by an elephant down there. I was never so scared in my life."

She stood and looked at the area for a long time, reminding me that was the same day her parents were murdered.

I helped her get the corroded batteries out of the old flashlight, and she took it with her. I put the old metal box in the car.

Slipping and sliding and throwing a lot of mud, the 4 x 4 Cherokee made the precarious climb back to the top of the plateau. It was late in the afternoon. At the highway, we stopped for a quick snack.

"I don't dare bring the box home with me, Matt. What can I do with it?" Stephanie asked.

"If you like, I'll keep it for you. If you don't mind, I'd like to show the letter from your Uncle George to Ann. Then I'll put it all in the hotel safe."

"I don't mind at all if you show it to her. I just appreciate you keeping it for me."

I drove Stephanie to the place I had picked her up. When I stopped, she smiled at me. "You're a wonderful guy, Matt. I wonder if Ann has any idea how lucky she is."

"I think I'm the lucky one," I said. "But thank you for the compliment."

"I mean every word of it, Matt." She leaned over the center console and kissed me on the cheek.

Stephanie opened the door, turned, and said, "Can I call you tomorrow? Or do you need a day off before we check those things in Bangkok?"

"Why don't you call me tomorrow afternoon. I'll make some appointments in the morning, and we'll go to Bangkok the next day. Maybe Ann will be well enough to go with us."

"Yes, maybe she will. Tell her I hope she's feeling better. Goodbye, Matt, and thank you again."

"Goodbye, Stephanie."

As I drove back to the lodge, I began to think . . . What happened to her Uncle George? No one knew he was coming home. Stephanie's parents died before he was to arrive, but he probably didn't know that. His brother John said George died in Israel. Was he lying? I wonder what happened to George and that map?

CHAPTER EIGHT

During the next week and a half, I drove Stephanie to Bangkok several times.

Ann still had a serious infection in her ankle. Despite taking antibiotics and doing everything the doctor told her to do, it was slow to respond to treatment. I was quite concerned, but at least she didn't have tetanus from the rusty chain. She insisted I take Stephanie and help her get everything done to claim her legal inheritance before her uncle came back.

"I had a visitor today," Ann told me.

I was helping Ann fix a meal for us in the kitchenette in her room. She used her crutch to limp to the small table.

"Really?"

"Yes, while you and Stephanie were having fun in Bangkok," she smiled shyly, teasing, "Jack Green brought me flowers."

"Oh, he did?" I replied with trepidation.

"Yes, they are beautiful. Didn't you see them?"

"Well, I did notice a bouquet of flowers, but I thought the lodge sent them. The staff is always doting on you, trying to please you. Don't think I haven't noticed the bellboys. They make every excuse they can to come in. They have to fix this or adjust that. They just want to see you. It's because you're so beautiful."

"Maybe they think I'll tip them well," she chuckled.

"Nope. They know I'll do the tipping when we leave here. They just want a glimpse of you. . . . What did Jack have to say?"

"He heard I was still having trouble with my leg and just stopped to see how I was doing. He's quite charming and very good-looking, even though he's a maverick."

"I wonder how he knew you were still having trouble with your leg? . . . Did he ask where I was?"

"Yes, I told him you were in Bangkok on business."

"Did he mention Stephanie?"

"No, and I didn't either. Matt, do you really believe everything Stephanie told us is true? I mean she said her Uncle John and Jack wouldn't let her do anything. They don't seem the type to me. Maybe she's exaggerating."

"I don't think so," I said.

"In fact, I don't think she told us everything. Some of the things she says don't add up . . . like she's holding some things back."

"Anyway, I'm back. If Jack shows up again, I will expect you to tell him you're already spoken for and throw him out." I smiled as I said it.

"I will not!" she said. "You're never around anymore. I get lonesome."

"One or two more days and I think Stephanie will have her business done. I've also been teaching her to drive. I think she could pass the driving test now."

"Good. Then I can have you back? I think my ankle is responding to treatment finally."

"I hope so. You've had me worried. Maybe we can do some more sightseeing when the doctor releases you. . . . By the way, was Jack doped up?"

"Well, I didn't want to mention it to you, but since you asked, yes he was. In fact, he tried to kiss me."

"You're kidding!"

"I just moved away from him, and then he left."

"I think Jack could be dangerous, Ann. Watch out for him."

"I can take care of myself," she haughtily replied.

* * * * *

A few days later Ann, Stephanie, and I had reservations for dinner in the restaurant at the lodge. Ann and I were seated at a table on the terrace. The sunset was remarkable. Ann looked stunning in her cream-colored sheath dress.

When Stephanie walked in, she waved at us from across the room. We were both astonished to see the transformation from an awkward adolescent to a stunning woman. It was the first time we had seen her in anything other than jeans or shorts. Heads turned as she crossed the room. The bright aqua, knee-length skirt and colorful blouse with jewelry to match complimented her long reddish auburn hair which fell in waves over her shoulders and down her back.

Ann turned to me before Stephanie reached our table. "Matt, why didn't you tell me she could look so beautiful?"

"I didn't know," I stammered.

"I haven't seen Stephanie since she came to ask for help almost two weeks ago. She didn't look like this that day," Ann said, giving me an inquisitive look.

I couldn't believe how much the two women resembled each other. Ann stood to shake Stephanie's hand, and I caught myself comparing them. Both were unusually lovely. They looked about the same age, although Stephanie was twenty-three and Ann twenty-nine. Ann's hair was a dark, shiny auburn-brown. Stephanie's hair was also auburn, but in the light a lot of red dominated it. Ann's complexion was smooth and blemish-free, a few shades darker than Stephanie's. Stephanie didn't have Ann's delicate features, but she had a well-sculptured face and full lips. Ann had enticing large brown eyes while Stephanie's eyes were a bright shade of green. At 5'10", Ann was a little taller than Stephanie. They both had narrow waists and shapely hips. Ann was the more beautiful of the two women. I had never seen anyone as beautiful as Ann Tyler, but Stephanie was certainly a great runner-up.

"With you two lovely ladies, I'll be in the envy of every man at the lodge," I said as we sat down.

"Thank you, Matt," they said in unison.

"Oh, I'm so glad your ankle is better, Ann," Stephanie said.

"No happier than I am," Ann laughed. "I love your outfit, Stephanie, and your jewelry matches the color of your blouse. It's beautiful."

"Thank you. Didn't Matt tell you he helped me pick it out?"

"No, he failed to mention that," Ann said as she looked at me a little accusingly.

Just in time, the waiter came to take our order.

While waiting for dinner, I asked, "Stephanie, can you think of anything else we can help you with?"

"Well, you helped me hire a lawyer. He proved my parents' will was valid. The banker didn't know of any other loans to my father and verified that fifty-thousand dollars was paid to my Uncle John. John still does all his banking there as far as the banker knew. The lawyer helped me claim my father's savings account. With all those years of interest, it had grown to almost twenty-five thousand dollars. That's how I was able to buy these new clothes. I also put a down payment on the new car you helped me pick out."

She smiled at Matt. "Oh, and Matt taught me to drive. I just passed my driver's test today. Now I have my license, and I am driving my new car." She smiled at me again and said, "You two will have to forgive me. I'm just so happy. Thank you, Matt," she said, looking adoringly at me. "You've been so wonderful to me. Oh, and thank you, Ann, for being so patient. I'm sorry I took up so much of Matt's time. I can't think of anything else I need help with, and I can't thank you both enough."

"Your lawyer felt sure he will have no trouble getting all the land your parents owned transferred to your name, Stephanie," I said. That will make you quite a wealthy woman."

"I know," Stephanie said excitedly.

"I'm sure your uncle and your cousin, who obviously had someone farming that land for years and telling you they had legal right to it, are not going to be happy when they learn what has transpired."

"I know. They will be furious. I don't mind admitting I'm scared, but I wouldn't change what I've done with your help for anything. I'll just face them and ask Uncle John why he has been lying to me all these years. But I swear I will never be their slave again."

"Ann and I will be here at the lodge for a few more days. We're going to do some research to see if your uncle ever arrived in Thailand and got his plane out of storage. If you want me to be with you at your house when John comes home, I'll be glad to. In fact I think I should be. I can help explain everything."

"No, no thank you. I'll be all right. I'd rather face him alone. If we can't settle our problems, I can now drive. I still need a lot more practice, but I can drive and I have my own money. I'll just move out. But thank you for offering."

"Let me know if you change your mind," I told her.

I was worried about Stephanie. If her Uncle John had been stealing from her all these years, things could get difficult when she confronted him with the truth.

CHAPTER NINE

"I didn't know there were so many small airports around Bangkok. We should have gone to the last one on our list first," I said, grinning. Ann and I were just finishing lunch. "Well, at least we know George did pick up his plane. He didn't file a flight plan, but we know he was heading for the private airstrip. The logbook noted he took his plane out of the storage hangar and took off just before dark in a light rain. If there was a light rain in Bangkok, it could've been raining hard fifty miles away at the airstrip."

"Could his plane have crashed, Matt?"

"I don't know. It's possible. If he landed and learned about James and Amy, he would surely have stayed for the funeral and helped search for Stephanie. No one ever searched for his plane. The only two people who knew he was coming were already dead. He took his plane out of storage July twenty-fourth. His lease on the hangar space was up in about two weeks, and no one reported him missing. The person who leased him the hangar space probably assumed he rented space somewhere else. I'm surprised they kept the rental records that many years back, but I'm glad they did," I said. "And now that I really think about it, I guess it is quite possible that his plane did crash. If George rented a hangar in another airport sixteen years ago, then returned to Israel and died there, he wouldn't have paid his hangar rent. I doubt they would have sold his airplane to collect a few hundred dollars' rent. I think they would have tried to contact some of George's family. They could have easily found John Green. John didn't know George even owned that plane, or he would have known his brother probably died in a plane crash somewhere around Bangkok, not in Israel."

"And what about the landing strip George asked his brother to prepare?" Ann asked excitedly. "James died the night he got the letter."

"You're right. That runway could have been in such bad shape that George couldn't land. It probably hadn't been used since he landed there the last time. It could've been full of ruts from all the rain out there plus tall bushes and weeds. George only had his landing lights to see the runway. One other thing to consider," I added. "His plane hadn't been flown in a long time. I'm sure he would have checked his fuel gauge, but the fuel could've been old. It's called pure speculation, but any one or all of those factors could have brought that plane down. He may have been trying to find another place to land in the dark and the rain and ended up crashing."

"You're right," Ann added. "It's all just speculation. But if he didn't crash his plane, where is it?"

"Yes, where is it? We know he didn't crash in Bangkok," I replied. "And small planes would probably follow the highway if they were flying over the jungle. If anyone found the crash site, they would have notified his brother, John. The area along the highway between Bangkok and the village is pretty densely populated. Maybe he didn't crash until he was almost to the airstrip. It's not very populated out there, believe me," I said. "I'm pretty sure that old airstrip was up on the plateau where the Greens are now farming the land. There's plenty of room up there. It would be a perfect place for a private airstrip. It's a long shot, but if his plane did crash and we could find the wreckage, assuming it didn't burn, maybe we could find the map he had with him. It's worth spending some more time here. Are you okay with that?"

"Are you kidding?" Ann said. "What could be more fun than spending time together in this exciting place? Besides, I enjoy playing detective. Do we have any more clues?"

"Well, we have the map showing the location of all known crash sites in this area."

"Yes, but they have all been identified, and we know George's plane was not listed."

"Yes, but I need that list. I've got an idea that might work."

Ann quizzically looked at me. "This is getting intriguing. Are you going to let me in on your plan?"

"Well, tomorrow I'm going to start hanging out in the bars."

"You're what?" Ann exclaimed. "I thought you wanted to hang out with me."

"Oh, believe me, I much rather be with you, but this is real detective work."

"Maybe you'd better tell me more, Detective Lane."

"Okay. I'm going to buy a few drinks back in the village and try to make some acquaintances with the hunting and fishing crowd. I'll let it be known I'm looking for an old airplane that crashed. An anonymous person is offering a one-thousand-dollar reward for the recovery of the pilot's remains, and I'm willing to split the reward. His family would like to give him a proper burial. If anyone says they know of such a site, we'll check if it is a known crash site on our list. If it isn't, maybe it's the one we're looking for."

"You're a regular Sherlock Holmes."

"Well, pretty lady, that's just one of the many tricks I know. Stick with me, and I'll show you some real detective work."

"I'm already impressed," Ann laughed.

"I won't be telling a lie," I said as we got in the car. "If George did crash and we find him, I'm sure someone would like to see him properly buried. I'll pay for it myself if need be."

* * * * *

The old man was skinny, but strong. The long sinewy muscles flexed under the tanned skin. Many years in the sun had deepened the lines in his face, causing him to look older than he really was.

After hours of sitting in the same position, he felt the now familiar aches and pains in his back and legs as he moved to tie up his boat and step onto the dock. It had been a hot day on the river, but the old fisherman had caught all the fish he needed. He walked the gravel path to the small frame house where he lived alone.

Jacob Hanover liked where he lived. He had been living here for years, no close neighbors and right on the river where he fished every day. He cleaned his catch and put them on ice in plastic trays in the bed of his old yellow pickup. Then he drove to the local fish market and sold his catch to one of the vendors for cash. Driving back to his neighborhood, he parked in front of the local watering hole, not too far from where he lived. He took a seat on his usual bar stool.

The big burly bartender smiled and said, "Hi, Jake. How's the fishing?" as he filled a mug and slid it down to him.

"Can't complain," Jake replied with his usual toothless grin. Then taking a big swig of the brew, he lit a cigarette.

Everyone who knew Jake liked him. He was always smiling and forever had a whopper of a tail to tell. Jake always just had a few beers, joked, and visited with the bartender or whomever was sitting close to him and then went home. The beer he drank in the evening never kept him from heading up river at the crack of dawn.

Today there was a buzz among some of his cronies about an American who was offering $500 if anyone knew where the crash site of a certain airplane could be found.

* * * * *

Three days had passed. About 8 p.m. the phone rang. The desk clerk told me there was a man in the lobby asking for my room number.

"It's okay, send him up," I said.

Answering the knock on the door, I was greeted by an old man with a sun-burnt face and scraggly, gray beard. I'd venture to guess he was in his late fifties or early sixties. He grinned at me, showing only four teeth, but his small squinty eyes were bright blue. He entered the room with his hat in his hand, a smoky aroma trailing behind.

"I understand someone is looking for a lost airplane," he said.

After inviting him to sit down, he asked if I might have a cold can of beer. I ordered one from room service, and it was delivered promptly.

"Do you know of an old crash site?" I asked.

"Maybe. What's in it for me, if you don't mind me asking?"

"Well," I said, "if it's a wreck that's not on this map, and if you would be willing to take us out to see it, I'll give you five-hundred dollars."

"Could you make it seven-hundred?" he asked. "And I get the money even if it's not the one you're looking for?"

Executing the bargaining skills I had acquired through my many travels, I countered with a six-hundred-dollar offer.

"It's a deal!" he replied with a grin of satisfaction.

The old man studied the map that showed all the old crash sites. "Nope, it's not anywhere near these places," he said.

* * * * *

By 10 a.m. the next morning, Jacob Hanover, myself, and Ann were in Jacob's old fourteen-foot aluminum boat with a forty-five HP Johnson motor creating a tall wake on the smooth river water. We were about fifteen miles south of the village. There were heavily entangled mangroves on each side of the river and jungle beyond that. The sun was bright, and it was getting hotter and more humid by the minute. The river was sixty to eighty feet wide and deep in some places. I could see the bottom through the clear copper-colored water.

"I'm surprised we haven't seen more large birds," Ann said.

"Wait 'til late afternoon. That's when they all come back to roost," muttered Jacob.

We had been on the slow-moving river almost an hour. Jacob was a man of few words. He didn't speak unless he was asked a question.

"Is the wreck in the jungle or in this river?"

"It's in the river."

"Are we getting close?" I asked.

"Not much farther," Jacob replied.

"How long has the wreck been here?"

"Well, let's see," he said, scratching his ear. "I started fishing these waters maybe ten or twelve years ago. It's been here all of that time."

"How deep in the water is it?"

"It's pretty deep. It's right around the next bend."

Jacob cut the engine and dropped his anchor. When the boat stopped moving, we started looking down into the water.

"Over by the bank," Jacob said.

My eyes followed where he was pointing. Ann and I saw it at the same time . . . a silver fuselage down about ten feet, partly covered in moss and not easy to spot. The nose was pointing downstream on the right bank of the river.

Ann said, "It looks like it only has one wing and the tail is completely gone."

"George's plane was a Piper Comanche. I can't tell what kind of a plane this is from up here." Turning to Jacob, I said, "If you have a rope, I could tie it around my waist so the current wouldn't pull me past it. Then I could dive down and get a closer look."

"I wouldn't advise it, Mr. Lane."

"Why not?" I asked. "I've been watching for crocs, and I haven't seen one."

"Well, there are plenty of them in here . . . Big ones! I almost always see them. I don't know why we haven't seen any yet today. They usually hide back in the mangroves." He pulled up his anchor while he was talking. "Just a little farther around the curve there is a kind of clearing along the river. They sometimes lay on the bank in the sun. Let's just see."

He didn't start the motor. Instead, he let the boat drift downstream with the current.

"There . . . there they are!" Jacob waved toward the shore.

Ann gasped. "There must be ten of them!"

Some were just lying in the morning sun, but several were fighting over what was left of a large animal they had killed.

Jacob said, "They probably killed that cow when she came to get a drink. Now do you see why nobody would go in the water here? I doubt if anyone but me even fishes up here. I've never seen anyone else in all the years I've been fishing this part of the river."

"Well, it looks like they're all down here, and probably full from feasting on that cow. I've got to see that plane up close. I'll give you another hundred dollars if you'll help me."

"Okay by me. I can use the money, but don't say I didn't warn ya." Jacob shrugged his shoulders and gave me an incredulous glance as he added, "Can you pay me first?"

I peeled seven bills from my money clip and handed them to Jacob.

"No, Matt," Ann cried. "Don't go in that water. There's got to be another way."

Emptying my pockets, I placed the car keys and money clip in her trembling hand. "There is no other way, Ann."

Within ten minutes, I had on the fins and a snorkel mask I had brought with me. We anchored the boat upstream from the crash site. I tied the end of a long rope securely around my waist. After reassuring a very frightened and protesting Ann, I quietly slipped over the stern, took a deep breath of air, and dove down forty feet upstream of the aluminum fuselage. The current carried me to the back of the plane. Grabbing the door handle, I stood on the left wing. The door would not budge, and the glass windows were too dirty to see through. I let the current pull me to the front windshield. *Maybe this is a Piper Comanche*. The windshield was not broken, but I couldn't see through it either. The current was pulling me downstream, away from the airplane. Jacob and Ann, both holding the other end of the rope, were trying to judge how close to the windshield I was, but they were giving me too much slack.

I surfaced for air. "Hold me tighter to the plane." We devised some additional signals by tugging on the rope before I dived down again. This time I was able to get a grip and rubbed my forearm across the moss and film on the windshield. I cupped my hands tight to the glass and looked inside. Alarmed, I instinctively jumped back.

Staring at me was a skeleton, still sitting at the controls with the seatbelt on. Shreds of clothing were waving in the reduced current. The sight was eerie, but my lungs were about to burst. I had to surface again. After several deep breaths, I recovered from the shock and submerged back into the water. This time I saw a small suitcase on the seat next to the pilot.

At the same instant, the rope around my waist went taunt, and I was spiraling up toward the boat. Jacob and Ann were pulling me up backwards. To my right, I caught the splash of a crocodile swimming toward me. I broke through the surface, gasping for breath. Turning I grabbed the stern of the boat. Jacob and Ann dragged me up into the boat next to the motor. My legs were barely out of the water when the croc surfaced.

I laid in the bottom of the boat, choking and trying to catch my breath. Jacob got the rope off me, pulled up the anchor, and gave the old Johnson full throttle, heading quickly back up river. I was a bit bruised, but otherwise unharmed. That was close . . . too close!

I had to go back down to that old airplane, but I needed help. I knew exactly the person I would call.

CHAPTER TEN

He was a young man, thirty-one years old, six-foot-one and very muscular. Right at this moment, his powerful arms were straining to hold his one hundred and ninety pounds in a level position on a climbing rope. Sweat had matted the black curly hair on his forehead and was stinging his dark eyes. Rivulets were running down the neck of his shirt. Just a little lower now, and the layer of pottery shards would be at eye level.

Carefully he tugged on a large piece. The dirt it was buried in crumbled and fell into the deep canyon below. It was a large piece of a very old clay bowl. Excited, he carefully put the piece in his pouch. Digging into the deep layer of packed dirt with a screwdriver, more large shards were revealed, plus several pieces of bone. The layer of pottery shards extended far to his left and his right. This has to be an ancient dump site, evidence of a people who occupied this area thousands of years ago.

He was twenty feet down from the top of the cliff where his rope was tied to the front bumper of his Jeep. He knew this was a very important find judging from how far below the original level of the terrain he was. This could be the oldest site ever found.

Slowly he was extracting a piece of bone when the loud mechanical melody coming from the little black magic box on his belt broke the silence around him. Gingerly he removed the satellite phone from his belt clip, being careful not to drop it into the canyon below.

In less than thirty seconds, a big grin came over his face. This site would have to wait. His best friend half-way around the world needed his help, and he couldn't wait to get there!

* * * * *

Someone was pounding on the door to my suite. With some trepidation, I open it. There, larger-than-life, stood Jim Morgan.

"You said you needed an expert scuba diver."

"Well, actually, I just need a mediocre scuba diver who I can use for crocodile bait! I think you will work out just fine."

"Well, whatever it takes to save your butt, here I am," Jim joked as we hugged each other.

We had been best friends since the seventh grade and were practically raised together. He was the brother I never had, especially after his parents were killed in an automobile accident by a drunk driver. The brown-eyed Casanova of Italian/French descent lived and breathed the adventure of our archaeological pursuits. His polite mannerisms and infectious smile were a magnet to young and old, male and female.

We were just sitting down when Ann came rushing in. She gave the young man a big hug, as she said, "The handsome one has arrived!"

Jim replied, "You're just as beautiful as ever. I hope this big lug is taking good care of you."

"Well, to tell the truth, he isn't. In fact, sometimes he just scares the heck out of me. We'll have to tell you all about it."

Before I met Ann, Jim and I were always trying to outdo each other by attempting to date the prettiest girls D.C. had to offer. The contest ended when I got to know Ann. Jim conceded I had won.

We had dinner at the lodge. Most of the evening was spent relating the story of everything that had happened to us, including our abduction.

"I can't believe you guys had all that fun and adventure and didn't save any of it for me," Jim said.

"Oh, don't you worry, buddy. We saved a really exhilarating and amusing experience for you. We'll show you in the morning."

Ann didn't laugh. She was worried.

By nine a.m. we were approaching the sunken aircraft. This time I had rented a larger boat with a powerful engine and the latest in scuba gear. I also hired Jacob to come with us just in case we needed the extra help.

Around the bend all the crocs were still lying on the bank basking in the morning sun. To play it safe, on the way to pick up the boat, we stopped by the outdoor market and bought several chunks of meat. When Jim and I were suited up and ready to dive on the wrecked aircraft, we moved back to where the crocs were and threw the meat as close to them as we could. The crocodiles immediately took the bait and started fighting over the treats, causing an electric display of waves splashing on the rocks by the shore.

Quickly we maneuvered the boat back around the bend and anchored where we had been a few days before. Jim and I quietly slipped into the water.

Just before I went in, Jacob tapped me on the shoulder. "Take this with you, Matt. I made it myself. I've never had to use it, but I always have it with me. This is what I call my last resort."

It was a double knife with a long blade on each end and a handle in the middle. I had my own hunting knife. I wasn't sure I wanted to be encumbered with the long heavy weapon. Each blade was about five inches long, and the handle between the blades was maybe six inches. There was a quillon between each blade and the handle. The total length of the weapon was around sixteen inches.

"You take this with you," Jacob insisted. He pulled a protective leather sleeve over each blade and attached the knife to my weight belt with a strip of Velcro.

"If one of those big crocs decides he's still hungry, you're going to be real glad you have this weapon," he said with an anxious look in those bright blue eyes. "Now you boys be real careful down there. Those animals mean business. You're in their territory, and they will kill you. I wish I had another knife for you, Jim."

"I'll be okay, Jake," Jim said grinning. "I'll just hide behind Matt."

Reluctantly, I left my knife in the boat.

Jim and I swam toward the pilot's door. This side still had the wing attached. On the other side, the wing had been ripped off by the bank and a tangle of mangrove roots when the plane crashed. Standing on the wing, I yanked on the door handle. It didn't budge. The current was strong, and it was hard to stay on the wing without holding onto something. Finally with both of us pulling on the handle, it started to slowly move.

As we labored to gain access to the cockpit, we kept a sharp eye out for crocodiles. Both of us had a rope tied around our waist. Ann was holding the end of my rope, and Jacob was holding the end of Jim's rope. If Ann or Jacob saw a croc in our area, they would warn us with three hard tugs.

The door was opening. Silt from inside the plane was so stirred up we couldn't see anything for a few seconds. Finally it settled.

The old skeleton was intact, head resting against the back of the seat like he was still flying the plane. I had warned Jim about the skeleton inside, so he was prepared. It was a chilling sight.

The only thing in the passenger's seat was the old small leather suitcase. I reached in over the skeleton to grab it, but the handle broke off. Struggling in the current, I accidentally bumped the skeleton. The bones which had been held together with decaying tissue began to fall apart. The skull tumbled down and rolled onto the seat next to the suitcase.

Pushing the skull aside, I lifted hard and fast and came out with the suitcase in both hands. It started to disintegrate so I handed it to Jim and motioned for him to take it up to the boat. Clutching it in both arms, Jim started his ascent.

I turned to look inside for something to identify the pilot or the aircraft. Not finding anything, I backed out and proceeded to close the door so the skeleton wouldn't wash out. The aviation investigators would want to remove it from the plane. As I closed the door, I felt Ann tug frantically three times on my rope and then three more times.

Like a re-occurring nightmare, there she was . . . an eight foot croc! She looked like the same one I had encountered just four days ago, but this time the monster was between me and the boat, swimming straight toward me. I could only retreat and try to avoid her jaws. I stepped backward off the front of the wing and squeezed under it. I slid feet first into a cramped hole of tree branches and mangrove roots. She pushed her snout hard into the roots trying to bite. I grabbed for the knife Jacob had given me. I got it free from my belt, ripped the blade covers off and begin slicing it through the water at her. She couldn't get me, but I also couldn't leave. She was violently tearing further and further into the mangroves toward my face!

Suddenly, looking beyond the croc, I saw Jim coming back down toward her tail. He had a knife in his hand. I knew if she turned around and attacked him, he would be a goner. I had the double-bladed knife, and the mangroves were protecting me, but Jim was in open water. Strong as he was, he would be no match for this killer. She would take him to the bottom in a death roll, and my best friend's life would be over.

My survival instinct and adrenaline triggered my immediate reaction. I stuck my right arm with the knife out of my refuge in the mangrove roots right in front of her nose. My timing had to be perfect. She lunged forward opening her jaws wide to bite off my arm. In one quick motion, I jabbed my hand into her mouth stabbing through her bottom jaw, holding the top blade straight up. I just knew I would suddenly be minus my right arm. She was lightning fast. As my hand went in, she snapped her jaw shut. The top blade sliced through between her two nostrils on top. I had somehow managed to stab her just behind her teeth on the bottom jaw. Her top jaw stopped when it hit the quillon dividing the blade from the handle but her teeth still bit into my wrist. My hand was shaking, but I was able to maintain my grip on the knife handle. Blood shot out from my wrist.

Bright red blood spurted from her mouth and nose. She jerked her head. I let go of the knife handle and pulled my hand out.

She turned and quickly swam away right past Jim, leaving a bright red trail of blood.

Tears were running down Ann's cheek as she hugged me.

Jim and Jacob started cleaning and bandaging my wrist. Her teeth had just sunk in a little on the top and on the bottom, no major damage. It would just be sore for a while.

Ann and Jacob had watched the whole scene from up on the boat unable to do anything to help, while Jim had risked his own life to try to save me.

Even old Jacob's eyes were moist as he excitedly helped Jim and me take off our gear.

I gave Jacob five $100 bills. "This is for the knife I lost."

Jacob shook his head saying, "You don't owe me anything for the knife. I'm just glad it worked."

I insisted he take it. "That's the best insurance policy I ever bought. Use the money to have a new knife made. Any man fishing in these waters should never be without one."

Starting the engine, Jim turned the boat around and started heading back up river, bucking the current and a strong wind.

We were anxious to examine the contents of the old suitcase. What would we find? Would the map be there?

CHAPTER ELEVEN

The suitcase collapsed as we opened it with optimal care. Its contents weren't in much better shape. As we sifted through the items we found tattered clothes, a shaving kit complete with an old rusty straight razor, a toothbrush with no bristles left, and a leather wallet. Nothing in the wallet was legible, nothing that would help us ascertain who the pilot was. Four hundred twenty-seven dollars in U.S. currency were still identifiable, but there was no parchment map.

With the tail section missing and most of the right wing gone, we could not identify the plane, but we were pretty sure we had just met George Green.

"I'm actually glad we didn't find the map," I said back in the room that night. "No map would have been decipherable after all those years in the water. We may still have a chance of finding it."

"Really?" Ann asked in surprise.

"Yes," I said. "Some of the Piper Comanches had a rear cargo door in the tail. He could have put the map in there. If the tail broke off before it hit the water, we may find it in the jungle near where the plane crashed. The down side is if the tail broke off when it hit the water and floated downstream, we'll probably never find it, and if we did, the map would be destroyed."

"I appreciate all you did today, buddy," I said as I gave Jim a bear hug. "You put your life on the line for me. Thanks, bro."

"Thanks to Jacob's double knife, you survived a bad situation. I'm glad I didn't have to take her on. When I saw she had you pinned down, I grabbed the first weapon I could see and headed back down. She probably wouldn't have liked me trying to cut off her tail with Jacob's old bait knife."

We all three laughed.

"Why didn't the meat we threw out keep her occupied?" Ann asked.

"Jacob said she probably had a nest of eggs or babies on the bank nearby. She was just trying to protect her young."

"Why don't you hang around the hotel tomorrow, Jim? Sleep off your jet lag. I've rented the only plane available and it's only a two-seater. Ann and I are going to go flying. Maybe we can spot the tail section in the trees."

"Good luck with that," Jim said doubtfully.

"I know it's a long shot, but I've played long shots before and won," I added.

"Well, you guys enjoy your plane ride. Don't forget your parachutes. I'll be spending some time at the pool."

Jim and I learned to fly single-engine airplanes when we were in our twenties. Later we both received our multi-engine license.

Even though Jim had logged hundreds of hours of flying time, he almost died in an aircraft accident last year. While flying over the rain forest in Borneo, his small plane caught fire. His life was saved because he had a parachute and was able to bail out.

When we left Jim after breakfast, he told me, "Two parachutes, Matt . . . one for you and one for Ann."

So I asked for parachutes when I came to pick up the plane I had reserved over the phone. I was given one and was told there was another one already in the airplane.

I turned to Ann as a rental agent handed me the chute. I laughed and said, "Jim insisted. After his experience in Borneo, he won't fly without one."

"And neither will I, Matt. Small planes make me very nervous. Especially small planes flying over jungle where there's no place to land."

It was a beautiful day. The sunbeams glistened on the river water, and the dense jungle was a brilliant green as far as the eye could see.

We had been flying low and slow, following the river.

"We should be coming up on the crash site any minute now."

"I think I see the big bend," she said, "where the crocodiles hang out."

I brought the plane down to just above the trees and dipped the right wing so Ann could get a better view from her side.

I banked right and made another pass over the trees along the river. I started about a half mile upstream of the aircraft.

"I see where you dove on the sunken aircraft, Matt, but there are too many overhanging trees to see the plane down in the water."

Ann intently watched the jungle below, but spotted no airplane debris.

"Circle the other way, Matt, and you look. I don't see anything."

"It's got to be here," I said. "He had to have hit the trees, breaking the tail off, and then plunging into the river."

"Someone could have found it, carried it out piece by piece, and sold it for aluminum scrap," Ann said.

"I don't think a person could walk through that dense jungle, much less remove the scrap aluminum. The foliage is too thick. The tail section may not have fallen all the way to the jungle floor. We have plenty of fuel and plenty of time. I'll make a few more passes, and each time I'll come in from a different direction."

Within fifteen minutes, Ann said, "There, Matt. I caught a flash of something. Go around again. I don't see it now."

Circling, I made another pass.

"I see it, Matt. It's not far from where the plane went in. It looks like it's hung up in the tree branches. The trees have closed in around it, so not much is visible."

I made another pass and spotted it from my side of the plane.

"That's got to be it. It's hung up in the trees, all right."

We were ecstatic and high-fived each other.

"I can't believe we actually found the tail piece, Matt. How are we ever going to get to it?"

"Remember how we were rescued off the glacier on Mount Ararat?"

"With a helicopter?"

"Yes, with a helicopter and a rescue winch. Jim is a licensed helicopter pilot now. He can fly the bigger ones better than I can. I'm sure he could rent one in Bangkok."

We made a few more passes so we would be able to find the exact spot again.

I said, "You can't even see it except for a brief second when we pass right over the top of it."

When we felt sure we knew exactly where it was, I gained altitude and headed back. When we were close to the village, I changed direction.

"Where are you taking us now, Mr. Aviator?" Ann asked as she handed me a sandwich and poured some coffee from the thermos.

"Let's just fly over the jungle for a few minutes. There are lots of small lakes down there. Maybe we can spot one that has a waterfall at one end and maybe remnants of a boat dock or possibly a camouflage net over a metal building on the other end. The local police still haven't contacted us about flying out in the plane they were trying to borrow. Maybe we can spot something ourselves."

Moments later Ann said surprised, "There's a plane coming up on your side. It is above and behind us."

I looked quickly to my left, but couldn't see anything. Then out of the blue the plane swooped down and leveled off right beside us. It was way too close.

"That's Tiny!" Ann screamed. "I can't see who the pilot is, but I'll bet it's Drake."

"It is Drake. I just got a glimpse of him in the pilot's seat."

Immediately I banked to the right, and the other plane disappeared from view. I knew we were in trouble. The other aircraft was much faster and more powerful than ours. We couldn't outrun them!

"Grab the parachutes," I told Ann, "and put one on."

In a couple of minutes, she had her chute on. "Oh no," she cried out. "There's something wrong with the other one, Matt. There's no ripcord."

I looked at it. The ripcord had been cut off on the one that had already been in the airplane.

"Someone knew I was renting this plane. They were worried we would locate the lake and trace it to the owner of the property, the man on the other end of the phone conversation."

"Matt, I'm scared. What can we do?" Ann pleaded.

"I'm thinking!" I said.

Nothing happened for a few minutes.

"Maybe they left," Ann said hopefully. "I don't see them."

I was gaining altitude and flying toward the mountains where the jungle wasn't quite so dense. I knew if Drake and Tiny got in a position to fire at us, we had no defense against them. If we had to bail out, I wanted to be as high as possible, and I couldn't land in the jungle. If we could make it to the foothills or at least a clearing in the jungle, we would have a better chance.

After a couple of minutes, Ann said, "I think they're gone."

"I don't think so. I don't think they dropped in to just say hello. That first flyby was just to make sure it was us flying the plane. I hope you're wearing a leather belt," I said.

She gave me a puzzled look. "Yes, I am, but why?"

"Well, don't panic, but if they damage this aircraft and we have to bail out with just one chute, I'll wear the good chute, and I'll strap you to me with our two belts."

Pulling off my leather belt, I handed it to her. Then I gave her my pocket knife.

"The knife is very sharp. Try to punch more holes in both belts and make sure my wide belt will go through your buckle."

"My belt is as wide as yours."

"Good. Now try to stab some holes crossways with the point of the knife in both belts. Stab it hard into the seat between your legs. Be careful not to cut yourself."

"I'm trying."

"Hurry, Ann!"

We both saw the plane above us at the same time. The right side door was partly open, and we were looking at Tiny aiming the large barrel of a rocket launcher at us. I dove instantly just as he fired. He missed!

I couldn't let them get in front of us again. They could only fire from Tiny's door, but their plane was much faster. So with my throttle wide open, I flew a zigzag course. I couldn't see them for a few seconds, until suddenly, there they were. They were right above us. I turned hard left and down. Something slammed into our tail and I lost all control. I pulled back on the yoke, but nothing changed.

Ann screamed as the plane plummeted. Without a second to spare, I jerked the parachute off her.

"Trust me, Ann," I said as I struggled to put on her chute. "Listen carefully," I shouted over the scream of the dying aircraft. "Put your belt back on, but don't buckle it."

Watching how she started the belt through the first loop on her pants, I mirrored Ann's movement putting my belt on in the same direction. There were now several holes in each belt to choose from. I knew we only had a few seconds, but if we could get out of the plane and pull the ripcord, I wanted Ann cinched tight to me. If I dropped her, my life would also be over.

The plane was screaming as we continued downward. I could see the trees and the ground through the windshield getting closer and closer. Finally we were ready. I still don't know how I did it, but in that tiny two-seat cockpit, I picked Ann up, moved into her seat and put her on my lap facing me. Cinching the two belts as tight as I could, I shouted, "Put your arms tight around my neck and don't let go. When we get out the door, clamp your legs around my waist before I pull the ripcord."

Terrified, Ann grabbed me. Without looking to see how close to the earth we were, I forced the right door open, held Ann tight, and rolled out.

When we cleared the airplane, Ann immediately wrapped her long legs around my waist.

"Hold on," I yelled as I pulled the ripcord.

The chute caught the air and billowed open above our heads. I felt Ann's weight pull down hard on my shoulders and waist as the chute began to slow our descent. She had her head buried into my shoulder, her arms tight around my neck. I saw the plane explode as it hit the trees not far from us. Looking down, the gap between the dense jungle canopy and us was quickly narrowing. We were still falling fast when we hit the trees, plowing through the light branches and leaves and then wrenching to an abrupt stop when the chute caught on a branch. Our feet were dangling fifteen feet above the jungle floor.

Ann had not made a sound since we bailed out. We just hung there swaying back and forth. I was trying to see how we were going to get down.

Suddenly Drake and Tiny's plane flew over the top of the trees. It was very low. We had to move fast before another rocket hit the tree we were in. I heard the plane making a turn.

"We've got to get down, Ann. They're coming back."

"Oh no," she cried. Then she opened her eyes. "Oh, my God," she said as she saw how high we still were. "Okay . . . okay, Matt," she said, "keep holding on to me. If I can unhook the belts, I think I can grab the branch behind you. Then you can turn around and grab the same branch."

The plane flew over again, just clipping the treetops, and they fired another rocket out the back side of the door. It hit the main trunk above us and exploded in a fireball. Burning debris started falling all around us. Ann got the belt unbuckled. I got the chute off.

We scrambled down through the tree as smoke burned our lungs. Dropping the last six feet to the ground, we ran for cover. I could hear the motor from their aircraft. They were still circling, but we couldn't see them. We hoped they couldn't see us!

We raced through the jungle toward a dirt road I had seen from the tree. Our hearts were pounding, and we were out of breath. We sat down on an old tree stump close to the road. The jungle was not nearly as dense here closer to the foothills as it was by the river. Ann and I were both badly scratched and bruised. I was bleeding from a gouge on my left calf, but neither of us were seriously injured. We couldn't hear the plane anymore.

Ann leaned against me, and I put my arm around her. We rested there for a few minutes. Then Ann turned and looked at me. "Matt, no one would believe what we've been through in the last few days. That's twice we've almost died. Let's get out of Thailand, Matt. Let's get out before Drake and Tiny finally succeed in killing us. The police can't help us! No one can! We've got to leave this country before it's too late!"

Dust swirled as we saw a parade of vehicles heading toward us. Soon we were surrounded by several people wanting to help, and within a few seconds, two policemen arrived. This time the police were real.

A group of neighbors were having an outdoor barbecue. They had watched in terror as our plane was hit by a rocket and plummeted from the sky. Everyone cheered when they saw a parachute open and were amazed when they realized there were two people clinging together on one lone chute.

Someone in the group called the police and an ambulance while others piled into their cars and raced toward the crash site. Among them was a paramedic who performed first aid on our abrasions and advised me to get some stitches for the gash on my leg.

Soon the ambulance arrived and took us to a nearby clinic where a nurse practitioner put some stitches in my calf and treated our cuts, abrasions, and a burn on my arm. She recognized us as the couple who had discovered Noah's Ark and had been kidnapped while visiting here in Thailand. No one could understand why someone would try to kill us.

The policemen filled out their report. We explained all that had happened, but could only identify our assailants as a Caucasian named Drake and a large Thai man they called Tiny.

It was late when a taxi dropped us off at the lodge. Jim was pacing in the lobby when we didn't arrive back on schedule. After describing the entire day to him, he said, "Sure, you guys leave me to waste my day in this lodge, sleeping by the pool with drinks, snacks, and a great lunch, while again you go out and have all the action and adventure. And I don't mean to be critical, but I'm beginning to think you two are having a hard time making friends down here."

Ann and I looked at each other.

"Do you want to kill him or should I?" Ann said.

Laughing, Jim said, "Believe me, I'm very glad you both came through that harrowing experience still in one piece. But why would those guys try to kill you two now, Matt? They know you have told the police all about them. I would think they would have hightailed it out of the country."

"They're probably worried we'll lead the police to the lake with all the bodies and find out who owns the property. He's probably in the higher echelon of the crime family behind the kidnappings and ransom schemes in Thailand. They certainly are taking great risks to protect him."

"Could anyone identify the plane?" Jim asked.

"That's a question the police asked everyone. We didn't see any numbers, and no one else did either. The police told us that type of plane is very common around here."

"Putting my arms around Ann, I said, "You pulled through like a real trooper."

"Oh, sure, it was you who saved us again, Matt. I was so scared I couldn't think."

"You did great," I told her. "Do you think you can stick with me a little while longer? Tomorrow we've got to pick up our car from the airport and deal with the insurance company on the aircraft we lost. That will take some time."

Ann just shrugged her shoulders in an apathetic response.

Nevertheless, I had a plan to return to the wreckage site. It would involve all three of us.

"Jim, I'm really glad you brought your aviation license with you. The license allowing you to fly a helicopter is going to really come in handy right now. How would you like to drive to Bangkok tomorrow? I'd like you to spend the night there, and make arrangements to rent a large helicopter. You'll need to pick it up about four a.m. day after tomorrow. Be sure it is equipped with a rescue winch and fly it back to Jacob Hanover's . . . that place on the river where we put our boat in the water. There's a clearing behind the buildings where you can land. I'll let him know you are coming. Ann and I will meet you there the day after tomorrow at around five a.m."

"Whatever you say, Matt, but you and Ann be careful. Some of your friends play a little rough. I wouldn't rent any more airplanes for a while," Jim said.

* * * * *

It was 9:30 p.m. the next evening. I had showered and put on my pajamas and the white terrycloth robe the hotel had provided.

Ann came from her room next door. She was concerned about my stitches.

We sat on the couch and as she leaned back against me, I held her in my arms. As I brushed the damp hair from her face, I couldn't help but notice how great she smelled and how beautiful she was in her flowing lounge dress. I wondered if this comfortable, contented feeling would endure through fifty or more years of marriage.

"I can't believe what we've been through since we arrived in Thailand, Matt. Can you?" She turned her face close to mine.

"No . . . No, I can't believe it either. It's been unreal. The sooner we can get out of here, the better off we will be. But tomorrow will be our last chance to find the map. If George Green was right, that map could lead to the greatest discovery of all time. I think it is even more significant than Noah's Ark. Just think of it, Ann . . . the Ark of the Covenant . . . the gold-covered, wooden box that holds the stone tablets God inscribed the Ten Commandments on . . . the rules he wanted all mankind to follow while on this earth. People have been searching for it for centuries."

"I know," Ann said. "And I know we can't leave now, not until we see if the map is in that tail section, but what then, Matt?"

"Then we can leave Thailand," I said, "and we will. If we do find the map, it really belongs to Stephanie, not her Uncle John and not her cousin. It was her father who helped finance his brother George. If we are lucky enough to find it, we will give it to her. If that really happens, let's just hope we can talk Stephanie into the four of us going to Israel to see where the map might lead us."

Ann wasn't as optimistic as I hoped she would be. She seemed to have lost her enthusiasm to continue the search, but who could blame her after all that had happened.

"You need a good night's sleep. Tomorrow will be a brighter day," I said as I walked Ann to her door. "Be sure to use the deadbolt and chain on your door. I still wish you would sleep in my bed. I could have the maid make up the couch for me."

"I can make up a couch, Matt. We don't need the maid," she said with a smile. "But I'll be fine. I want you to sleep comfortably in your own bed. Besides, the police have stationed a man in the lobby all night as long as we're at this lodge."

"Well, that is some protection. I'm glad they at least did that, but I also know we're on the gang's hit list. They don't want us to find the place the kidnappers have been using. If they get half a chance, they'll kill us."

"Just promise me one thing, Matt."

"I already know what you're going to ask," I said. "If the map is not in that tail section, we're catching the next plane out of here."

"You got it," she said as she gave me a quick kiss on the check and closed the door. Ann was really anxious to leave Thailand.

"The map will be in that tail section," I thought. "It has to be!"

CHAPTER TWELVE

The horizon was a palette of brilliant pink outlined in slate blue with silver and gold highlights. It was breathtaking. Somehow I had a feeling . . . Today was going to be a fabulous day!

The sound of the rotors hovering over the trees was deafening. Jim had picked us up early as planned, and we were already at the site. He and Ann were communicating with me through the headsets on their helmets. Ann was standing by the cargo door operating the electric winch, lowering me about forty feet down just above the tail section in the dense foliage. I could barely see her. There was very little wind at this early hour, but the wash from the chopper blades was whipping the vegetation all around me.

"It's the whole tail section," I said over the squawking mic. "It's wedged between the main trunk and two major branches. It looks pretty beat up. The small branches and some climbing vines have almost covered it up. Bring me down slowly, Ann . . . Now forward a little, Jim . . . Okay. . . . Steady," I directed. "I've got to cut away some foliage."

Hacking away the vines with a machete was tedious work while hanging from a cable. Jim was doing a great job of keeping the helicopter steady. Finally, I had carved an opening to the front of the tail section.

"Good news," I shouted into my mic. "There is a cargo door."

"Great," Jim said. "I hope it's not locked."

"It's not locked, but it's pretty bent and corroded. It's not opening easily. Let the wench down a little more, Ann . . . Good . . . Stop . . . Okay, it popped open. Guess what? . . . I have another leather suitcase in my hand."

"Did you really find a suitcase?"

"Yes, I really did."

"That's fabulous!" Ann shouted into the mic. "Don't drop it."

"I've got a good grip on it. Bring me up real slow. There's a lot of branches and vines above me."

When I was clear of the trees, I said, "Start reeling me in."

Within fifteen minutes, we were in front of the cargo bay of the big chopper. Jim had set down on some vacant land where the jungle was being cleared and burned. It was about 6:30 a.m., and there was no one around.

Ann and Jim watched intently as I used my pocket knife to pry open the rusty catches on the suitcase. It was full of more clothes, but there was also a round leather tube that extended from corner to corner. The tube was about three inches in diameter, with a tight fitting leather cap on each end.

We all held our breath as I pulled the round cap off one end. Inside was a piece of old rolled-up leather. I pulled it out and carefully started to unroll it. The aged leather was dry and cracked, but still somewhat pliable.

Under a blank protective sheet of papyrus was the old parchment map. The humidity in the air and the leather cover kept the parchment from totally drying out, and the plane's cargo door had been facing downward so rainwater had never gotten in.

We all three gazed at the old faded map, gingerly opening it only a little at a time. The lines and marks which had been inked centuries ago were badly faded.

"This is going to take some studying," I said. "It's not showing much."

We found two other smaller rolls of papyrus inside the map. They were letters written in ancient Hebrew. Since Ann was familiar with that language, she began to decipher the writing.

"I am Benjamin Shalev of Jerusalem. Our land is in the hands of a cruel enemy. All who knew where the treasure is hidden have been slain. I am hunted and may soon be found. David, my friend, was accidentally left to watch over the treasure."

Then a second letter must have been written many years later.

"I am Benjamin Shalev of Jerusalem. Our land is still ruled by the enemy. The treasure cannot fall into their hands. I am very old now. The map and this letter will be returned to the place where I've kept it all these years. I pray the Lord will guide some righteous people to this hiding place."

We turned our attention back to the ancient map. It was so old and faded that it was very hard to decipher. It showed a lot of squares all in one place and some lettering that Ann recognized as the Hebrew word for Jerusalem at the top of the map. An arrow pointed to a series of five wavy lines. We decided the wavy lines depicted canyons. Next to the arrow were words. The words translated to *"two days' ride."* Then a crude sketch of two stick-figure horses pulling a cart was facing the five wavy lines. The lines ran on an angle to the bottom left corner of the map.

"Wow," Ann said. "This map doesn't quite pin down the exact location, does it? Were all five wavy lines really drawn on the parchment? . . . Or are some just creases, not really drawn by anyone? Everything is so indiscernible. It's hard to tell."

"To someone very familiar with that terrain and those canyons, it might make more sense. George Green probably understood it. His letter indicated he thought with the help of some laborers digging in the sand, he could find it. We'll need to enlist someone we can trust, and someone who has searched that area before," I said. "And I know just the man."

"Professor Kempson," Jim interjected.

"Exactly," I replied.

"But I thought he was in a wheelchair," Ann said.

"The last we heard, he had undergone laser surgery on his back and is much better now," Jim said. "He's out of the wheelchair and walking. The professor spent years in Israel searching for artifacts. If the treasure has already been found, he would know that."

"I'm sure the Ark of the Covenant was never found," I said. "That would have made news all over the world."

"Just like when we discovered Noah's Ark," Jim said.

"Yes," I answered.

"I wonder why George said he was sure the Ark of the Covenant would be found with the treasure. The old letters written by Benjamin Shalev never mention the Ark of the Covenant," Jim said.

"Unless the Ark was stolen at an earlier time, it would probably have been hidden with the treasure. The Ark of the Covenant was not casually talked about in ancient Jerusalem," I reminded them. "Benjamin Shalev may not have called it the Ark of the Covenant. Maybe he just called it the 'treasure.'"

"What do you think Benjamin Shalev meant when he wrote his friend David was accidentally left to watch over the treasure?" Ann asked.

"I don't know," I replied. "This is really exciting. The map doesn't pinpoint the location of the treasure. Hopefully, the treasure is the Ark of the Covenant, but it really narrows the search. It has to be hidden in a cave in one of the five canyons south of Jerusalem."

In a pocket inside the suitcase we found a bundle of old letters.

"We'll read these letters tonight," I said. "Someone could have been watching all of our activities over the past few days. Jim, you take the chopper back. Ann and I will trade the Grand Cherokee in for a different car, and we'll move to the new location we talked about."

I was concerned. The mystery voice on the cell phone had to be the one behind all of this. It appears he has connections everywhere. How else would he know when we rented the airplane? He probably knows where we are staying. He may even know what car I rent next.

We have to be vigilant at all times. None of us are safe.

CHAPTER THIRTEEN

We each took a letter and started reading. After nearly an hour of reading and discussing what the old letters were all about, I summarized.

"Besides the personal letters from his brother James telling about their move into the old bamboo hut and how big Stephanie was getting, we found letters from local banks about his past-due loans. But, best of all, we know how he got the map."

"Yes," Ann said enthusiastically. "And it makes it much more credible."

"The map was in Jericho most of that time, hidden in a box under the stone floor of an old house," I continued.

"Can you believe it?" Jim said. "New houses have been built on that old foundation over the centuries. Tile floors were laid over the stone floor, but no one knew it was there until a new bathroom was installed. A plumber with a jackhammer found the old leather tube and handed it to the owner who was watching him work."

"The owner and his sons tried to find the treasure," Ann said.

I replied, "Yup, for years they secretly searched the canyon area, but could never find anything. They finally decided to sell the map and sought George out. He paid them the equivalent of five-thousand dollars for the map. The family who sold it to him were poor and needed the money, but they were also honest and warned him that they had searched the area and could not find anything."

"Amazing what we have learned just reading this old correspondence," Jim said. "But can we find the actual hiding place? It must be in a cave or a cavern in one of the canyons south of Jerusalem, but the map is so cracked and weathered, how can we decipher which canyon? There isn't an X marking the spot."

"We have more resources than that family had," I replied. "George felt confident he could find it. I think we have a good chance," I said, "especially with the assistance of the professor, who is quite knowledgeable about that area. The notes on the map indicate there were two maps. Ben, who made this map, referenced a second map made by a man named Levi. Levi's map was hidden somewhere else."

"Who knows," Jim said. "That other map could have surfaced a couple of hundred years ago. The treasure could be long gone."

"You're right. But if the Ark of the Covenant is with the treasure, I'm sure everyone would know where it was," I replied. "We wouldn't even be searching and neither would George. I'm betting the other map has never been found. Who knows whose ancient stone floor could be hiding that map?"

"Yes," Ann said, "or it could be hidden in a clay pot in a cave in the desert like the Dead Sea Scrolls, just waiting for a stray sheep to wander in."

"Well, if this map doesn't produce some kind of lost treasure, maybe we should take up sheep herding," Jim laughed. "Maybe one of our sheep would stumble upon it!"

"Maybe we should," I chuckled, "but I'm putting my money on the map in hand."

* * * * *

I was dreaming I could hear a phone ringing. It seemed like a long way off. Then it stopped. Then it started ringing again. I finally realized it was my cell phone. Quickly I got to it before it stopped ringing again, muttering a drowsy hello.

"Oh thank God, Matt. Are you still in Thailand? This is Stephanie."

"Yes, we're still here," I replied, trying to wake up.

"I'm sorry to be calling so late."

"That's okay, Stephanie. What time is it?"

"It's twelve-thirty a.m. I'm so sorry."

"That's okay." I could tell she was crying. "What happened?"

"I need to ask a big favor again."

"Sure, what do you need?"

"I need a place to sleep. I can explain later, okay? I called the lodge, but they told me you had checked out. Then I remembered you put your cell phone number on my phone. I was afraid you and Ann had gone home."

"We are leaving in a day or two, but we just moved to another resort. Come over here, and I'll get you a room."

"Oh thank you, Matt, but are you sure they have a vacancy? Everything else is full."

"If they don't, I'm sure Ann would let you sleep on the couch in her suite."

"I hate to bother Ann in the middle of the night. Do you have a couch? I really need to talk to only you."

"Okay, yes, I have a couch."

I gave her the name of the resort and the address.

"I'll catch a cab and be there soon."

"Wait, what's wrong with your car?"

"I'll tell you about it when I get there."

I put my robe on over my pajamas. Then I put on some coffee. Stephanie was right. All rooms in the city were full. I opened the bed built into the couch and got a pillow and sheets from the closet.

When I opened the door, Stephanie stumbled into my arms. She had bruises all over her face, neck, and arms. One eye was almost swollen shut. Her lip was cut and bleeding. Obviously, someone had beaten her up. The wet blood on her clothes told me this had happened within the last couple of hours. I helped her to a chair.

"Who did this, Stephanie?"

"I can't tell you, Matt. He'll kill me."

"No, he won't. Was it your cousin Jack?"

She trembled at the mere mention of his name and looked at me in surprise. She was shaking, almost hysterical.

"Just a hunch," I said. Holding her, I kept reassuring her she was safe now. The monstrosity of such a savage beating had me seething with anger.

A good half hour later, the tears abated and Stephanie spoke as the story began to unravel. "Yes, it was Jack. He gave the cook and housekeeper the night off. I should have told you what he is really like when we first met. I would've told you, but I was afraid of what he would do to me if he ever found out. In fact, if he knew I was here right now, he would kill me. He'd kill us both."

"But why, Stephanie? He didn't seem like that kind of person when I met him, and Ann thinks he's nice."

"That's because you don't know him. He can really charm people, especially women. Believe me, that's all an act. Inside he's a monster. When he's high on drugs like he is now, he's mean and cruel. You wouldn't believe he was the same person. He beat me up before and not just once or twice. He hates me. He tried to molest me when I was young, but my aunt always protected me and kept him away from me. After she died, I've managed to make sure I never end up alone in the house with him. Thank God we have live-in servants. One time when Jack was drunk, he put a rope around my neck. He tried to strangle me, but I screamed and fought him off. He quit because he was afraid some of the servants would catch him. When my uncle dies, I know he'll kill me. He has already told me he would."

It must have been a nightmare for Stephanie, having to live in constant fear like that.

"Tonight it all started when I told him I can drive now and have my own car. He flew into a rage when I told him I was moving out. He beat me up and took my car keys. I ran out of the house. He got in my car and chased me down the street in the dark. I got away by running through the block between houses. I caught a city bus to take me into the village."

She started to cry again, pleading, "I've never told anyone any of this before. Please don't let him know I told you."

"Tell me, Stephanie," I said. "This is just a hunch, but does Jack have a couple of friends named Drake and Tiny?"

"I don't know who his friends are. I know he has some friends who take drugs with him. I've overheard enough of his cell phone conversations to have figured that out, but I've never heard him say their names. Jack's been using drugs for years. He's always desperate for money. He steals from everyone, even his friends. I heard him screaming at someone over the phone, denying he stole from them.

But knowing Jack, I'm sure he did. Once he took some of the ancient artifacts from our collection, removed the gold, rubies, and emeralds, and sold them. Then he paid someone to duplicate the original gold pieces out of brass with a thin gold plate and replace the precious gems with colored glass. I thought my uncle was going to kill him when he discovered it. But now Uncle John is an old man, and Jack just runs over him."

It was almost 1:45 a.m.

"Stephanie, why don't you go take a shower. You'll feel better. I'll get one of my T-shirts you can wear to bed. You need to get some rest."

She was dead on her feet but followed my directions, much like a zombie. After she showered, I helped her into bed and sat on the edge holding her hand.

"Again you saved me, Matt. I don't know what I'll do when you leave and I don't have you anymore." She paused." . . . to help me, I mean. Thank you, Matt."

"You're welcome, Stephanie. Now try to get some sleep."

Within minutes, an exhausted, innocent Stephanie drifted off into a fitful sleep.

How could anyone mistreat another human being like this? Somehow I have to make sure Jack never touches her again. I left the room making my way to the couch. It wasn't very comfortable, but tonight I wouldn't notice.

CHAPTER FOURTEEN

As Ann entered my suite the next morning, she quickly noticed the unmade sofa bed.

"Why were you sleeping on the couch, Matt?"

Before I could answer, Jim was knocking on the door. Entering the room, he immediately raised his eyebrows but didn't ask any questions.

"Who's at the door, Matt?"

The feminine voice surprised both of them as they turned to see a disheveled Stephanie limp through the bedroom door wearing my T-shirt.

It took a couple of hours and a pot of coffee to explain it all. I introduced Stephanie to Jim, and then called room service and ordered breakfast.

Ann loaned Stephanie some clothes and helped cover her cuts and bruises with makeup. She gave her a pair of sunglasses to hide the now very black eye. After examining her cut lip, Ann assured her it wouldn't leave a scar.

Jim helped Stephanie to a chair at the table, attentive and trying to make her comfortable. Obviously, he was mesmerized by her beauty and sat next to her.

I think Ann was skeptical about Stephanie's story, but couldn't deny she had been beaten up.

After breakfast, I said, "Stephanie, we found your Uncle George's plane."

"You what?" she said surprised. "Where? How?"

I proceeded to tell Stephanie where we found the plane and showed her the parchment and the letters. She was overwhelmed. Tears came to her eyes as she read her father's letter to George.

"It sounds like my dad was proud of me," she said with a lump in her throat.

"Stephanie, the map does not really belong to us. Your Uncle George bought it, and he may have used some of your father's money to help him buy it. You have more ownership in this map than anyone. What would you like to see done with it?"

She didn't reply.

"Would you want to tell your Uncle John and your cousin Jack about the map and share it with them? They are not good people, but they are all that is left of your family."

"Heavens no, Matt! Jack beat me up, but Uncle John was in the next room. I know he heard me screaming, but he didn't try to stop him. He has never tried to stop him. I think that in his younger years, he was just as mean as Jack is now. No! I don't want either of them to even know the map exists. But Matt, what is this map supposed to lead us to?"

I told her all I knew about the treasure, and the unsubstantiated stories of it being taken out of Jerusalem and hidden to prevent the invading Babylonians from finding it.

"But what about the Ark of the Covenant?" Stephanie asked. "Was that hidden with it?"

"Some people believe it was. Apparently your Uncle George thought it was hidden with the treasure, and I think so too. But no one really knows."

"What do you know about the Ark of the Covenant, Stephanie?" Ann asked her.

"I know a lot about it. I read everything I could about it in the Bible and on the internet after you and Matt were at our house that evening. It's what's in the Ark that's important. I would love to find it and see the stone tablets."

"The treasure, if there really is one, and the Ark of the Covenant still belong to Israel," I said, "and if we find it, we intend to turn it over to them. So unless the Israeli government wants to give us a reward, we won't end up with any of the treasure."

"I see," Stephanie paused. "But finding the Ark of the Covenant would really be something special, wouldn't it, Matt?"

"Yes, it would. I think it is the most important of all the biblical artifacts. Just like when we found Noah's Ark. It would be another witness that the old stories in the Bible are true."

"Just imagine actually holding the stone tablets in your hands," Jim said, "or examining how the letters were cut, using an electron microscope. Did God cut them with a laser? Did he have that kind of power in his hands or were they just scratched into the stone with some kind of a tool? I'd love to know."

"If you believe the stories in the Bible, I don't think you had better touch them," Ann said. "According to the Bible, several people died from just touching the Ark. One man named Uzzah died when he reached out to prevent the Ark of the Covenant from falling."

"What do you think should be done with the map, Stephanie?" I asked her.

"Before you answer, Stephanie," Ann said, "I think you should know what having this map means. It could be the key to one of the largest treasures ever found. We believe it is possible that some of the artifacts that are made of gold could date back to King Solomon himself."

Jim added, "When Solomon reigned, gold was so plentiful that it may have been weighed in pounds, not ounces, as we weigh gold today. The annual income of Solomon's government was twenty-five tons of gold. . . . Just think, every year twenty-five tons of gold. Solomon had two hundred men who served as his bodyguards. He had two hundred shields made for these men out of pure gold. Each shield weighed seven pounds. He also had three hundred smaller shields for the palace guards that he had overlaid with three pounds of gold each. All of Solomon's goblets, plates, and bowls were made of pure gold. Once every three years, Solomon's special fleet of ships would return from foreign lands laden with gold, silver, ivory and other treasures."

Ann said, "So you see, Stephanie, a lot of people would love to have this map, and many would kill us all for it. I just thought you should be aware of that."

"Wow!" Stephanie said. "I didn't know that."

"It's in the Bible," Ann said rather smugly.

"Well, let's just hope the next generations of Israelis didn't spend it all," Stephanie said, "and that it was all hidden before Nebuchadnezzar invaded Jerusalem in five-eighty-seven BC."

We all stared at her. We were surprised.

"I've been reading the Bible quite a lot lately," she said laughing. "And since you guys say it's my map, I'd like to be a part of the expedition . . . if that's agreeable with you three. Let's go to Israel and find the treasure and the Ark of the Covenant!"

We all cheered and raised our glasses to our success.

* * * * *

It was going to take Stephanie an extra day to talk to her lawyer about the land and get ready to leave for Israel with us. She was excited! Terrified Jack was going to find her, she couldn't go home so she slept on the couch in Ann's room. I drove her everywhere she needed to go. Ann helped her buy some clothes and items she would need for the next few days.

Jim flew on ahead to Israel. I asked him to rent us a place in Jerusalem and to talk to Professor Kempson about joining our team. Professor Kempson was one of our archaeology professors when we were in school. He was a brilliant researcher and scholar, but above all, a close friend. His research led us to the place where Noah's Ark was built in ancient Mesopotamia, and we hoped all his years of investigating and exploring for the Ark of the Covenant in Israel would be just as productive.

CHAPTER FIFTEEN

It was 8:30 p.m. I tucked the three one-way tickets to Tel Aviv in my pocket. The red-eye flight would leave Bangkok at 11:45 p.m.

"I'll feel much safer when we are out of here. Jack has friends all over this village and Bangkok too," Stephanie said as she snapped the lock on her suitcase. "If he hears I'm going to leave the country, he'll try to stop me. He'll kill me! And if he knows about the map we have, he will stop at nothing to get it. You heard what he said about the Israeli treasure when you were at our house."

Ann and I tried to calm Stephanie down. I pulled out the ancient parchment. "Before we go, let's all three try to memorize the map, just in case someone does get it away from us."

I grabbed a piece of stationery from the desk by the phone. Roughly outlining the most important features of the map, I folded the sketch and put it in my wallet.

It was dark and quiet. It had rained earlier, and the streets were wet. A half moon was mostly hidden by the clouds. I had just pulled out of the resort parking lot, turning right onto the narrow one-way street. Ann was beside me in the BMW, and Stephanie sat behind her in the back seat.

"How long will it take to get to the airport?" Ann asked.

"About an hour," I replied.

There were several cars parked parallel to the curb on our right in front of us. Between the parked cars and the resort buildings was a well-manicured lawn with a sidewalk next to the street. On the left next to the street, a tall formidable block wall had been built.

We passed a familiar vendor's food cart chained to a light pole between the cars and motorcycles. The small enterprise was closed for the night. Jim and I had bought rice and dumplings for lunch there just a couple of days ago.

Suddenly I had an uneasy feeling. My intuition alerted me that something was wrong. Two black Chevy Suburbans were parked ahead of us, a few cars between them. Maybe there was no problem, but I hadn't noticed even one big black Suburban in this village before, much less two of them.

I could see someone's face in the driver's side window as we drove past the first car.

"There were men in that car," Stephanie said, her voice apprehensive.

"I saw them," Ann said suspiciously. "And there is another car just like that one up ahead," she added, clearly alarmed.

I watched in the rearview mirror.

"Damn!" I said.

"What, Matt?" Ann asked.

"The headlights on the Suburban we just passed came on."

Both Ann and Stephanie turned to see the big car pull away from the curb.

They followed behind us about a half a block back. Just then, the other Suburban in front of us turned his lights on and pulled into the narrow street ahead of us.

"We've got trouble," I said.

Both girls already knew that.

Stephanie in the back seat was starting to panic. "Oh God. It's Jack! I know it is. He's going to kill us!"

"No, he isn't, Stephanie," Ann said trying to calm her down. "Maybe he just wants the map."

"He wants more than the map. He's crazy and if he's high on drugs, he won't stop at stealing the map."

Just then the taillights lit up on the car in front of us, and it came to an abrupt stop. In the rearview mirror, I saw the car behind us speed up, quickly closing the distance between us.

"It's a trap!" Ann shouted as I hit the brakes.

"Get us out of here, Matt!" Stephanie screamed.

The street was too narrow to turn around. We only had one alternative.

"Hold on," I said as I jammed the big car in reverse. I spun the steering wheel hard right. Burning rubber, I backed in an arc between the parked cars where the Suburban in front of us had been. Jumping the curb, I hit the brakes and shifted to drive simultaneously.

With two wheels on the lawn and two wheels on the sidewalk, we shot past the car that had been following us.

"I wish we had a weapon," I shouted.

There are strict laws regarding weapons in Thailand, and our request for a gun permit had not yet come through.

At a driveway, I got back onto the street and gunned it. If we could turn right at the next corner, and then another turn, we would be on the main street where, by some miracle, we might encounter a police car.

Just as the corner was coming up, Ann pointed, "Matt, that white pickup . . . It's blocking that street!"

I had already seen it. A large crew-cab pickup was in the middle of the street where I wanted to turn. Now I couldn't turn right and left would put us back into the dead-end parking lot, so I continued straight ahead down the residential street at sixty mph. The pickup, sliding as it rounded the corner, turned in behind us.

We raced through the residential neighborhood. Finally I chanced turning right onto what looked like a major thoroughfare. It was a dead end. I was desperately searching for another escape route when a burst of machine gun fire blew out both our rear tires. A second volley hit the top of our rear window spraying glass all over. I knew the next round would be lower and would probably kill one or all of us! I was forced to stop.

Ann locked the doors, but a man on each side of the car smashed the windows.

Yanking the doors open, they roughly jerked us out of the car and shoved us into the Suburbans. They put me and Stephanie in the backseat of one car and forced Ann into the back of the other one. Without a weapon, I couldn't do anything to protect the girls.

They hadn't taken time to tie our hands or blindfold us. Was this a clue to our eventual fate? If no one cared that we could see where we were being taken, they probably weren't worried that we would live to tell anyone.

I had gotten in a few good punches when a Thai man pulled Ann away from my arm and loaded her into the other vehicle. Unfortunately, another muscular brute had struck me from behind, rendering me helpless.

The road was steep with multiple switchbacks. About two thirds of the way to the top of the mountain, the road ended.

Stephanie was holding my arm, trembling with fear. "They're taking us to the mine," she whispered.

We pulled through a gate, down a narrow driveway and into a large flat graveled yard. The area was enclosed with a tall chain-link fence on all sides, with security wire around the top. The side facing the valley and the jungle below was extremely steep. I could see the lights of the village way below, and a ribbon of lights moving on the main highway leading to Bangkok.

As we were taken out of the cars, one of our captors came toward us with a rope. Ann and I made it a point to put our hands out in front of us so he could more easily tie them, mimicking what we had done when she and I were abducted before. Again I didn't want him to tie our hands behind our backs. I nudged Stephanie who started to resist, trying to get her to do the same. Finally she understood and extended her hands in front of her.

I looked around for any conceivable way to escape. We stood next to a steel building with an open-air repair shop. It was dark. I heard a generator start up and suddenly fluorescent shop lights lit up the whole area. An old dilapidated pickup was parked next to a rusty front-end loader by the side of the mountain. The moon had appeared from behind the clouds, and the air was cool. Beyond this abandoned maintenance building was a shabby mobile home. Off to our left a pair of heavy wooden doors opened to the mine entrance. Antique ore cars lay on their side next to the railroad tracks coming out of the mine.

I figured this was the original tin mine Stephanie had so vividly described to us. The area was vast. I estimated the entrance to the mine was almost the length and width of a football field away from the shop and the mobile home. Between the old pickup and the front end loader was a large industrial evaporative cooler mounted on a stand, with a short length of ductwork spanning the distance to a rock wall. I assumed that was to force fresh air into the mine or at least part of the mine.

Two of the men had found the map and were studying it under the fluorescent lights. One was talking on his cell phone.

"What are they going to do with us?" Ann whispered.

Before I could reply, a white Mercedes sped into the yard. The driver hit the brakes and slid to a stop. The driver's door flung open. We were silent as we waited, dreading the appearance of our latest arrival.

Minutes passed before the fluorescent shop lights illuminated a big ugly man with a ponytail . . . Drake!

The passenger door opened and out stepped Tiny . . . our two nemeses who tried to kill us at the lake and shot our plane! Our predicament just went from bad to worse.

"Hold him," Drake said as he walked toward me. Two men grabbed me from behind. Without warning, Drake hit me twice in the face with his fist, then two hard blows in my stomach. I was forced to my knees where Tiny kicked me in the face.

Both Ann and Stephanie screamed. "Stop hitting him!"

Then they dragged me to my feet. My nose was bleeding, and my left eye was swelling fast.

I was mad. If I wasn't being held by two killers who had my hands tied, I would have tried to kill them both. I was really worried about the two girls. I cursed myself for allowing this to happen.

The rear door of the Mercedes slowly opened. No one appeared for a long time. Then a man staggered out. He was either high on drugs or had been drinking or both. He and Tiny conversed in hushed voices.

"It's the devil!" Stephanie said, seething with anger.

He was well dressed in a light blue suit, but his back was to us. We still hadn't seen his face. As he turned, Ann gasped, "Jack – it's Jack!"

Jack's movements were slow and his speech slurred, but there was no question who was in charge as the rest of the men followed his orders. "Put Ann in my car and keep her there. Close the door. Then do what I told you. Bring Lane and Stephanie over here."

Ann clinched my arm, but when one Thai started to pull her away from me, she kicked him and scratched his face. Infuriated, he put a knife blade to her neck and the other man put a gun to my head. Reluctantly, she moved away with them. I saw the terror in Ann's eyes as they forced her toward Jack's car. I was powerless to help her.

Jack turned his attention to me and Stephanie. "Surprise, surprise! Huh, Lane?" he laughed.

"I'm not surprised, Jack. I was pretty sure when you beat Stephanie up that you were the one behind this." No longer able to contain my anger, I warned him, "If any harm comes to either of these girls, I'll kill you, Jack!"

"You're in no position to threaten me, Lane."

"It's not a threat. It's a promise," I said.

"Well, I don't think a dead man can keep such a promise, Lane. It's because of you that Stephanie has that black eye, you know. It's all your fault. She tells me she has a car and she has some money. She wants to be independent. You helped her with all that stuff, Lane. It's your fault I had to knock some sense into her."

Jack was on a roll. We were his captive audience as he droned on. "By the way, cousin, after you got away from me, my old man decided he didn't like the way I treated you. Can you believe that, Stephanie? I was surprised to hear that coming from a man who had his own brother and sister-in-law murdered."

"Murdered? What do you mean? Are you saying Uncle John was involved in my parents' murder? But why?"

"Money, of course. The mine played out. He needed money. I heard him give the order myself. You're lucky the men he hired couldn't find you. I guess they figured the elephants would take care of you."

"How do you know he had them killed?"

"I told you. Dad brought some rough-looking guy into his office in the house one night. I was just a kid, but I listened outside the door. He gave the orders and paid the guy to get it done. He told him no knives or bullets, just a blow to the head while everyone was asleep. Then he was to stampede the elephants through the hut to make it look like an accident. Your dad had just paid him the money he owed on the loan. With your family out of the way, Dad could fake the deed to your land.

What a surprise when you showed up on his doorstep. He had no choice but to feign being the benevolent uncle and take you in."

"I can't believe Uncle John would do such a thing," Stephanie said.

"Well, believe it, cousin, 'cause he did. He gave the order to kill all three of you, three members of his own family. He did it for money. It's amazing what some people will do for money. Anyway, you don't have to worry about him anymore. He's out of the picture now," Jack gloated as he laid out ugly detail after detail.

"What do you mean?" Stephanie asked.

"I mean he's out of the picture."

"What are you talking about?" she asked him again.

"I mean he's dead. Stephanie, he's dead!" Jack yelled.

"What did you do to him, Jack? What did you do?"

Jack staggered a few steps away from us. He stood with his back to us for a few seconds. Then he slowly walked back. I couldn't believe what I was seeing under the stark white fluorescent light from the shop. We could clearly see the tears. Jack was crying.

"Oh hell, I might as well tell you. You're not going to tell anyone anyway." Jack took a deep breath and looked up toward the sky. He said, "Last night when I told him all I knew, and that he was a worse person than I am, we got into a fight. He fell down the stairs and broke his neck. He wasn't quite dead from his unfortunate fall, but he is now."

"You're crazy!" she screamed at Jack.

"Well, I couldn't just have him suffer now, could I?"

"You are sick, Jack, really sick," I said to him.

"Maybe I am," Jack said wiping his eyes with his sleeve and trying to regain some of his composure, "but now I may also be very rich. I now have my uncle's treasure map. Maybe it will lead me to the hidden Israeli treasure. I'll inherit my dad's estate and yes, your estate, Stephanie. You're a desirable woman. It's too bad you weren't a little nicer to me over the years. I would be taking you and Ann in my private jet to Israel. Now it will just be Ann. And you, Lane . . . You escaped once. You won't escape this time. Actually I guess it was good that you did escape the drowning. Because you got away from us, I now have Ann, and I have a treasure map. You see it pays to have friends in key places. No, no, maybe I should say . . . I pay, therefore I have friends in key places. Yes, that's it. I had spies watching your every move."

Looking at his watch, Jack said, "Sorry I can't stay. Oh by the way, Matt . . . may I call you Matt?" he said, grinning. Jack's whole demeanor had suddenly changed. "Ann is a beauty. I'll take good care of her. She'll live like a queen. I look forward to having fun with her. Just like the movies, a happy ending . . . I get the girl!" he laughed.

As Jack turned to leave, I shouted, "Ann will never have anything to do with you."

Jack stopped. Turning he stepped quickly to within inches of my face. He was irate.

Shaking, he shouted, "I shouldn't tell you my little secret, but you're never going to see tomorrow anyway. Ann's already asleep in my car. She's going to stay asleep most of the way to Israel. A little heroin does wonders. That beauty is going to be my personal possession. Once addicted, she'll do my bidding. She'll give me anything for another fix . . . anything! She's mine. Do you understand me, Lane. She's mine!"

Stopping to regain his composure, he said, "Sorry I have to run. By the way, Drake usually just takes people back in the mine. There he shoots them in the head and pushes their bodies into the deep shaft and dumps some lime on top. He is going to try something special with you. Anyway, you will never escape from the mine. No one has ever escaped. If his little experiment doesn't work and you should manage to live through it, I've left instructions. I'm afraid you'll still have to be shot. But your old acquaintance Drake thinks his method will be a harder way for you to die. Something about revenge for his friends you killed at the lake. We had to do a lot of scrambling after you and Ann got away. They're not at all happy about that."

As Jack was walking away, I saw Drake and Tiny put some plastic buckets in the back of the old pickup. Now they were backing it up to the evaporative cooler.

"Just so you know," Jack turned and said, "There will be a couple of guys in the mobile tonight. They will collect and dispose of your remains at five in the morning. I've told them to use lots of lime."

My head was spinning. How had I let this happen? I should have been more careful. I have to stop this. I have to save Ann and Stephanie. In my mind, I was praying for a way out. I was living a nightmare, but I knew it was real.

Stephanie screamed at Jack, "Please don't do this, Jack. Please. I'll do anything you want. Don't kill us, Jack!"

"Too late, Stephanie," Jack said as he got in the back seat of the Mercedes with Ann. "You know too much. I have someone who can forge a very convincing will. By the way, you left everything to me, your only living relative. . . . You know, I guess I'm not that different from my father. I'm having you two killed and for what? Money! It is truly amazing what some people will do for money."

The car door slammed shut.

CHAPTER SIXTEEN

With guns in hand, Drake and Tiny shoved us through the mine doors. Bare light bulbs dangled every few yards from an electrical cord strung along the walls of the mine.

My mind was racing. "Find an escape route! The lights are a plus! Locate the ductwork that comes from the cooler while the lights are on! Look for anything I can use to plug the air duct!"

My eyes darted around the tunnel. I couldn't see the cooler vent. It must be farther in the mine.

We forged ahead, walking on the wooden ties between the steel tracks. The tunnel opened up into a round cavern. All the ore had been removed, leaving a dome-shaped cavity of black rock, wet from seepage. The colossal room spanned roughly two hundred feet across and was forty feet high at the center. Vertical beams helped shore up the roof. Small pools of water had formed here and there from the seepage on the walls. They were like mirrors on the black dirt, reflecting the image of the light bulbs.

Three dimly-lit tunnels led away from the main cavern. I mentally labeled the tunnel on our right, tunnel number three.

I couldn't see how far it extended, but being closest to the outside wall, I surmised it had to be where the duct came in. Narrow railroad tracks led from each tunnel to the main cavern where they were switched to one track that continued under the main doors. I was trying to size up the odds for or against us.

Drake and Tiny forced us down the third tunnel. About fifty feet in, a narrow tunnel intersected it. We turned right and were pushed into the branch tunnel. It was blocked with mine timbers forming a wall. In the center of the wall was a heavy wooden door. Using a key to open the padlock, they forced us inside.

Once inside, Drake pulled Stephanie aside. "You're lucky we have to catch a plane. You're the first woman we've had in our little house of horrors."

Tiny giggled at Drake's remark.

"Tiny and I could have lots of fun with you, couldn't we, Tiny?"

"Ya, we could think up lots of fun games to play," he sneered. Looking at his watch and pointing his gun at my face, he said, "Don't we have time for just one quick little game, Drake?"

"I wish," Drake replied, leering at Stephanie, "but we have to finish outside, start up a certain cooler, and be on that plane with Jack. Maybe when we're in Israel, the boss will trust us to guard Ann. Then we can play some games with her."

"That works for me," Tiny said. "It's always good to have something to look forward to."

With those chilling parting words, Drake and Tiny backed out and snapped the padlock. Seething with anger and fearful for the safety of Ann and Stephanie, once again I found myself desperately trying to cut a rope off my hands. My eyes darted around what must have once been an office. The room was about twelve feet by fifteen feet. The floor was black dirt . . . the walls and ceiling dark rock.

Above our heads was the air duct protruding through the rock wall. A dirty register was screwed to the end of it. There was a beat-up wooden desk and chair under the duct. The desk only had one thin pencil drawer.

We tried to untie each other's hands, but it was impossible and we were running out of time. A tall metal cabinet with two vertical doors stood against one wall. With our hands tied, we struggled to open it. Our hopes were dashed as we discovered only an old pad of yellow paper, a few pencils, a couple of old books, and some rags. Stephanie held one vertical door while I sawed at my rope on the raw sheet metal edge. The edge wasn't sharp, but it was working. I pushed as hard as I could trying to make every stroke count. It took over five minutes to get my hands free. I untied Stephanie's hands and looked around for any kind of a tool we could use. All I could find was a rusty metal file almost buried in the soft damp dirt floor.

"As soon as Drake and Tiny get everything rigged, they are going to pump some kind of gas through the ductwork. Grab anything you can find . . . books, rocks, cloth, anything. We've got to plug up the duct to keep the gas out of this room."

I heard Stephanie tearing some cloth. "Here!" she shouted handing me a piece of dark blue material. "Cover your nose and mouth." We both tied a piece around our neck. We saved the rest to put in the duct.

"We look like bandits," she shouted as she turned to search for anything else we could use.

In any other circumstances, we would have laughed at that remark. But when you're about to die, it's difficult to even manage a smile.

There was one light bulb in the room. It hung over the desk. No tools . . . no hammers . . . no time to try to break out of the room. Everything was rock except the door, and it was solid wood.

I shoved the desk under the register and stood on top of it. Grabbing the light cord, I held the bulb so I could see back into the duct. I knocked out the remaining blades of the register with the file.

"Damn! There are steel bars where the duct goes through the rock wall. We can't get out through the ductwork. It's not big enough anyway."

Again our spirits were daunted. It was then I got my first whiff of a pungent smelling gas.

"There is gas coming in," I shouted. "The evap cooler is not on yet. It's just starting to seep in. I think the gas will rise. Stay low!"

"What are we going to do, Matt?" Stephanie was frantic.

"We will have to use our clothes to plug the duct. They won't blow back at me when the cooler comes on if they're wet."

Still standing on the desk, I looked again around the room.

"There is a puddle of water over by the wall," I pointed. "Start with this," I said handing her my shirt and pulling off my khaki pants.

Frantically I pulled open the desk drawer. There were only a few pieces of tablet paper, some small pamphlets, and one wooden pencil. The drawer itself was too large to fit into the duct, so I broke it up and used the pieces.

"What about these, Matt?" Stephanie was pointing to some ore samples and other rocks on the floor by the wall. One of them was pretty big. "That should plug part of it," she said.

"Great," I replied. I lifted the large cylindrical ore sample onto the desk, climbed back up and pushed it into the duct.

Stephanie handed my wet pants and shirt back to me.

"Oh no," I said.

Stephanie knew what was wrong. The evap cooler had started. She could smell the gas. We both started to cough.

"Don't breathe deep. Keep that rag over your nose and mouth," I shouted.

I didn't take time to look around. I was too busy stuffing everything Stephanie handed me around the big piece of cylindrical rock.

When there were no more clothes, she handed me the rocks. They were smaller, and they were just rocks, but I used them no matter how small some were. I had most of the duct filled, but the gas was still coming in, so she started handing me dirt, double handfuls of black, wet dirt from the floor. I packed as much wet dirt as I dared. I knew much more weight would cause the joint where the duct came through the wall to break. If it broke at the wall, we couldn't stop the gas at all!

Again I started searching the room for anything else we could add to the barrier built of paper, rocks, clothes, rags, wood, pamphlets, and wet dirt. All I had left were my boxer shorts. Everything else I had already stuffed in the duct including our shoes and socks.

The gas was very noxious. It burned our eyes and our lungs.

I hesitated to look at Stephanie. She had already passed me most of her clothes including her shoes. I knew she had to be down to her underwear. I was going to add both hers and mine if I still smelled gas because that's all we had left.

I once again stuck my head into the duct. Cautiously I pulled my handkerchief covering my nose down. I couldn't smell much of the gas in the duct, and there was no air coming past the barrier. It looked like Stephanie's blouse and pants plus the dirt had finally stopped it. I cautiously sniffed the air in the duct again. This time I couldn't smell any of the gas, but the cooler was still running, still trying to pump the poison gas into our space.

I felt Stephanie touch my legs. I looked down. She was standing by the desk in her pink bikini panties and bra. She saw my neckerchief was down, so she pulled hers down also.

"That's all I've got left, Matt. I can't find anything else. Do you need my underwear? That's all there is left to give you!"

She was exhausted, breasts rising and falling with every breath.

"No." I said."You can keep your underwear on. I think we finally got it stopped."

I got down off the table. She put her arms around me and pressed her cheek to my chest. I could feel her warm body tight against me. She was shaking. I put my arms around her and held her tight.

After a few minutes, she looked up with tears in her eyes and a catch in her throat. "We're going to die in here, aren't we, Matt?"

"No, we're not, Stephanie," I replied trying to sound convincing.

"When they find us alive in the morning, they are going to shoot us and throw our bodies down that shaft."

"Not if I can help it."

"But that's just it, Matt," she said, looking me straight in the eye. "You can't help it, and neither can I. We're going to die in a few hours. Face it, Matt. Even if we were to get out of this office, we could never get out of this mine. I'm convinced, even if you're not, that in a few hours we will be dead. We will, Matt. I know we will."

Neither of us said anything. We were tired and not feeling our best after breathing some of the poison gas. We needed to rest. Stephanie was quiet. I still had my arms around her.

I started to release her, but she said, "Wait, Matt." She looked up again, searching my eyes. "I need to tell you something. This is not the time to tell you. This is not where and how I had hoped I could tell you. Everything is wrong. You're probably going to think I'm terrible or crazy. I guess I really can't even imagine what you're going to think."

I didn't say anything, a bit bewildered at her ramblings.

She took my hand, "Please don't say anything. I have to say this . . . I have to. I want you to know this before we die. I love you, Matt. I really love you. I have tried hard not to love you. I knew it could only end in heartache for me. I've loved you since we first met."

I started to speak, but she put her fingers on my lips.

"Don't say anything, Matt. If we weren't about to die, I don't think I would have ever told you."

I just stared at her. I didn't know what to say. I was totally dumbfounded! Maybe Stephanie was delirious and exhausted from all the energy we expended to block the gas. Neither of us said anything.

Now hypothermia was our immediate danger.

I finally said, "I think it's time to get out of this mine."

"I don't believe we can. I don't think there is any way we can stop them from killing us. Without any weapons how can we possibly stop them? Please tell me how?"

I turned and searched her face again. Then I smiled and said, "A beautiful young woman just told me that she loved me. How often is that going to happen in a man's life? I'm sure as hell not going to let them just come in and shoot us, not without a fight! Now let's get out of here!"

CHAPTER SEVENTEEN

I had dried blood on my face and a cut on my chin from where Drake hit me. Stephanie wet my neckerchief and washed it off.

"I can't believe the lights are still on," she said trying to help me.

I was working on the door with the file.

I replied, "The lights, the evaporative cooler, and probably the mobile home all run off that generator. When the generator runs out of gas, the evaporative cooler fan will stop running. The gas will stop being pumped in, and the lights will go out. Let's just hope whomever Jack left to get rid of our bodies in the morning are asleep in the mobile. Otherwise, they'll check out the generator and the evaporative cooler. If they smell a lot of gas and realize the gas isn't going through the duct, they will come in to find out why."

With the old file, I continued prying on the door frame. It took hours of gouging the wood plus brute force before we finally got the door open. At last we were out of the small room we now referred to as "the gas chamber." Our underwear offered little protection from the bitter cold.

Stephanie was right behind me, the ore on the floor pricking our bare feet. Stephanie snuggled up to me as often as she could to get warm. We were racing the clock. I was just as cold as she was. Every few minutes, we held each other, warming both body and soul.

The big double doors at the entrance were built with heavy lumber, hinged on the outside onto a huge timber frame. A steel plate the width of the opening was buried in the ground, preventing us from digging under the door.

"What time is it, Matt?"

"It's almost two-fifteen a.m."

"Matt, we have less than three hours to live! What are we going to do?" Stephanie was out of answers. "We've looked everywhere in this mine. There's nothing we can use to help us get out of here! Nothing!" she said in defeat.

"We can't give up! We've been in two tunnels and part of tunnel number three. We've never been past the gas chamber in tunnel three. Jack said there was a hundred-foot-deep shaft, and we haven't found that yet. Let's go."

As we passed the gas chamber, I went in to check the duct work to see if gas was still being pumped in. Carefully moving some of the wet clothing, I felt an immediate blast of gas, making me cough and my eyes water. But as I struggled to put the clothes back in place, I detected fresh air blowing in my face, not gas.

Stephanie was right by my legs as I stood on the desk. "Quick. Close it, Matt. The gas is still coming in."

"No, it's not. The air coming in now is free of gas. The gas that was trapped in the duct has dissipated. I think the gas is probably all gone."

I looked down at Stephanie from the desk where I was standing. She was shivering from the chilling cold. The evaporative cooler was still blowing cold air.

"Our clothes are still wet and cold. We have to start a fire. We need to warm up and try to dry our clothes."

"How, Matt? I can't see where you could have a match in those boxers?" Stephanie smiled nervously.

Pleased that she still had a sense of humor, I grinned at her. "No, but there's a plastic disposable lighter in my pants pocket. I almost always carry one in case of an emergency."

"I saw a can of motor oil," Stephanie said excitedly.

"Great! We can use rocks and the file to splinter off pieces of railroad ties."

Using some of the motor oil on the splinters and pieces of wood from the door and railroad ties, we built a fire in the large cavern. The smoke hugged the roof and some escaped around the entrance door. While Stephanie dried our clothes, I went exploring farther down shaft number three.

It was dark. The weak light bulbs were few and far between. Being careful where I stepped in the dark, slowly I continued, following the old rusty railroad tracks back into the tunnel, looking for anything that might help us get out of here.

Disheartened, I began to worry. "Maybe I can't get us out this time. This is the third time Jack Green has tried to kill me, twice with Ann and now with Stephanie. Maybe the third time, he'll get it done. It's not looking good!"

Just then an apparition ten feet ahead gave me a glimmer of hope. An old miniature steam engine with one ore car attached was leaning on its side beside the track.

The old engine had been used to haul ore out from the shaft to the dump area in the yard. Abandoned years ago, it had been pushed over to make it easier to get past. The wheels on one side were still on the old track, with the engine leaning against the wall.

A little farther beyond was the deep shaft which was to be our burial place at the end of the tunnel. Just then I heard a noise behind me, giving me a start.

"What have you found, Matt?" Stephanie asked, handing me my shirt. She only had her blouse on.

"Our pants are still drying," she explained.

"I'm hoping it's our way out of here," I said as I put my shirt on.

Moving closer, Stephanie put her arms around me to get warm again. It felt good to have her arms around me, too good. I held her longer than I should have. She stopped shivering. Suddenly she kissed me. Without thinking I returned her kiss, long and passionately. I couldn't help myself. I guess all the stress we had been under for so many hours finally had to find a release.

I held her for a few more seconds. Then reluctantly I moved away and forced myself back to the steam engine. She knelt beside me watching intently as I examined the burner on the old engine. We never said a word about our kiss or our feelings.

We got the ore car uncoupled. Using brute force and all the strength we could muster plus leverage from a pry bar we found behind the ore car, we finally got the old rusty engine tipped back upright on the track. I poured some motor oil on the bearings and levers and the main piston shaft. Using the heavy pry bar, I chipped wood from old railroad ties and some support timbers and loaded the fire box. I poured some of the oil on the wood in the fire box and on the extra pile of wood we had ready.

Using a bent piece of sheet metal and some empty oil cans to scoop drainage water from shallow pools, we finally got the heavy steel boiler full of water. The boiler leaked a little around some of the rivets, but Stephanie poured more in to replace what seeped out.

All at once the lights dimmed and went out. We were thrust into total darkness . . . another fly in the ointment!

"The generator has quit running," I said. Feeling my way, I poured oil on one end of a piece of wood and lit it for a torch.

Stephanie moved closer to me. "I'm cursed. I'm so sorry I got you involved with my family," she said. "What time is it, Matt?"

"Three-oh-five."

I kept adding oil, lubricating the rusty throttle handle and anything else I thought should move, while Stephanie held the make-shift torch so I could see.

"This old engine is really corroded, Matt. It hasn't been used for years. Even if we succeed with our project and make steam, it will be a miracle if this hunk of rust will ever turn a wheel. Every single part looks rusted solid," Stephanie said.

"Oh ye of little faith," I said. "Wait till this rusty steel gets hot. This old workhorse will come back to life and hopefully save ours, but if you have a better idea, I'm all ears," I said.

"I'm afraid I'm fresh out of ideas," Stephanie confessed. "But I'm glad you're not."

"Let just hope this works," I said.

We lit the wood in the firebox under the boiler, put the rest of our clothes on, and warmed ourselves while the fire heated the water.

The pressure gauge had no glass in the face and we had no idea how accurate it might be if it did work. At last the needle started to move.

"We'll only have one shot at this," I said. "We'll have to hit the doors really hard to do any good at all. That impact will probably damage the steam engine beyond repair."

It was 4:15. We didn't have much time. The clock was ticking. It seemed like the cold water would never heat up, but finally steam began escaping from the bolts on the end caps of the boiler. The gaskets were shot, and we had no wrenches to tighten anything. Steam was shooting out everywhere. It sizzled at first, but as the water got hotter, the steam began to whistle as it rushed to escape. We stayed clear of the jets of steam so we wouldn't get burned. Stephanie put her hand over her ears to block out some of the noise.

"The steam gauge is stuck at 180 pounds of pressure," she yelled at me.

"There's a lot more pressure than that," I said. "Listen to the sound of the escaping steam. It's getting louder and louder. In fact," I shouted, "it's a high-pitched scream. That means she's geared up to turn her wheels."

Sitting behind the six-wheeled engine, I pushed the lever that delivered the steam to the pistons. Nothing happened. There was just too much rust. Frantically I continued to oil and scrape rust from the piston arms, and Stephanie raced to keep the boiler full of water and wood in the fire box.

It was 4:50. We were almost out of time. After a long period of frozen pistons refusing to budge, slowly they moved and the main drive wheels started to turn. We both cheered. I worked the lever back and forth starting and stopping the pistons and making the wheels do a few complete revolutions.

The time had come. I put more wood in the firebox. Soon the eight-hundred pound engine, seven-feet long, four-feet high, and two-and-a-half-feet wide was ready to go and had a full head of steam.

"Let's get out of here!" I shouted at Stephanie.

"Yes . . . yes!" she yelled back.

"Be prepared to run. If this screaming steam hasn't already awakened them, they will be wide awake when we go through that door."

"I just hope it goes through the door," she yelled. "This is our only chance."

She gave me a hug and a kiss. "Go for it, Matt."

It was just 5 a.m.

Stephanie followed as I slowly drove the old engine out of the tunnel. The light from the fire in the firebox cast an eerie yellow glow on the walls and support beams in the main cavern.

Stopping, I tried to judge the curve in the track.

If I gave it full throttle now, would it go around the curve too fast and tip over? I had no choice. It was now or never!

I shoved the throttle forward. The engine was using a lot of water and losing some steam. I had to hurry while it still had enough pressure. The old engine started chugging like a real steam engine. It was gaining speed fast. I feared it was going to tip over as I rounded the curve in the middle of the main cavern and I leaned to the opposite side, but it miraculously clung to the track.

Just before the engine hit the straight track, I shoved the throttle forward as far as it would go and jumped off, tumbling as I met the black ore of the mine floor. When the engine straightened from the curve, it gained more speed. It must have been going forty miles an hour when it hit the doors. The bolts anchoring the hinges to the frame split the timbers, breaking down the heavy doors, and the little engine went screaming into the yard. Finally jumping the track, it lurched onto its side fifty feet from the mine entrance.

Grabbing Stephanie's hand, we ran out into the darkness and found shelter behind the metal building as we waited for all hell to break loose.

Excruciating minutes passed as we watched, but no one came out of the mobile home. The only sound was the steam coming from the engine. Soon the steam stopped escaping, and all we heard was a deathly silence.

Armed with the pry bar, we carefully made our way to the mobile. Sneaking inside, and using my plastic lighter to see, we determined no one was there. Ashtrays were overflowing, empty beer cans were strewn around the room, and a half-empty bottle of Jack Daniels sat on the counter.

"It looks like they had a big party when they knew Jack, Drake, and Tiny were leaving for Israel. I think they went to town, probably to a bar."

"Let's hurry before they come back," Stephanie said.

"We've got to find our passports."

"Got them," Stephanie said as she picked them up from the counter. "And here's my purse."

"I've still got my wallet," I said. "Let's see if our suitcases are here." They were not.

The only vehicles left at the mine were the front-end loader and the old pickup. There were no keys in either. We searched the pickup and all the obvious places – the floor mat, the visor, under the hood, on top of the tires. Finally Stephanie held my lighter, while I hotwired it.

Precisely as I got the pickup running, we heard a car coming up the mountain and saw the glow of headlights shining on the trees as the only car on the isolated road kept coming. When the vehicle got to the gate into the property, it stopped. Voices and the clank of a chain on the steel gate told us Jack's hired killers were back. . . . Another roadblock to our freedom!

We could hear them drive through, closing and locking the steel gate behind them, before driving down the steep road. I killed the engine. We slipped below the line of sight in the cab. Headlights lit up the inside of the old Dodge pickup for a second as the car swung into the yard. We heard two car doors open and close.

"What the hell?"

Apparently they had spotted the still hot steam engine lying on its side in the yard.

I made out excited voices speaking a combination of Thai and English. Peeking out over the bottom of the window on Stephanie's side I watched two men with flashlights and machine pistols run toward the mine.

The black Chevy Suburban they were driving was facing the steam engine and the headlights were still on. I was hoping that in their haste the driver had not pulled the keys. The car was parked less than forty feet from us.

The doors creaked as we climbed out of the cab of the pickup. Stephanie and I, keeping low, ran toward the Suburban. Just as we reached it, the two killers came out of the mine. It was still very dark. These men knew they would be in a lot of trouble if their captives got away. If the local police found out what went on in the mine with all the decomposing corpses at the bottom of the shaft, they were dead men.

"They have to be here! They couldn't have gotten out of this area with barbed wire at the top of the fence. Look in the pickup. If they're not there, look in the house. I'll walk the fence."

One man went to the pickup we were just in. Not finding us, he headed away from us, walking toward the mobile home. The other man went toward the fence in the opposite direction, searching the tall weeds with his flashlight as he went.

Crouching by the door on the driver's side, we could not be seen by either man. Suddenly the headlights went off. I peeked through the driver's side window to see if by chance the keys were still in the ignition. It was too dark to see. We had no choice!

Carefully I opened the door. The dome light inside lit up, and a chime sounded. But finally a lucky break . . . The keys were in the ignition!

As I jumped behind the wheel, Stephanie climbed in the back seat. I turned the ignition, the engine roared to life, and the headlights came on. I backed away from the steam engine and then slammed it in drive. With the wheels throwing gravel, I headed up the road to the gate. Bullets destroyed the rear window just as we plowed through the chained and padlocked gate. At the top, I turned right onto the mountain road. We were free, at least for the time being!

I exceeded the speed limit through the village, and all the way to the international airport in Bangkok. We didn't have any idea when we would be able to catch a flight to Israel. After parking at the back of the airport parking lot, we walked into the terminal at 6:45 a.m.

We knew how grimy we were from the black dirt in the mine, so we went immediately to the restrooms. My face looked bad with the cut chin and swollen eye and purple bruises. After I washed up, I looked a little better except for needing a shave and a replacement for my mud-caked clothes. Stephanie's black eye was covered by her sunglasses. She used some makeup from her purse to cover her bruised face and cut lip.

Anxious to see how soon we could catch a flight to Tel Aviv, Stephanie went to the ticket counter. The next flight was at 9 a.m., and there were still seats available. The ticket agent eyed her with suspicion because she purchased two tickets but had no luggage, and her clothes were so wrinkled and dingy.

Trying to be as inconspicuous as possible, we waited for a clothing shop in the terminal to open at 8 a.m. Doing our best to explain why our clothes were in such bad shape and my face was so bruised, we told the clerk we had been in an accident on our way to the airport. Hurriedly we picked out the bare necessities, paid for our purchase, and left the shop. Assuming the police would soon be arriving to further investigate our story, we ducked into the nearest restrooms again to change into the new clothes.

The clean clothes felt good. Of course, Stephanie walked out of the ladies' room looking great. We tried to melt into the throng of people milling in the waiting area.

There wasn't much time. Hurriedly I used a pay phone to call both Jim's cell phone and Ira in Washington D.C. Our cell phones were taken when we were first yanked out of the BMW.

Jim didn't answer and his mailbox was full. Leaving a brief message for Ira in Washington D.C., I asked him to alert the police in Tel Aviv that Ann had been kidnapped and had probably already arrived in Israel in a private jet, either owned or leased by Jack Green. I asked Ira to tell Jim we were on our way, but we would be going directly to the police station when we arrived in Tel Aviv.

We devoured the light breakfast served on the airplane, since we hadn't had time to grab anything to eat at the airport and we were famished. It was the first food we'd had since lunch yesterday.

After the meal, Stephanie covered herself with a blanket the stewardess gave her, rested her head against my shoulder, and slept most of the way to Tel Aviv.

We had eluded our captors, but right now my number one priority was to find Ann and rescue her from Jack.

CHAPTER EIGHTEEN

Ann was struggling to wake up from a bad dream. Recalling a few floating moments of reality, she remembered Jack Green's face, twisted with anger.

Someone had roughly punctured her arm with a needle, and it hurt. Slowly a euphoric warmth had spread through her body and she became so mellow, so relaxed. Now that seemed like a long time ago. That marvelous feeling was now changing to pain and agitation.

The curved ceiling was trimmed with wood. Lying on the soft, light blue, leather couch felt like she was floating on a cloud. Four plush chairs close by matched the color of the couch.

Jack was sitting in one of the chairs, talking in a muffled tone to someone. Ann was disoriented, and the room swirled around her as a continuous hum droned in her ear. Surveying her surroundings, Ann realized she was on plane, a private jet. Her head throbbed. Raising up on one arm, she was immediately confronted by three faces . . . Jack, Drake, and Tiny. Recognizing the danger, she screamed, "No! No! Stay away. Get away from me!"

Jack's distorted face pressed even closer. He was smiling and saying something. Ann struggled to get away from him, but someone was holding her arm. There was that pain again on the inside bend of her elbow. Soon she began to relax. Again the blissful intoxication enveloped Ann as she drifted off to sleep. Nothing mattered anymore.

* * * * *

Ann woke up again. How long had it been? She wasn't in the plane anymore. She had to get away. Where was Matt? Why wasn't he here? It was a nightmare!

She was wet and cold. It was raining and dark. Ann spied the big house up the slope across a wide expanse of lawn. Sprinting in the opposite direction trying to escape from Jack, her heart sank when the path was blocked by a tall red brick fence. It was too high for her to reach the top. Crouching under some bushes, Ann found relief from the rain, but it was short-lived. Hallucinations of spiders and snakes sent her dashing along the wall, her arms flailing at the imaginary monsters. There were streetlights on the other side of the wall and traffic noise could be heard over there. Huge trees loomed ahead, some of their branches reaching over the wall. Abruptly, night turned into day as security lights lit up the vast yard. Men were shouting, and dogs were barking. Ann was riveted in place, unable to budge!

He was a raving maniac, unleashing a tirade of profanity. Ann was terrified. Jack slapped her across the mouth, splitting her lip. Then he grabbed the top of her blouse and ripped it down to her waist. Again she endured the pain as the needle went into her arm. Fog rolled in as the world again became a wonderful place.

* * * * *

The red brick, colonial house presented a tranquil appearance to the outside world. Manicured vegetation covered the grounds. A tall, red-brick fence around the entire estate set it apart from the rest of the upscale neighborhood.

Inside, an existence of anguish and agony was Ann's fate in the locked basement bedroom. She screamed, but no one heard her. The couple Jack had hired to watch her and administer the drugs kept a vigilant eye on her. There would be no second breakout or they would suffer Jack's wrath.

In the quiet of the afternoon, Jack, high as usual, sat on the back porch with a vodka tonic. He was deep in thought. There were many important things to review. His father's death would be ruled an accident. The housekeeper would find John's body at the bottom of the stairs when she came back from vacation in a couple of days.

The note he left in the kitchen in Thailand would explain his trip to Israel. He went over the note in his mind.

Dad,

Stephanie and I must leave for Israel. It's about that business opportunity we spoke of yesterday. We'll be gone for a couple of weeks. We'll see you when we return. Stephanie says for you not to forget to take your pills.

Jack's father would have known Stephanie would never go anywhere with him. She was afraid of him, but the police would not question it. And now both of them were dead.

Rising from the step with drink in hand, Jack staggered down the path into the gardens, mumbling to himself.

"I'll be fine. I've got all my bases covered. Stephanie's and Lane's bodies will never be discovered. The lime will do its job. The Thai police will contact me in Jerusalem and inform me of my father's fatal accident. I will direct the local funeral home to put his obituary in the newspaper and to cremate the body."

Taking a sip of his drink, his thoughts turned to Ann. "It's really a shame to turn her into a junkie, but one way or another, I'm going to have her. Soon she will be so desperate for a hit of heroin, she'll do anything to please me.

"I'll have to watch my temper. I didn't mean to slap her so hard when she tried to escape. I can't let that happen again. In a few more days, she will be begging me for another fix. Maybe someday she will really love me.

"The plan I have will take a lot of money. The chances that the map will ever put a lot of money in my pocket are slim. The map does not even tell me which canyon to search in. On the other hand, the reward for actually finding the treasure with Uncle George's map could be fabulous. It's worth looking for.

"Even if we don't find it, I still won't have to resume our kidnap and ransom game back in the Thai jungle.

"I'll have my Thai friends at the mine mail Stephanie's passport to me. There's a man here in Jerusalem who can forge an Israeli immigration stamp. Then I can prove she entered Israel with me. Perhaps we went for a swim and she was caught in a riptide. I couldn't save her. Her body was never recovered. As next of kin, I will inherit all her property. Everything is going very well."

Jack smiled and took a long sip of his drink.

CHAPTER NINETEEN

Stepping out of the cab, we entered the police station and were taken immediately to the chief of police who had already assigned an investigative team to the case. We spent several hours with two detectives detailing the events that happened to the three of us after leaving our resort two nights ago. We gave descriptions of Jack Green, Drake, Tiny, and their Thai friends at the mine.

Stephanie assisted with the telephone calls to the police in Bangkok, explaining where the John Green residence was located. She spoke the Thai language fluently and explained on the phone what Jack had told her about killing her Uncle John, as well as the location of the mine.

Dead on our feet, we finally left the police station. I had a taxi drive us from Tel Aviv to the house Jim had rented in Jerusalem. Exhausted from jet lag and several hours with the police, Stephanie slept most of the way. I was too wired to sleep. I had to find Ann.

The police in Tel Aviv were trying to find Jack's immigration form. If he hadn't lied on the form, it would tell them where he intended to stay while visiting Israel. Jack had no reason to lie. He believed anyone who could accuse him of any wrongdoing was dead, except Ann. Landing at a small airport, they could have transferred Ann to a private car on the runway without anyone even knowing she was in Israel. Therefore, Jack probably had obeyed Israeli law and filled his immigration form out correctly. We were counting on that.

I looked over at Stephanie, still sound asleep. It was a miracle we had escaped from that mine. As I sat there thinking about it, I knew it wasn't me that got us out of there. Having just enough materials to plug that duct, stopping the poison gas, finding the file that got us out of the gas chamber, and discovering that old steam engine and bringing it back to life were just too many coincidences. In addition, the men assigned to kill us had gone to town and were not there to shoot us at 5 a.m. Then I thought about how Ann and I escaped the drowning. If Chi hadn't been high on drugs, he probably would have been able to dodge that concrete block and shoot me. What about our surviving the plane crash? There was no doubt in my mind we had somehow received all the help we needed to escape those deathtraps. Someone was watching over us.

Stephanie woke with a start. Then she smiled at me. "We'll find her, Matt. I know we will."

The house Jim had rented was perfect. It was two stories with five large bedrooms and four bathrooms in an upscale area of Jerusalem. It wasn't very far from the walls of the Old City. From this house, we started our own search for Ann. I prayed Stephanie was right, and that we wouldn't be too late.

* * * * *

I was not sleeping much at night. It was 11:15 p.m. We had searched for Ann for weeks, but still hadn't found her. There wasn't time to eat or sleep. Every day was consumed with searching for her. I would kill Jack with my bare hands when we found them.

Stephanie, lying beside me, stirred in her sleep. Her pale yellow nightgown emphasized her beautiful reddish hair fanned out on the pillow. She had been by my side every day, buoying up my feelings of despair.

I got dressed and went out. The streets outside the walls of the Old City of Jerusalem were dark, wet and cold. It had just stopped raining. Pulling up the collar of my windbreaker, I walked for blocks in deep thought. *Why couldn't we find her? Why hadn't the police found her?*

I continued walking for more than an hour. I left the residential area and continued along the dark sidewalk in front of some stores, all closed. There was no traffic on the street at this hour of the morning.

I walked past a store with a large pane of glass. There was a night light above. My reflection in the glass caused me to stop and look at myself . . . gaunt, thin, unshaven. . . . I hardly recognized my own face.

How could I have failed Ann so? How could I have let this happen? She must have waited and waited for us to come, all the while succumbing to Jack's control. But we never came. By now Jack had probably tired of her and had turned her into a prostitute.

I had been so deep in thought I didn't notice the woman at all, but suddenly she was standing right beside me. I looked harder at the reflection in the glass. Her hood was up on the long black raincoat she was wearing, hiding her face.

Speaking softly, she asked, "Can I show you a good time, mister?"

The voice! . . . I recognized the voice! I turned quickly toward her as she turned toward me. Gently I pulled her hood back. I couldn't believe it at first, but there she was! I had found Ann at last. I put my arms around her, pulling her close.

Pushing back slightly, she stared at me. "Matt . . . Matt," she said. "Is it really you?"

I hugged her close to me again. We were both crying. I kissed her face and we kissed again.

"Oh, Ann, I found you!"

"Matt . . . Matt," Ann said over and over. "Matt, oh I love you. I love you! ... Why didn't you come for me, Matt? . . . Why couldn't you find me? . . . Now it's too late."

Stepping away, she turned and started to leave.

"Ann, don't go," I cried. "Don't leave, please . . . "

* * * * *

"Matt . . . Matt." Someone was shaking me. "Wake up. . . . Wake up, Matt. You're having a nightmare."

Suddenly Ann was gone. I sat up on the edge of the bed drenched with perspiration. I was shaking. The lamp beside my bed was on. Stephanie, in her pajamas and robe, was sitting on the edge of my bed. She put her arms around me.

"It's okay, Matt. You were having a nightmare. I could hear you screaming way over in my room. You must have been dreaming about Ann. You were calling her name. Everything's okay. We just got here last night, Matt. We'll find her."

Jim burst into the room. "What's going on?"

"Matt's been dreaming," Stephanie said. "He'll be okay now. Won't you, Matt?"

"Yeah, I'll be okay. . . . I can't believe how real my dream was."

After a few more words of reassurance, Jim slipped out of the room and went back to bed.

"Do you want me to stay here with you? I'll be glad to."

"No. I'll be fine, Stephanie. Thanks for waking me up."

"You know I would do anything for you, Matt."

"I know, Stephanie, and I appreciate that."

I turned and looked at her. The soft light from the lamp by the bed enhanced her natural beauty even more.

"With all the police and detectives working on the case, I'm sure they will track Jack down and find them soon. I want her to be found safe too."

Stephanie rose and slowly crossed the room. She turned, smiled at me, and closed the door. I turned off the light and lay there in the dark, wide awake until dawn.

CHAPTER TWENTY

We had been in Jerusalem for two days. I hired a private detective firm to help us find Ann. We had no idea where to look. All of us were consumed with worry about her. We were sure Jack flew into Tel Aviv, but even our hired detectives couldn't find any airport that had a record of their landing. It had been almost four days since Jack took her.

Finally the immigration office found the form Jack had filled out when he arrived. The address he listed as his temporary residence while he was in Israel was in Jerusalem.

* * * * *

It was dark now. Jim and I were in the back seat of the lead detective's police car. We were parked on a side street facing the only gate into the estate. A street light on the corner lit up the gate and several feet of the tall red brick fence on each side. We had been ordered to stay in the car no matter what happened.

The police wanted total surprise. I counted six police cars and two armored vehicles parked behind us. Jim and I watched through the windshield as four men dressed in black scaled the wall and dropped into the grounds.

When the gate opened, we barreled across the street and up the driveway. We screeched to a halt in the drive. The armored vehicle stopped under the huge portico. Bright headlights and red flashing lights lit up the front wall of the house. Two men in Israeli SWAT team uniforms were at the door with weapons drawn. We watched from the squad-car as two more SWAT team members ran under the trees toward the back of the house, their flashlight beams dancing in the blackness.

Suddenly we heard dogs barking in the backyard. Then a loudspeaker demanded anyone in the house to come out with their hands up. The demand was broadcast a second time. When no one responded, the men broke the door with a heavy steel battering ram and entered the house with guns ready to fire. We could see flashlights through the front window rapidly moving in the house.

I was a nervous wreck. Would she be there? Would Jack try to hold her hostage to prevent being arrested?

A woman screamed and men were shouting, but no shots were fired. Anxious moments ticked by as Jim and I waited. Soon a police officer came out of the front entrance. I jumped out of the car running to the house with Jim on my heels.

"We've got her," he said as he restrained me from entering. "She's unconscious. She was locked in a room in the basement. There's an ambulance on the way."

I grabbed Ann's hand as they brought her out of the house on a gurney, and I rode with her in the ambulance to the hospital. She was unconscious. She looked gaunt and malnourished.

The paramedics gave the doctor all the narcotics they found in the room with her. I overheard one of them mention heroin.

"We didn't find Jack Green or the men you said were with him," the officer with us at the hospital told me. "The older married couple staying in the house were acquaintances of Mr. Green. They were hired to keep house and watch Ann. He had apparently been in Jerusalem before and rented this same house. That's how the couple met him. He had hired them when he was here a couple of years ago while he explored Jerusalem. This time they were paid extra because of the girl. He told them she was his patient, passing himself off as a medical doctor. His instructions were to keep her sedated with the drugs he gave them until he returned. Mr. Green and the other men living here left early this morning. He told the couple they would return before six o'clock tonight. He didn't say where they were going."

I looked at my watch. "It was eight-thirty when we arrived at the house. It's nine now. Could he have gotten word about the search?"

"I don't think so. We received that address about seven-thirty. By that time Mr. Green and his men were already an hour and a half late. The house will be kept under surveillance, and we will arrest him and his men if they return. We are holding the couple at the station, initially charging them with kidnapping. Those charges may not hold up. We'll know more when we take Jack Green into custody and question him."

We thanked the officer and his men for the great job they had done in finding and rescuing Ann. They promised to keep us informed of their pursuit of Jack and his two companions.

I knew Jack was probably too smart to go back to his place. He didn't know Stephanie and I had escaped the mine and were now in Israel trying to find him, but I've learned to never underestimate Jack Green. He was smart and cunning. He was pure evil and had well-paid informants even among the law enforcement department.

I worried where Jack Green would turn up next.

CHAPTER TWENTY-ONE

I had been at Ann's bedside all night, hoping and praying she would recover. She had to be all right! The doctors told me that only time would tell if she would recover completely. She had not been sexually assaulted, but being held prisoner while they forced drugs into her blood stream had to be a horrific experience.

It was early morning while I was holding her hand that I noticed some twitching movement. Calling her name, I begged her to open her eyes, but I was not prepared for the hysteria that followed. Wild, wide-eyed Ann was screaming and fighting to get away from me and the nurse who had rushed in to assist. Reality was evasive and traumatic for her those first few minutes. We had to repeatedly reassure her she was safe . . . that no one could hurt her here.

During the next few hours as doctors came and went, monitoring her progress, I responded to the barrage of questions she asked. I related the events that had happened to Stephanie and me after she was forced into Jack's car. I told her we had been locked in a room at the mine. Interjecting some humor into the part about patching up the old steam engine and breaking down the doors with it, I compared it to the children's story of "The Little Engine That Could," hoping to elicit at least a smile.

I minimized the danger we had faced. There were other details I omitted like how we used our clothes to stop a gas flow or anything else that happened between Stephanie and me in that mine. I hoped she wouldn't ask.

I told Ann, Jim had rented a five-bedroom house, and I had hired a lady to cook and clean for us starting tomorrow.

"And Professor Kempson arrived last night," I concluded.

For the first time, Ann's face brightened. "Oh, great. I love Professor Kempson. It will be wonderful to see him again. The house Jim rented sounds nice, but why so many bedrooms?"

"Well, the three of us men each have our own room with Jim and I sharing a bathroom. You will have your own bedroom and bathroom, and so will Stephanie."

"Oh, did Stephanie come with you? I assumed after all she had gone through in the mine and her uncle dying, she was still in Thailand." Ann sounded disappointed.

"No, she detested her uncle almost as much as she despised Jack. She came with me."

"What about Jack, Matt? Where is he? Have they caught him yet?" She was starting to get anxious again.

"The inspector said he rented a black Hummer a few days ago. They're staking out the house and where he rented the car, ready to arrest him when he comes back, but no one has seen him."

"That's really strange."

"Yes, it is. I'm sure they will catch him soon, Ann," I told her, not really believing a word I said.

"Oh, I'm so glad you got me out of there, Matt. It was horrible. It was a total nightmare."

"I know it must've been terrible for you, sweetheart," I said.

* * * * *

Ann gave me a big hug as I opened the car door for her in front of the house. She was making a remarkable recovery and was ecstatic to be out of the hospital.

"What time do you need to take your medicine?" I asked concerned, fearful of a relapse.

"Not until noon, Dr. Lane," she laughed. "Don't worry. I'll be sure to take all my meds. When do we start searching for the treasure?"

"Not for a few days. We have some arrangements to make, and besides, the doctor said you should get at least two more days of complete rest."

"I feel good enough to go tomorrow."

"I'm glad you're so eager after your ordeal, but we'll go after you have had a little more time to recover." My tone left little room for negotiation.

"I guess you're the doctor." Ann gave me a big grin as we walked arm in arm up the sidewalk to the house.

Jim, Stephanie, and Professor Kempson were waiting by the entry to welcome Ann. Jim swept her off her feet and whirled her around in a big bear hug. Ann laughed for the first time since her abduction.

Dr. Ronald A. Kempson was a gracious, soft-spoken man in his early sixties. He was bald on top with a nicely trimmed gray goatee and mustache, six feet tall, much heavier than Jim or I. He asked that we just call him Ron, but we seldom did. The title "professor" seemed to be more appropriate, more respectful, more fitting for this knowledgeable, seasoned archaeologist.

Ann gave him a big hug and a kiss on the cheek. "The professor and I are old friends, Stephanie," she said. "I met this charming man when we were trying to find Noah's Ark."

Stephanie handed Ann a fragrant bouquet of lilies. "I met him last night when he arrived at the airport. He promised to take us all on a tour of the Old City as soon as we have time. I'm so looking forward to that."

* * * * *

Two days passed quickly.

"That was a great meal, you guys," Ann said to them. "Much better than the hospital food."

"Yes, it was delicious considering Jim gave the housekeeper the afternoon off so he could cook a special dinner for you," I added.

"Thank you," Ann said. "That was really nice of you, Jim."

"Well it was my idea, but I couldn't have pulled it off without Stephanie helping me. Anyway, we're glad you liked it. Aren't we, Stephanie?" Jim said. "Because since we cooked . . ."

"I know," I said. "I have to do the dishes."

"You got it," Jim replied laughing.

"I'll help you, Matt," Stephanie blurted out, quietly adding, "I don't mind doing the dishes. I'm just so excited to be here."

Ann and Jim caught up on the news from D.C. as Professor Kempson relished relating the inside scoop on the government officials. My father, Senator Clifford Lane, was working on a budget bill.

Stephanie and I returned with a plate of cookies after finishing the cleanup.

Ann was telling Jim and Professor Kempson about her abduction. "Well, I now know why people get hooked on drugs. When you're high on heroin, it's a euphoric feeling. But when it wears off, you think you are going to die. A few more days of that and I would've been totally addicted. As it is, I was out of touch with reality. I don't know much about what's been going on. Matt gave me a brief overview of what happened, but I'm short on details. So forgive me if I seem a little lost."

"Join the club. I've not been given a lot of details either," Jim said, shooting an accusing glance my direction.

Rushing to reply before Stephanie could speak, I blurted out, "Ann feels she is well enough to start the search."

"Are you sure, Ann?" Stephanie asked.

"I'm more than ready."

Stephanie walked over and gave Ann a big hug. Then with tears in her eyes she said, "I'm so sorry Jack has done all these terrible things. I've known since I was seven that he was a horrible person, but I had no idea he would resort to murder and kidnapping. He's got to be insane. I'm so sorry, Ann."

"This was no fault of yours, Stephanie," Ann replied. "Jack is a monster! All three of them are. I hope they didn't come back because they died somewhere!"

"I'm sure we all hope Jack gets everything he deserves," I said, hoping to soften the sullen direction the conversation was leading.

"But looking forward to our search, the professor and I believe a good four-wheel-drive vehicle with air conditioning will be best where we are going. It may be a little crowded, but we'll see how it works out.

"And, professor," I asked, "you've been very busy studying the maps. What do you think?"

Professor Kempson rose and walked over to an easel with several sketches and maps attached. "Yes, I have been studying the rough sketches you copied from the map that this Jack Green now apparently has in his possession. I was hoping for a little more detail," he chuckled.

"We were too," Ann laughed.

"Sorry, Professor," I added. "I'm afraid that's the best we could do."

"I was most pleased to find the area where the map takes us is the exact place I have theorized the Ark of the Covenant was hidden. South of Jerusalem is the most logical place the Israelites would have chosen. There are limestone and sandstone canyons there. Those stones are porous and can be easily carved. There are also some natural caves like the ones where the Dead Sea Scrolls were found.

"I've been in all of these canyons at one time or another over the last several years. After comparing your sketch with some maps and charts of the canyon lands that I brought with me, I am hoping we can eliminate four of the five canyons your sketch shows.

"From bits and pieces I have read over the years, I am convinced the cave or cavern we are looking for was designed by King Solomon himself. The hiding place would have to be a cavern in the side of a high vertical canyon wall, far removed from the city . . . probably a natural cave. King Solomon could have used expert stonecutters to enlarge it and shape it to match his design. Concealing the entrance would have been a paramount problem. The stone used to conceal the entrance would have been very unique. It had to blend into the natural canyon wall. It couldn't be like the movies. In the movies, huge entrance stones are hoisted up or slid sideways using counterweights with ropes and pulleys behind the scenes. Any rope made at that time wouldn't have lasted more than a few hundred years. The stone couldn't be made like a stone wheel to be rolled open and closed the way they used to seal a tomb. It would be too easy to notice. A lot of engineering had to be put into that closure stone. After years of research, I believe the stone that covers the entrance has to be a tall, thick slab, leaning and pressed tightly against the canyon wall. The canyon walls are not smooth. They are very rough in texture and full of vertical fractures. The closure stone had to be so well designed, shaped and blended, it would be impossible to distinguish it from the craggy wall of the canyon. That's why no one has ever found it. The top must pivot right or left to reveal the entrance. Horses or a team of oxen may have been used to pull the top of the leaning stone to the right or to the left as you face it. That would open or close the entrance.

"My guess would be that any map showing the location of that special cavern was kept by King Solomon. As kings lived their lives and died, the map would have been kept very secret and passed down to each succeeding king.

"The cavern might have even been empty most of the time. The Ark of the Covenant was in the Holy of Holies at the Temple, and Israel's great treasure was stored in the treasury in Jerusalem. The prepared hiding place was for emergencies only. It may have never been used until the Babylonians invaded Jerusalem. That was more than three hundred years after King Solomon died. I'm sure the Ark of the Covenant and the great Israeli treasure would have definitely been moved out of Jerusalem and hidden at that time."

The professor was truly excited. "I'm hoping we can eliminate all of the canyons except one on our first search. There is one, in particular, that I believe is our canyon. I formed that opinion years ago, and your rough sketch confirms I was on the right track. We should start the search there first."

"Why do you think it might be one particular canyon?" I asked.

"I accidentally came into possession of a very rare manuscript many years ago. It was a rainy afternoon. I was in an antique book shop in the Old City. Back in a far dusty corner of the shop, I found an ancient journal. I purchased it because it was so old. The owner didn't even know it existed. It wasn't on his inventory, so he didn't know its origin. As I studied the old book, I came across a very interesting article. It appeared to be a copy of something that had originally been deciphered from a papyrus scroll written centuries before. The old scroll was a partial accounting of expenditures sometime during King Solomon's reign. I deciphered enough to believe the king had appointed one of his most trusted friends to be the watchman over a newly built, remote storage cavern. He gave this man sixteen cows, two bulls, one hundred sheep, fifty goats and a variety of seeds in bags. The king paid for a well to be dug on a plateau. He gave him many tents and everything he would need to raise his family. He placed this man he trusted and his family on the flat lands above a canyon. He and his family were to live at the top of this canyon and be vigilant to see that no one ever tried to find the storage cavern. I am sure the cavern had to be in the canyon below."

"What about the workers who originally worked on the cavern, those who made the stone door?" Ann asked.

"They were probably murdered to keep the secret. Then they could never be tortured to tell where it was or describe the closure stone. King Solomon could not afford to take any chances. I believe the chosen family . . . secret sentries . . . lived there for generations, father to sons, generation to generation, similar to the Knights Templar. After that discovery, needless to say, I spent a lot of time on the plateau above the canyons south of Jerusalem. I searched for a place where a canyon below would be quite visible. I searched for signs of someone having lived above one of the canyons."

"Did you find anything, professor?" Jim asked.

"Yes, as a matter of fact, I did. I finally came across the perfect spot. I searched the sand carefully and found small pieces of pottery shards everywhere. After some digging, I found rock foundations under the sand where dwellings had once been. I also uncovered an ancient brick-lined cistern, mostly filled with sand and a strange ring of rocks that I believe was the top of a water well. Wheat and corn could have been raised there. There was also an old trail leading down into the canyon. The trail down was rugged, but a team of horses coming from Jerusalem, even pulling a large cart, could have gone down into the canyon on that old trail. That canyon is my first choice. I never told anyone about the area until now. I believe when the Babylonians invaded Jerusalem in five-eighty-seven BC, the Ark of the Covenant and the treasury from Israel were moved into that remote storage cavern. King Solomon had it built for that very reason over three hundred years before. Unfortunately," the professor said, hesitating, "I have already searched both sides of that canyon to no avail. The canyon is fairly wide at the bottom of the plateau, then narrows as it continues down to the flat land. It is rough terrain. I was a lot younger and on horseback when I searched the area, but I never found the closure stone. If it has not changed in the past thirty years, we might get to the bottom in a Hummer H3 on that old chariot trail. That would be the fastest way into the canyon from Jerusalem. I don't think we could come back up that way though. It's too rough and steep to try to climb back up over those rocks on that same trail. We will have to follow the canyon on down to the bottom, then turn left across the rough terrain to the main highway that runs beside the Dead Sea. That highway will bring us back to Jerusalem."

I stood up. "Thank you, professor. I think your years of research may have finally paid off. Your research and our sketch were exactly what was needed."

"We can find that cavern," Jim said with conviction. "I know we can!"

An air of optimism filled the room. At last we were getting close to the greatest biblical treasure of all time . . . the Ark of the Covenant.

CHAPTER TWENTY-TWO

It was a little after 5 a.m. The girls and the professor had not come down for breakfast yet. I had the yellow Hummer packed with a cooler full of drinks and sandwiches. The sun was starting to rise when Jim joined me on the patio with two cups of coffee. Handing me one, he said, "I thought I heard you on the phone with Ira last night. How's he doing?"

"Well he was understandably a little perplexed. Apparently the insurance company can't understand how I could lose a Jeep Grand Cherokee, crash a Cessna, and not turn in the BMW I had rented. They found the BMW in a village outside of Bangkok with bullet holes in it, the rear window and the rear tires shot out. He asked me if I could perhaps call the insurance company and substantiate what happened. He also mentioned something about me being a little more protective with the rental cars here in Jerusalem."

"Well, I guess I can't blame him," Jim said. "Considering your recent auto and aircraft experiences, I'm apprehensive about getting into a vehicle with you."

We laughed. "I think he was pacified when I told him about my letter to the insurance company explaining what happened, including a copy of the police reports."

We slowly walked away from the house toward the rear of the large acreage.

"By the way, how did your meeting go with the Department of Antiquities yesterday?" Jim asked.

"Well, besides getting the permit to search in the canyon, they addressed me as Dr. Lane and treated me to a very nice lunch."

"I knew I should have gone with you," Jim said, feigning regret.

"I tried to get you to go, remember?"

"Well, don't listen to me next time. You know you always have to coax me to do those things."

"Yes, and you're always glad when I do."

"Yes, dad. You're right. Next time force me to go. Okay? I could use a little ego building about now."

"Oh, why is that? I've never known you to have a problem with self-esteem."

Jim stopped walking and turned to face me. He was smiling, but I knew he was baiting me.

"Well, it could be that I can't find a girlfriend, and you have two."

I gave Jim a quizzical stare. "I only have Ann, Jim. Ann is my girlfriend, maybe even more than just a girlfriend. I'm almost thirty-two years old."

"Don't remind me, partner. I'm thirty-one."

"We're getting a little long-in-the-tooth to have girlfriends."

"Maybe," Jim said. "But I'm not ready to settle down yet. It's you, my friend. I am beginning to worry about you. I think you might have a problem."

"What kind of a problem?"

"Stephanie . . . you know Stephanie . . . the girl from Thailand," Jim said, looking me straight in the eye. Now he had a serious look on his face.

"Yes, I do seem to remember a girl named Stephanie," I kidded him."What about Stephanie?"

"Well, let's just say, I don't know what happened in that mine, but something must've happened."

Ignoring the mine comment, I paused and then said, "You're right. I have a problem, but it's one a lot of men would love to have, something I've seen you struggle with a few times. Two girls seem to like me at the same time."

"No, Matt, you're wrong. The key word here is not like. The key word is love. Both Ann and Stephanie are in love with you. Don't tell me you haven't noticed Stephanie. It's obvious to everyone."

I turned away from Jim's penetrating stare.

"Don't get me wrong. Stephanie is a very beautiful girl. She is smart, sophisticated, poised. What else can I say? But when it comes to you, she makes any excuse to be around you, volunteering for everything as long as you're there. I'm surprised she didn't go with you to the Office of Antiquities. Mark my word, Matt. Sparks are going to fly between her and Ann. It's imminent."

I turned to face Jim, not knowing how to answer. "Stephanie is very special. I won't deny that. There was an incident in the mine that could complicate things, but right now I can't cope with it. I just thank God Ann is safe and recovering from her ordeal. I think everything else will work itself out."

Quickly changing the subject, I said, "What I am excited about right now is the Ark of the Covenant. It's in one of those canyons. I know it is, and we're very close to solving the puzzle."

"I know, Matt, and I agree. With the map and the professor's help, we may actually find it. But we're also close to an explosion of human emotions." Turning away, Jim leaned against the tall block wall that enclosed the estate. "We've shared everything since we met in seventh grade, Matt. I just wanted to be sure you were aware."

"Thanks for your concern, buddy," I said smiling, "and you're right. If something doesn't change soon, present circumstances could wreak havoc on my future with Ann. I don't know how to handle it. I have strong feelings for both girls. Ann is the love of my life, and I shouldn't have any such feelings for Stephanie, but I do. My emotions are in a turmoil. I have to get a grip on my own feelings. Then I can tackle the situation and deal with it. But not right now, not when we are so close to our goal."

An uncomfortable silence prevailed for what seemed like an eternity. Finally I said, "By the way, a woman from Antiquities has been assigned to be our contact. During our lunch, the head of the department patiently told me about all the people who have searched for the long-lost Ark of the Covenant. All seemed to possess a map of some kind. I don't think my rough sketch on stationery from the resort in Thailand impressed them very much."

"No, I don't suppose it would," Jim laughed.

"I didn't tell them what the professor added to the equation, or that he knows which canyon might be our first choice."

"Good," Jim replied.

"Our contact is to be with us if we investigate anything of interest. This is a good thing. If we find any important artifact, she will catalog each item. Then no one can accuse us of stealing it."

"I agree," Jim said. "That's good. Who is our contact?"

"They haven't told me her name yet."

"Maybe she's young, cute and single. And since you already have more women than you can handle, the field is clear for me. That is assuming, of course, you don't think you need three girlfriends."

"Very funny! But you'd better be on your best behavior. She may be the woman I saw in the office when I was obtaining our permit. If that was her, she exudes refinement and is extremely attractive. Definitely not your type," I joked. "Oh, and did I mention she may have a husband?"

Jim gave me a strange look, as if he were wondering whether I was kidding or if I was serious.

* * * * *

The sun was just rising, but it was already heating up the plateau. Without a cloud in the clear blue sky, the day would get much hotter.

We were south of Jerusalem as I drove slowly eastward on the flat sandstone, parallel with the rim above the canyon floor. The area below was a series of north to south canyons, each one separated by a plateau as high as the one we were driving on. The canyons ran adjacent to the rim. We had looked down the length of three of the canyons as we drove along the rim, and I could see more ahead of us. Each looked to be a few miles long with rough, hilly terrain where the plateaus finally started to slope down to blend with the desert floor. We hadn't seen a sign of civilization since we headed east off the dead-end dirt road, not even a shepherd's camp.

The cracks in the flat sandstone were getting deep, so I moved a little farther from the edge where there was more sand and brush. Professor Kempson was in front with me leaning out the window, his eyes straining to examine the terrain, trying to locate the place he had discovered years ago.

"Stop right here," he shouted. "This is it. This is the place I found."

He bounded out the door and jogged over to the edge of the canyon with the rest of us trailing in his wake.

"See right here," he pointed. "The old cart trail starts right here. It's cut into the sandstone cliff and goes clear to the bottom of this canyon. And look back there," he said excitedly walking back away from the trail apex. "These stones are not natural. They form a rectangle. I think they were a foundation for a stone building of some kind, probably a guard shack. It wasn't very large, but you can see the entire canyon from where it was constructed."

There it was . . . just as the professor had described. From where we stood, it seemed to be the only area where the cliff did not have a sheer drop-off. The sandstone sloped out enough to allow a zigzag trail all the way down. The old horse and cart path was in such disrepair with rocks, deep ruts, and brush, that it was hardly recognizable, but centuries before it had been used as a narrow road down to a canyon between two escarpments.

I wasn't sure a horse could pull a cart back up because it was so steep, and I had qualms that our Hummer H3 could even go down without plummeting over the edge. The crumbling roadway hadn't been used for a long, long time, and I doubted a motor vehicle had ever attempted the descent. The professor was the first to suggest we abandon his original idea of driving down that trail. He said it was much narrower than he remembered.

We followed the professor away from the rim to a large flat expanse of land. At first we didn't see anything. Digging and sweeping wherever the professor pointed, we began to uncover the remnants of a large ancient village, complete with two rings of stone. One was small, four or five feet in diameter. As we dug down in the center, we knew this one was once a well. The other ring was large, about twenty feet in diameter, and the flat rocks all around it under a layer of dirt sloped toward the center. We theorized this one had been used as a cistern to catch and hold rain water.

We found stone foundations everywhere, and the sand was full of tiny pottery shards. This ancient site had never been excavated. We sat down by a large rock to rest for a few minutes.

The professor was ecstatic. "That old book I told you about created a sense of urgency in me," he said. "I was about thirty years old and by myself. I rented a saddle horse and a packhorse, bought a tent, some camping gear, and enough food for two weeks. A piece of pottery sticking out of the sand prompted me to start searching here. Digging around the piece of pottery, I found the cistern . . . then some of the foundations. In one area I even found arrowheads, spearheads, and human bones. There was no doubt in my mind there had been a battle here. The bones were very old. I reburied them. Then when I looked over the edge and encountered the old trail to the bottom, it whet my appetite to explore more. I just knew this was the place described in my book . . . a perfect spot. They had water, land that would produce food, and a trail down to the canyon. I rode my horse down and then back up that old trail several times.

"Below is the canyon where King Solomon had a large storage vault built with a special stone to hide the entrance, and this settlement was set up to guard it. I'm sure of it."

By now, we were just as excited as the professor. We covered everything we had found with sand and agreed to come back later to excavate the entire area. Who knows what else might be hidden under this sand, but right now we were heading for the canyon floor.

I drove to the edge where the trail started. It looked wide enough for a cart or a wagon. Our Hummer was questionable. The trail was in extremely bad shape. Everyone tried to talk me out of trying it, but it would save hours of time if we could get to the bottom of the canyon this way. Taking a deep breath, I started down. I had everyone get out and walk while I drove over the eroded, most dangerous areas alone. The Hummer was too wide in some areas, and we all lugged loose rocks to fill in the road. After a half hour of slipping and sliding over brush, rocks and gravel, we arrived at the bottom. From there we could look back up and see the top of the pass where we had started our descent.

Jim hopped in the passenger seat at the professor's insistence.

"Jim has younger eyes. Watch the rock wall as we drive next to it down the canyon." Professor Kempson was sitting between Ann and Stephanie in the back seat. "The cavern has to be in this canyon. Of course, I usually have better maps to work with!" The professor chuckled, and before long we were all laughing at his wild tales.

The professor was a soft-spoken, charming man. Both girls found his stories fascinating. Jim and I had been in some of his classes on archaeology. Last year Professor Kempson had given Jim and me a map that led us to a cave above the Tigris River. There, a pictorial history of Noah and his sons constructing the great Ark and loading all the animals had been carved into the rock wall. From evidence we uncovered, we determined Noah's Ark had been constructed on the land below. That was in ancient Mesopotamia, now occupied mainly by the country of Iraq.

I continued to drive slowly down the rough terrain of the canyon. Craggy vertical walls of stone towered above us on both sides. The area reminded me of the canyon walls in Petra, but this canyon was wider.

We searched for hours examining the walls on both sides, riding in the Hummer. Finally we parked the vehicle, and everyone but Ann walked another couple of miles down the canyon and back. It was very hot. I had convinced Ann to wait in the shade by the car since she was still weak, much to her chagrin.

We studied the vertical crevasses in the ancient stone looking for a large slab that was not quite natural. The distance between the two canyon walls got very narrow at the bottom. We found nothing.

Discouraged, we drove out of the canyon until the vertical walls flattened into small barren hills. Then we turned left and picked our way across the rough terrain. We didn't encounter a person or an animal. We followed our compass, hoping to find the main road that showed on our map. The constant bouncing and jostling was hard on everyone, especially Ann who winced in pain when we hit hard in spots. We all sighed with relief when finally we found the paved road that took us back to Jerusalem.

That night after dinner we told the professor about our trip to Thailand. I again somehow managed to avoid telling any details of what happened in the mine. I never even mentioned the gas chamber. Stephanie listened intently to every word, but added nothing. Ann watched intently as I rushed over the story.

The professor marveled at our ingenuity and survival skills. "Judging from the cut you still have on your chin, Matt, and your bruised face, I'd say you got the worst of it."

"This guy Jack, Stephanie's cousin," I added, looking at Stephanie and trying to read her thoughts, "he's really something. He and his friends are hardened criminals. I'm relieved we didn't run into them in the canyon today. Something really does not add up. They have the original map, and they had a four-day head start on us."

"The map is pretty vague," the professor said. "There are many canyons in that area. They could easily be searching in the wrong one. I feel we are in the correct canyon only because of my previous research."

"Well, tomorrow we're going to take a different approach," I said. The room got very quiet as the group was caught off guard by my declaration. They all looked at me in surprise. "I reserved a small helicopter. We're going to get a view of that canyon from higher up. That worked for Jim and me once before when we were searching for the entrance to a tomb in Africa. Remember, Jim?"

"Do I remember? Yes, I remember. A lion almost ate us. I've got a boot with claw marks to prove it." Everyone laughed at Jim's outburst. "But you're right, Matt. Good idea."

"We may see something from a higher elevation, something we can't see from the canyon floor. Sorry, girls. They didn't have a chopper for rent that was big enough for all of us."

Stephanie made a grimacing face, but then turned and said, "Would you like to go shopping, Ann?"

"Sure," was the disappointed reply.

*****

Jim, the professor, and I were in the air by eight.

When we arrived in the area, I hovered and moved slowly in front of the rock wall on both sides of the canyon. The lower part was almost too narrow in a few places to fly the helicopter through, but I was very careful and we made it all the way down the long canyon.

"What about that section right in front of us?" I said as we hovered in front of the wall. "From up here, it looks a little unnatural."

"You mean that portion that protrudes out from the wall? There are lots of areas that look like that," Jim said.

"Yes, but it's about the size I would expect it to be. It looks to be about eight feet wide at the bottom and twelve to fourteen feet tall. It probably protrudes out twelve to sixteen inches, maybe even a little more in some areas."

"I remember this area," the professor said. "It blended perfectly standing in front of it yesterday, but I'll admit it looks a little different from up here."

I moved the helicopter back and forth and higher as we studied the stone through the clear plastic cockpit.

"Look closely at the top. It's narrow and pointed. It also looks like there is enough space behind it to allow for the thickness of a rope. The rope could slip down quite a distance. If a deep hole was dug in the sand at the base so it could be pulled sideways, pulling hard at that point wouldn't break the top off.

"All the vertical cracks in these rocks slope up to our left, but maybe with a strong rope and a team of horses, the peak of that stone could have been pulled over to the right. If what we are looking at is really a slab of rock leaning against the wall, and not just a protruding part of the mountain, the entrance could be right behind it."

"Maybe," Jim said, sounding rather doubtful . . . if it really is a separate piece and not part of the rock wall. If it's part of the wall, a D10 caterpillar couldn't move it, and from down lower, it just looks like a craggy protrusion from the solid rock wall. There are a lot of slab-shaped rocks that don't look much different from this one."

We were in the widest part of the canyon, right at the bottom of the ancient trail we had driven down yesterday.

"Well, it's the most promising possibility we have seen yet," I said. "If we don't find anything that looks more like a separate closure stone, I'm going to ask our Antiquities Officer if she wants to witness us possibly making fools of ourselves when we try to pull it open."

"Let's try it," Jim said, "but we may look pretty stupid trying to move a piece of solid rock wall."

We all laughed in agreement.

We flew on down the canyon again, searching for a more positive location. At the bottom, I rose up probably 250 feet, turned left, and flew out over the next plateau.

As I made my turn, something strange caught my eye. "I think I just saw something. I'm going back."

I turned again and flew back over the narrow canyon next to the one we had been searching in.

"Look," I pointed. "There's a car down there."

"I see it," Jim said.

"I can't get down. This canyon's too narrow. It's a black Hummer. Maybe it's the one Jack rented."

"It looks from here like it's sitting in a gravel wash. There are some big boulders around it," the professor said.

"It's not moving, and the driver's side door is open. I don't see anyone around.

"It may not be Jack. There are a lot of black Hummers in the city. You think someone may be in trouble down there, Matt?" Jim said.

"It's a bad area to get stranded in," Professor Kempson said. "It can get very hot down on that desert floor, and if you don't have plenty of water, you can die in only a few hours."

"This entire canyon is too narrow for me to land," I said. "If anyone is down there, they surely would be waving at us if they need help. We'll notify the police, and they can follow us back out here this afternoon. We don't know for sure anyone is in trouble. They may have had plenty of water and hiked out yesterday."

"Do you think that could really be Jack's car, Matt?" Jim asked as we flew back to the airport.

"Could be," I replied. "That would explain why he didn't come back to the house he rented."

We knew we would come back that afternoon to see if anyone needed help. If it was Jack, at least we would know where he was.

CHAPTER TWENTY-THREE

Ann watched Stephanie put her Gucci handbag on the chair next to her, mentally noting she had one just like that. They were having breakfast in a restaurant in Jerusalem, prior to going shopping. This was to be "Girls' Day Out" and Ann and Stephanie looked stunning.

"Look," Stephanie said, pointing out the large window. "There's the Damascus gate. That's one of the busiest gates into Old Jerusalem. Isn't that interesting, Ann?"

This was the first time the girls had been together with no one else around.

"Yes, it is," Ann replied trying to sound as excited as Stephanie, but she had other things on her mind. "The professor promised to take us into the Old City while we're here, remember?"

"I know. I can't wait," Stephanie said excitedly. She took another drink of water and smiled at Ann, who was looking out the window.

They continued to make small talk, but something was wrong.

"I just hope they find the entrance to the cavern today," Ann said. "The professor was so sure they would find it in the canyon we were in yesterday. He eliminated several canyons. If he's right, and he feels sure he is, that will save a lot of time."

"If only we had the original map," Stephanie wistfully mused.

"Matt copied exactly what was on that old map. I helped him." Ann sounded a little defensive. "The original map is just so old and dried out."

"Oh, I know. The mark that once showed the location in the canyon just faded out, but I agree with the professor. It's got to be in the canyon they're searching right now. I wish Matt could have rented a larger helicopter. I'd love to be with him . . . ah . . . them today."

"So would I." A scowl briefly passed over Ann's face. Quickly avoiding an ugly moment, she said, "Shall we order?"

* * * * *

The housekeeper poured them some iced tea and left the room. They sat on the couch in the living room. It was much too hot outside to enjoy the patio.

Stephanie sensed Ann watching her. Her palms became sweaty and her mouth was dry. Would this be the moment of confrontation?

"Stephanie, can I ask you some questions?"

"Of course," Stephanie replied cheerfully, trying to hide her nervousness. "What about?" she said, facing Ann and forcing a smile.

"I think you know, Stephanie." She paused. "What happened in that mine?"

"What did Matt tell you, Ann?"

"Nothing. He tells me nothing. I have to know, Stephanie. It's very important to me."

"Maybe you shouldn't know, Ann."

"What do you mean?"

Stephanie slowly stood up. She wore high heels and a short skirt, and her hair hung down to her shoulders . . . a stunning woman indeed! She turned to face Ann. "This is very hard for me." A lump caught in her throat and tears starting to form in her eyes. "I knew you were going to ask me, and I've been dreading it. Just the thought of that mine still terrifies me. I don't like to talk about it. I don't even like to think about it."

"I know, Stephanie. That's how I feel when I think about Jack Green, but I have to know. Please tell me."

Stephanie hesitated. "Well, first they beat Matt up. You've seen his face. It is still healing, and some of his black eye is still visible."

"I know," Ann said. "Please go on."

"They locked us in a room in one of the mine shafts and started pumping poison gas in."

"Poison gas? Matt didn't tell me anything about poison gas."

"We had to use our clothes to stuff in the duct work and keep the gas from killing us. We had already been told that if we survived the gas, we would be shot at five a.m. and our bodies would be dumped down a deep shaft. It was cold, we were practically naked, and we knew we were going to die." Stephanie's voice was quivering. She couldn't hold back the tears. "We had to hold each other tight to get warm enough to keep trying to find a way out. We had to hold each other tight often." She glanced at Ann to see her reaction. "I was so sure we would never get out of there alive, that when Matt was holding me to get warm, I kissed him, and he kissed me back. We thought we were going to die. I knew we would be shot in a few hours. I love Matt, Ann. I'm sorry. I can't help it or hide it. I love him! And since we were going to die, I told him I loved him. I'm sorry, Ann. Sometimes things just happen."

"Okay stop, Stephanie! I understand. You don't have to tell me anymore. It must've been horrible."

"It was, Ann. It really was. Matt found an old steam engine that they used to haul out the ore. It was a miracle he got it running and used it to break down the door. Matt was wonderful. I was a nervous wreck. I was sure we would die, but Matt never panicked. He just kept searching and using his ingenuity until he got us out. I'm sorry, Ann."

"I know you are, Stephanie. I'm sorry too. I'm even sorry I asked," Ann said, wiping her eyes and trying not to show how shocked she was.

Just as she started to say something more to Stephanie, they heard the car doors close in the front drive.

With tears streaming down her cheeks and pain in her heart, Ann ran to her room and closed the door. She couldn't face Matt right now. Not right now.

CHAPTER TWENTY-FOUR

Joanne Zivah was nervous. The petite twenty-six-year old blonde had been summoned to the director's office in the Department of Antiquities. She entered the office and took the only chair in the room in front of the director's desk.

No one else was in the room. She checked her watch to verify she was on time, not too early, not too late. The clock on the wall behind the director's chair above a long mahogany credenza confirmed it was exactly 10 a.m. Had she done something wrong? Although she had been working in this department for almost eighteen months, she had never met the director, Dr. Levi.

The three-story building was very modern. All the walls were mostly glass. A wide corridor opened to offices on both sides. In the atrium, the aromatic floral scents in the air and the happily chirping birds in the emerald green canopy of trees provided a tranquil atmosphere away from the hustle and bustle of work. A stream with a small waterfall wound though the wooded area with a smattering of benches along the sidewalk.

The cafeteria was in the atrium. Joanne often purchased a sandwich or brought her lunch from home and ate it here. The sounds of birds and smells of the cafeteria were gentle reminders of how blessed she felt she was at this time in her life. There were places on each floor where one could stop and view this beautiful garden through tall glass panels.

She liked working here. Her hours were 9 to 5, each day spent in a large portion of the ground floor. Her cubicle was a standard eight feet by eight feet. The people she worked with were friendly and fun, but she missed being out in the field, actually down on her knees in the sand, excavating a primitive site, hoping to find some ancient writings perhaps on a piece of pottery or a clay tablet – a glimpse of life from an ancient civilization.

The clock now read 10:08. Had she misunderstood where the meeting was to be? Was she in the wrong office? She got up and went to the glass wall. Pushing the heavy glass door open, she peered both ways. No one was in the corridor or in the office across the corridor. She confirmed the number on the door read 3100.

She sat back down. Maybe they were going to dismiss her. She knew about the tightening of budgets all over Israel, and several people in her department had already been laid off. That had to be it. A secretary would soon come in with a pink slip.

She began to worry. How would she pay her portion of the rent at the apartment she shared with her best friend Talya? She and Talya had been friends and roommates for years. They were both so much alike. They shared everything, even their clothes. If Talya had a date, she would often borrow a dress or some jewelry from Joanne and vice versa. She began to think where she might get another job. There aren't that many positions for female archaeologists in Israel.

Joanne was born in upstate New York. Her Israeli father and American mother moved to Israel when she was sixteen years old. It wasn't easy for an American to adjust to such a change of culture, but with her outgoing personality she easily made friends. After high school, she attended the Israeli Archaeological Field School in Omrit, Israel. Then there were the five exciting years of exploring archaeological sites from the Sea of Galilee to the banks of the Dead Sea. She loved archaeology.

Her thoughts were jarred back to the present as a nice looking, dark complected gentleman in his mid-fifties, wearing a suit and tie, burst through the glass door. Joanne snapped to attention and quickly rose when he entered. Obviously out of breath, he sat his briefcase on the credenza and hurried to shake her hand and introduce himself.

"I am so sorry I am late, Miss Zivah," he apologized.

Dr. Levi was an energetic man, dedicated to his position. His main job was to see that anything of archaeological importance that was excavated or found in the sand by a citizen, a tourist or an expedition was cataloged with the location of the find and properly registered. It was also his responsibility to see that these items were not taken out of Israel. Too many wonderful artifacts had been smuggled out of the country over the years and were either still being sold and traded on the black market or were already in someone's private collection. The Department of Antiquities wanted all of these items to be displayed for everyone to see and enjoy in Israeli museums. Dr. Levi worked tirelessly in this effort.

Taking a moment, Joanne made some quick observations. Dr. Levi was about five-feet-eight inches tall, serious, but generous with his smile. His dark curly hair was gray at the temples, but his brown eyes were bright and alert.

He sat down behind his desk and got right to business. He told her she had been highly praised by her supervisors, and they had recommended her for a field assignment that had just opened up. He said he would understand if she declined the job as it would require much of her time away from the comforts of an air-conditioned office, and her hours may be long on certain days. Dr. Levi explained the job thoroughly.

Joanne Zivah did not even think about not taking the job. She immediately reached out to shake his hand, thanking him for the opportunity and accepted the new position, vowing to do her very best.

Dr. Levi felt good about his choice and added that even though these were tough times for the Department of Antiquities, she would be receiving a modest increase in salary and benefits. She would also be wearing an official badge and would be formally addressed as Officer Zivah.

CHAPTER TWENTY-FIVE

I turned off the highway that paralleled the Dead Sea and drove out across the rough terrain. We knew most days in this area at this time of year would be hot and dry, and today was no exception. The landscape crossing the barren hills below the canyons was parched with very little vegetation, but the sky seemed to be always a brilliant blue.

I followed the tire tracks we had made the day before when we drove across the south end of the canyons looking for the highway. We finally arrived at the canyon where we had seen the wrecked Hummer. Two four-wheel-drive vehicles were following us. The one directly behind was a police Jeep with two Israeli police officers. They were coming to investigate the abandoned vehicle and possible injured or stranded travelers. The yellow Jeep Wrangler I was watching in my rearview mirror as we zigzagged around obstacles was the person from the Department of Antiquities, Officer Joanne Zivah. She was a cute blonde. Joanne's bouncy personality enhanced her blue eyes and big smile. There was no hesitation on her part after what we had described about a possible hidden cavern. She was not wearing a ring, which pleased Jim immensely.

I noticed both Ann and Stephanie were unusually quiet. Neither girl hardly answered when Jim asked how the shopping went. I knew something was wrong.

As we entered the bottom of the narrow canyon, the terrain became very rough. Huge boulders and a dry riverbed were in the chasm between the vertical cliffs. We led the three-car caravan slowly. I picked out the best route I could, mostly in the rocky riverbed. Four-wheel-drive was not an option. . . . It was imperative. It was the only type of vehicle that could climb over the rocks and make it up the canyon.

We continued slowly and steadily until we could see the black Hummer about a half-mile ahead, facing us.

Jim said, "Maybe they had made their way to the high-end of this dead-end canyon and were coming back out when they broke down and . . . ."

His conversation was interrupted by Ann's shout from the back seat. "Stop! Back up a little, Matt. Look to your right. There's someone behind that big rock. I can see his boot sticking out."

Jim and I jumped out and ran to the area. There were two men behind the large boulder. They weren't going anywhere. . . . They were dead!

Ann recognize the first man as one of the two Thai men who came to Israel on Jack's plane. His body was bloated, a grotesque look on his face. She looked, then turned quickly away. I put my arms around her. His eyes were still open. I was surprised the body was not in an even worse state, as I watched several large birds circling overhead. He was lying in the shade of the rock with one small empty plastic bottle by his side.

The other man was lying on his stomach. The police officers rolled him over. After searching papers in his wallet, they were quite sure he was also from Thailand. Due to his decayed condition, Ann couldn't be sure if he had also been on the plane with them.

The license plate confirmed that this was the car Jack Green had rented.

"The heat in this canyon is brutal. They probably died the first day out," one of the officers said as he wiped the sweat from his face with his handkerchief.

"That would have been four days ago," Jim replied.

"Knowing Jack," I said, "these two would have been the ones he elected to not share the water with. It looks like their Hummer struck a rock a long way back. Look at the oil trail. It punched a hole in the side of the oil pan."

"That had to be a freak accident. The Hummer has skid plates to help prevent punching holes in the bottom," Jim commented.

We searched the vehicle. I found some white powder on the black leather rear seat.

"They were very likely too high on drugs to notice they had a flat tire and were leaking oil until the engine seized."

We spread out and started looking for any more bodies. About half a mile from the Hummer in the ravine we had just driven up, Jim found the leather tube. The map and letters were still inside.

"Jack probably tried to carry this out with him but finally gave up and just tried to save himself," Stephanie commented.

Jim handed the leather tube to Officer Zivah. She looked at the policeman in charge who knew her. He told her it would be okay for her to take it.

For two hours we helped search for the other men. It was getting late. I told the officer in charge if Jack, Drake, and Tiny made it out of this canyon and started out across the open desert, they could be anywhere. The police called for a helicopter to start searching the wide area between the base of the canyon and the highway. They thanked us for our help. They were sure the helicopter would locate the other three bodies. Without much water, they could never have made it to the highway.

We searched the canyon again as we slowly made our way back. We found nothing. Finally we left the officers and headed in the opposite direction of the highway. We continued picking our way across the rough barren hills. Officer Zivah . . . Joanne as we were all calling her . . . followed in her yellow Wrangler, but she wasn't alone. She had asked Jim if he would help her drive. When Jim got out of the front passenger seat, Stephanie, who had been sitting behind him, rushed to take his seat next to me. I could see Ann's face in the rear-view mirror. She did not look happy.

We headed up the next canyon, the one we had searched by chopper earlier that morning.

"This is the canyon! I'm even more sure of it now," the professor shouted from the back seat. "I've looked up the other canyons as we crossed them. This is the only canyon King Solomon would have chosen for his vault. That huge rock we spotted from the chopper has got to be the closure stone . . . It just has to be," he added, mostly to himself.

* * * * *

Jim and I took turns digging the sand away from the base of the rock we had spotted from the helicopter earlier. The professor helped. The more we exposed the base with the odd-shaped bottom, the more it became evident that the stone was really hiding the cavern entrance. Our digging now took on an air of excited frenzy.

The sun was casting long shadows across the canyon. The top of the canyon wall opposite where we were working was a glow of brilliant shades of crimson and gold, but huge thunderhead storm clouds were gathering.

After removing almost four feet of sand we knew this was the stone we had been searching for, and now we understood how it was designed to function. What a marvel of engineering!

We determined the massive closure stone was like one single hand on a very large clock. The hand only moved between the ten o'clock and the two o'clock positions. A large hole chiseled through the stone near the bottom, slipped over a round stone post, which protruded out from the canyon wall about three feet below the level of the canyon floor.

When the large stone, functioning like a clock hand, was at rest in the ten o'clock position, as it was now, the entrance was concealed. We theorized that if we pulled the top of the stone to the right completely over to the two o'clock position, it should open up and reveal the entrance to a cavern. At least we hoped it would. Excited, we all started pushing sideways on the mammoth stone, but it didn't budge. It was much too heavy.

Not discouraged, we devised another plan of attack to move the barrier between us and what we hoped was a cavern. I positioned the Hummer with the passenger side parallel with the rock wall. Standing on top of it, Jim looped a heavy wide nylon strap I had purchased between the slab and the canyon wall. I secured the strap to the tow hook under the front bumper closest to the wall. It was now getting dark, and a few raindrops were starting to fall. Our time frame was quickly closing.

Ann hopped in the vehicle and turned the headlights on. On my signal, she slowly started to back up, staying close and parallel with the canyon wall. The strap tightened. Jim, I, and the professor all pushed on the stone. Joanne Zivah and Stephanie stood back and watched as the strap stretched even tighter. Just as I thought the strap was surely going to snap, the top of the stone moved just a little. Continuing to apply steady pressure, we were able to slowly move the stone. It made an eerie, low-pitched, grinding sound, protesting as it moved against the mating surface of the flat canyon wall.

Like magic, an opening in the wall began to appear. Everyone, including Officer Joanne, cheered. It was only a small dark triangle at the lower left corner at first, but the triangle began to enlarge as the top of the stone moved. When I determined the stone had reached its balance position at twelve o'clock, I instructed Ann to stop pulling and shift into low, maneuvering forward ever so slowly. The nylon strap went slack. The stone appeared static in that position.

A man could pass through at this point, but the entrance wasn't fully open. I had Ann back up again. Suddenly, without warning, the heavy slab began to move under the power of gravity. The nylon strap went slack again as the top of the stone picked up speed in its arc until it struck a stone ledge with a loud thud. It came to rest at the two o'clock position, revealing an opening in the mountain about four feet wide and seven feet high. The entrance to King Solomon's hidden desert vault was open!

Jim and the professor grabbed six flashlights from the back of the car just as a bright flash of lightning lit up the sky. It was getting darker by the minute. Black clouds covered the entire area, and the wind whistled up the canyon as the storm approached.

We couldn't step across the hole at the base of the dark entrance until we shoveled most of the sand back into the hole. Finally I turned on my flashlight and shined it back into the entrance of the tunnel. The foreboding blackness revealed little to its intruders. Cautiously, I stepped into the tunnel with the other five following close behind.

The floor sloped uphill a little. The stonecutters must have done that so rainwater seeping in would run back out. We could see the chisel marks on the walls. A light layer of fine sand covered the floor.

"Something's not right," I said out loud.

"What is it?" Ann asked as she came up beside me.

"The foot prints in the sand," I said, as I stopped and shined my light on the floor in front of us. . . . They don't look like sandal prints, but rather more like boot prints."

Moving on, we emerged from the entrance tunnel and stepped into a large cavity. We all shined our lights around the room. The space was empty except for two crates. The crates were made out of a rough form of plywood.

Ann shrieked as her light beam landed on a skeleton sitting on the stone floor in a corner. The torso was still upright leaning against the wall. As we made our way to the skeleton, we paused to look in the two crates. Both were full of old tarnished pieces of silver . . . goblets, candle holders, trays, and many more things. Two marble busts were sitting on the floor next to the crates. It looked as though whoever was here before us left in a hurry. Puzzled, we moved to the skeleton. Remnants of tattered clothing were stuck to the bones. Dry skin and hair were still attached to the skull.

Joanne Zivah was down on her hands and knees using her flashlight to examine the skeleton more closely.

"I don't know for sure, but I don't think he was very old. Look at the black hair and shape of the skull – maybe just a young man. He must have somehow been trapped in here. He wasn't tied up; his hands and feet were not bound. Maybe it was an accident. What a terrible way for a young man to die."

"He looks like he's been here a long time," Jim said.

"That's probably David," Ann said. "Remember the ancient letter that Ben Shalev wrote. He said David was accidentally left to watch over the treasure. That was twenty-six-hundred years ago."

"Look at this," I said. "Most of the walls and the ceiling are naturally formed sandstone walls. Only two of the walls are flat. They were cut to enlarge this room which looks to be about twenty feet by thirty feet. The ceiling varies between twenty to thirty feet high."

"Where is the rest of the treasure?" Ann said.

"Where's the Ark of the Covenant?" I said. We all stood in total shock and disappointment. Finally I said, "There are some tunnels leading off this room. Let's look in them, but all these boot prints are telling me someone beat us to the Ark and the treasure."

"Well, we know it wasn't Jack," Stephanie said.

"No, it wasn't Jack." I answered. "The plywood crates are rather primitive and old. The wood is all dried out. It has been here a long time. Plywood was first made in the 1940s," I said. "Someone came here seventy or eighty years ago with plywood crates to remove the treasure."

I moved down a wide passage shining the flashlight ahead of us.

"What a shock," Stephanie said as she followed behind Ann and me. "What do you see in front of you, Matt?"

"I think there's a room up ahead."

"Maybe the Ark is in there."

I entered first. Stephanie screamed as she saw the grotesque face in my flashlight beam. The body of a man was lying on his back next to a wall. This man was wearing a blue sailor's uniform. His hands had been placed across his chest, with his hat by his side. The body was mummified.

"I don't think this guy was very old either," Ann said as she knelt by the body.

"I wonder what happened to him?" Stephanie remarked. "Two young men died in here. This is horrible. This is the fourth dead person we have seen today."

Jim put his arm around Stephanie to help calm her, as she was visibly shaken.

I knelt beside the corpse. Being careful, I went through all the pockets and found them to be empty, but under the body I found a small paper card. It was a faded rust color after years of exposure. "Look, I think this may be a pass of some kind. The writing looks like Italian to me. What do you think, Ann?"

"It is Italian," she said. "I think this is a pass to get food on a ship or on a base. There is a name printed here, but it is too stained to decipher. I'm guessing he was an Italian sailor, maybe early World War II," Ann said.

"Wait a minute," I said. "I see part of a brass pin on his uniform under his hands."

As we were talking, Jim, Joanne, and the professor ambled into the room. They were surprised to see the second body. We told them what little we knew about the sailor. They had found only a large pile of very old wood. They speculated that some of the treasure may have been in ancient crates.

Anxious to find at least one more clue, I said, "Let's go ahead and search for anything we might find. I won't try to remove the pin. I'll let the experts do that, but I'm really curious."

Professor Kempson, who had been moving about the room, said, "If you look closely, the walls in this room are all covered in plaster. It is a perfect match to the color of the stone. And look at this alcove in the wall above the dead man."

We all looked at the wall. There was a carved indentation in the wall about four inches deep, starting about four feet up from the floor. It was about eight feet wide and four feet tall with a slight arch at the top. The ceiling was rough natural stone about twenty feet high.

Professor Kempson shined his light up on the wall. "I think there is writing in the alcove, but it's not very visible."

We all rushed over to look, being careful not to step on the corpse. It was too faint to read. I redirected my light at an angle across the letters which improved the visibility.

"The words seem to be written in a very ancient Hebrew," the professor said.

Ann, Jim, and I all tried to help the professor interpret the text, but only the professor was able to translate it.

Professor Kempson studied the words for several minutes. "This is really old writing. I think it's the oldest I have ever seen. I believe it says, 'If ye seek real treasure, look up toward God's heaven.'"

We all stared at the inscription.

Finally Jim said, "I guess someone was trying to say getting into heaven is the greatest treasure, and we are not supposed to be disappointed if we don't find this one."

The next hour was spent searching the entire cave. We carefully looked in each of the four rooms and tunnels. Then we examined the walls for any outline of a sealed chamber, but found nothing.

A violent thunderstorm was raging outside. Lightning flashes reflected on the walls inside the main room, followed by thunder.

We came back to the skeleton. This time we found some words scratched into the wall. The writing was very old, but not as ancient as the engraving in the other chamber. Ann could also read this.

"I think he may have written part of this in the dark," Ann said as she aimed her flashlight on the scratched message and began to read.

"I am David of Jerusalem. Being sealed in this cavern was an accident. Tell my mother and my sisters that I love them."

Remnants of an old reed torch lay near the body.

"How alone and afraid he must have felt when the torch finally went out," Ann said.

Saddened and disappointed, it was time to leave. The storm prevented us from closing the entrance stone. We agreed the find would be safe until we came out in the morning with Joanne and her colleagues from the Department of Antiquities.

We drove back to Jerusalem in silence. It was still raining when I stopped at a corner under a street light and picked up Jim, who had driven Joanne's vehicle.

Our hopes were dashed, but I knew this wasn't the end. We just had to follow the clues. What did the Italians do with whatever they found? If they took it back to Italy even though it was war time, someone would know. Maybe the dead sailor still had a tale he could tell.

It was almost impossible to believe, but we suspected the Israeli treasure had probably been in that cavern for centuries. Then somehow the cavern had been found and its treasures stolen by members of the Italian navy during World War II.

Could this turn of events lead us to another country . . . to yet another piece of the puzzle?

The Italians may have found the gold and silver, but we didn't believe they found the Ark of the Covenant. If anyone on earth actually possessed the real Ark of the Covenant, we were sure the whole world would have heard about it by now.

That meant it's still hidden somewhere . . . but where?

CHAPTER TWENTY-SIX

Early the next morning, I introduced the others to Officer Joanne Zivah's boss, Dr. Levi, who was in charge of archaeological preservation.

We drove Dr. Levi and his team out to the cavern. They pored over the site like forensic scientists. Both skeletons were gingerly removed. The team photographed, cataloged, and boxed the items found in the two crates and the two marble busts. They were also very interested in the pile of ancient wood and carefully removed every scrap, including the wood dust.

Every detail of our discovery and the events leading us here was recorded. Though disappointed that the Ark and the treasure had not been found, Dr. Levi showered us with gratitude for finding the cavern. He was encouraged that maybe there really had been a lot more treasure hidden there. The cavern was certainly large enough.

When I introduced Stephanie to Dr. Levi, together we told him that the map and the letters that led us to the cave had belonged to her uncle, who had spent several years researching the lost Ark of the Covenant. He had been positive it would be found in that cavern. If he was correct, whoever took the treasure also may have the Ark of the Covenant. Stephanie donated her uncle's map and the letters to the Israeli Department of Antiquities.

Dr. Levi asked if we would be able to stay in the area for a week or two. He informed us that he would mount an investigation to try to find the perpetrators who had taken whatever had been in the cavern. Tomorrow he was going to contact a colleague in Rome. Everyone agreed to stay, except Professor Kempson. He had a prior commitment to give a series of lectures on archaeology at the University in Washington D.C. He was reluctant to leave and made us promise we would keep him informed.

Dr. Levi thanked the professor. Shaking his hand, he said, "I've been told that without all of the research you have done, the cavern may never have been found. Thank you for that and rest assured that should the stolen treasure ever be tracked down, you will be remembered as one who helped find it."

* * * * *

Before he left, the professor fulfilled his promise to take us on a tour of the old walled City of Jerusalem. It was amazing. We spent the entire day there with the professor showing us the highlights.

That evening after dinner we gathered in the living room. Everyone was talking about the day's events and all the things we had experienced in Jerusalem . . . the Via Dolorosa where Jesus carried the cross, the place where many believe the Last Supper took place, the Garden of Gethsemane and the rock where Jesus prayed to God, the place Jesus was taken before his trial. It was a religious pilgrimage unsurpassed by any other.

"By the way," Jim remarked, changing the subject, "what a great housekeeper you hired, Matt. She's young and full of energy, not bad looking either." He grinned.

"She is an excellent cook," Ann said as she sat down on an overstuffed chair.

Stephanie sat down next to me on the couch. "I love this house, Jim," Stephanie remarked. "I'm so glad you were able to rent it. Can we just stay here forever, Matt? All of us, I mean," she stammered. "This is perfect . . . this house, this country, and we are only a short distance from the walls of the Old City of Jerusalem. I still can't believe we walked the same streets that Jesus walked. He was crucified and placed in a tomb not far from where we are sitting right now. This is magical for me."

"It's magical for us all," Professor Kempson remarked. "I feel the same way, Stephanie, every time I come to this country, and I've spent a lot of my life here. We are just very lucky we could actually be here. Often Israel is a dangerous place to be. But every time I am here, I get the strong urge to try to live my life a little better. I believe if we are really judged in a future existence, that judgment will be based on how we lived our lives and how much we tried to help others."

We all concurred.

"Well," the professor said, "I really hate to leave you. I think you may be on the cusp of another great adventure. And how I love a great adventure!" he chuckled.

Ann, sitting closest to the professor, gave him a big smile. "We are going to miss you, professor. We wish you didn't have to leave us."

"Thank you for all you have done, professor," I said. "We probably would never have found Solomon's treasure vault without your diligent research."

"Well, it's too bad someone else found it first," he replied. "I have to assume that the map the Italians discovered was much more detailed than the old map we had. In all my years of research, I don't remember meeting any Italian archaeologist. The map they had in the 1940's must have pinpointed the cavern."

We all agreed.

"But where is the treasure?" I said. "And why didn't they take everything?"

"Maybe it's like the movie we all saw a few years ago," Jim commented. "They only wanted the Ark of the Covenant. Maybe that's all that was in that cavern . . . the two crates of silver, the two old busts of ancient leaders, and the Ark of the Covenant. Maybe the Ark of the Covenant was all they wanted."

"I don't know," I replied. "Italy needed money to keep the war machine going, yet they still left all that silver. Maybe there was a lot of gold, and they took the gold but left some of the silver. That could mean they couldn't carry it all. They closed the stone and filled in the sand. They probably planned to return for the rest of it, but they didn't. It could be that everyone who knew the location was killed in the war. Maybe we will never know."

As we all said good night, I noticed Ann was the first to leave the room. She had done that often lately. I had no doubt now. Ann was trying to avoid being alone with me.

* * * * *

Jim and I were talking when the phone rang. When I hung up, I had a grin on my face.

"Dr. Levi's team uncovered enough information from the uniform, the pin, and the chow pass to lead them to believe the sailor was from an Italian navy cargo ship, the 'Brenero.' They are pursuing the naval archives regarding that ship to see what happened to it and will call me when they learn anything."

"That's great news. They're moving fast," Jim replied.

"I think our discovery really got someone's attention," I said.

The following afternoon, I got another call from Dr. Levi. "Dr. Lane," he paused. "I'm afraid I have bad news."

"That's not what I wanted to hear," I replied.

"No," Dr. Levi agreed. "We are all quite disheartened. As you know, the sailor whose body you discovered in the cavern was stationed on the 'Brenero.' Unfortunately, the Italian naval records list the 'Brenero' as being sunk off the coast of Israel in 1940. The only survivor told authorities they hit a mine. All hands were lost, except for one sailor. He was found unconscious in a lifeboat several days later by an Italian patrol boat. The ship now rests on the bottom of the ocean, but no one knows exactly where."

"That is bad news," I said, disappointed. "What about the Ark of the Covenant? Do you know if it was on that ship?"

"We believe it could have been. From what we have learned at this point, we believe a vast treasure was removed from that cavern. We began by tracing the dead sailor you found. He died from the bite of a poisonous snake. He had only been on the ship for nine days. He came aboard July 11, 1940. The next port the ship came into was Haifa, Israel. The ship was moored at Berth #3 at the Haifa shipyards. The records from the shipyard reveal that on July 20th, ten large Italian army trucks with unspecified cargo were loaded on board. The ship pulled out that evening. It sank the night of July 21, 1940. We believe the treasure was in those trucks."

"What about the sailor who survived? Is he still alive?"

"No. Unfortunately, he was killed two months later when the next ship he was assigned to was also sunk."

"Did he have a family?"

"He had a wife. She is still alive, living on a farm in the country. The nearest city is Florence, Italy. She is in her early nineties. I hope you don't mind, Dr. Lane, but I took the liberty of having my liaison officer contact her and ask if she would be willing to meet with you. She agreed, but I'm told she may have a little dementia so she may not remember very much. She probably doesn't know anything that would help us, but you never know."

"No," I said, "you never know."

* * * * *

I drove the rental car up the narrow, rutted dirt road. It was 6 p.m. Ada Marino said she would be home at 5:30 p.m., and asked if six would be too late. The cloudy skyline was a dreary gray, and the wind whipped the large pine trees lining the drive. The branches lashed at us, delivering a foreboding message.

I parked in front of the old farmhouse almost hidden behind tall trees that formed an umbrella over the house. There was a large barn at the end of the yard.

A vicious sounding bark startled Ann and me as we reached the gate of the picket fence that enclosed the yard. A big German shepherd tugged the chain attached to his collar as he lunged toward us. Fortunately, it stopped him just short of the walk leading to the front door. The door opened, and an elderly woman beckoned us up the walk. She invited us in after cautiously scrutinizing our identification.

Soon Ann and I were seated at a wooden table in a warm comfortable kitchen with coffee and a substantial piece of apple pie. A fire in the stone-faced fireplace in the small living room next to the kitchen warmed the old house on this blustery evening.

Ada, a frail, wrinkled woman, understood and spoke a little English. She wore a gingham apron over her modest dress, and her long gray hair was done up in a bun at the back of her head. She sat at the kitchen table with us while her husband, Roberto, sat in the adjoining living room in front of the fireplace smoking his pipe. The sweet smell of tobacco permeated the air. The old man was friendly and smiling, but could not speak or understand any English. He had a full head of gray hair, and his heavily lined face sported a large mustache. He looked to be quite fit, slim, and still muscular, for a man in his mid-nineties.

Ann interpreted Ada's mixture of Italian and English.

"You said on the phone you wanted some information about Bruno. He was my first husband, you know. He died in the war a long time ago. We were only married a little over two years when he died. After the war I married Roberto. We've been married sixty-eight wonderful years. I have tried to forget about Bruno. I should have never married him. He was mean to me, you know."

With age comes the liberty to speak your thoughts, and Ada was not mincing any words as she described her first husband.

"Yes," she said, "he even hit me a couple of times."

"I'm so sorry to hear that," Ann replied.

"Well, it was a long time ago. I don't think about him so often, but I do remember some stories he told me. I'm not sure they are true. Is that why you are here asking about him?"

"Yes, if you could tell us about him and his stories, we would love to learn more about your first husband."

"Well, I'm sure you know Bruno survived the sinking of the first ship he was on. He was the only one who survived."

"Yes, we found that in his record," I said.

"He came home for a while after that first shipwreck. He told me there were truckloads of treasure on that ship. He was such a liar. He lied to me all the time, especially when he was drunk. I'm sure he made those stories up. Once when he was really drunk, he told me when the ship was docked somewhere in Israel, he watched them load some army trucks down into the hold of the ship with a dock crane. No one was allowed to go down into the hold. He said it was off-limits, but he talked to a sailor in the mess hall who told him one of the trucks was full of gold coins. Others had precious gems, and some had other kinds of ancient artifacts. The sailor told Bruno he had helped carry them from a cave in a canyon to the army trucks.

"He told me he was friends with the radio operator. They were together in the radio room when the ship struck a mine. They tried to radio their position before the ship sunk, but there was no power and it sank too quickly.

"Bruno somehow managed to find a life raft. He was injured and almost died himself. He was in the life raft almost a week before an Italian patrol boat spotted his life raft and picked him up."

Ada remembered a surprising amount of detail that Bruno had told her a long time ago for a person who has a "little dementia."

"When he got out of the hospital, he came home for about two weeks. He was stinking drunk most of that time. I avoided him as much as possible. When he was drunk, he told me he knew the position of the ship when it sank, but he didn't tell anyone. He said after the war, he was going to try to find it and see if he could get some of the gold if it wasn't too deep. Just before he shipped out again, he sobered up and he said he was sorry he had told me such stories. He said he had lied about the trucks and the treasure. He said he was drunk, and he was just trying to impress me.

"When he went back to sea, I never saw him again. Good riddance, I said. The next ship he was assigned to also sank. He was reported lost at sea.

"I have an old shoebox full of his stuff in the basement. Bruno told me to take good care of it until he got back. Would you like to have it?"

When Ann told me what she said, I was astounded. I told Ann to ask if she was sure she wanted to give it to us.

She said, "I have already taken everything I want out of it. When we move out of this house, the people who move in will just throw it in the trash. Roberto and I have sold our farm, and we will soon be moving into assisted living. We have to get rid of everything but our clothes and pictures. Neither of us ever had any children, and all of our friends and family are dead."

Then she told us again that Bruno had survived the sinking of the first ship he was on. He was the only one who survived, but died soon after on another ship. She watched intently as Ann told me what she said. Then she smiled at me, knowing I understood.

Ada went down into the basement. I offered to help her down the stairs, but she waved me off, stating emphatically that she still could do the stairs and needed the exercise. Soon she came back with an old cardboard shoebox she handed to me.

"Roberto has been after me to get rid of this old box for years. Please take it. I don't think you will find anything of value in it. I think there is something about his ship in the old newspaper clippings that are in there. If there is, you're welcome to it."

There wasn't much in the box . . . an old pocket knife and a few matchbooks advertising various bars. Most of the redheaded paper matches were still intact. There was an old photograph of several men posing for a picture. All the men were wearing Italian navy uniforms.

Ada said, "Bruno was not in the photo." She thought he might have taken the picture. There were also several old, yellowed newspaper clippings and a paper notebook. I started thumbing through the notebook hoping Bruno had written down the ship's position he had memorized, but it was not there.

Ada helped Ann read what Bruno had written. He kept track of his winnings and losses playing cards on the base before he boarded the ship. At the back of the book he had written about the ship striking the mine, his terrible ordeal in the water, how he was rescued, and names of some of his friends who died when the ship sank. Some were badly burned, and many were devoured by sharks.

After scrutinizing everything in the box, there wasn't anything to tell us where the ship sank. No reference was made to the latitude and longitude he supposedly had memorized.

The wind howled in harmony with the big dog as we stepped out into the cold, dark night. Ada offered to put us up for the night, but we declined the invitation. We shook hands and thanked her for her hospitality and left.

We drove in silence, disappointed. We had not found the clue we were hoping for.

*****

Ann fell asleep. I moved the rearview mirror so I could see her in the soft, reflective glow from the instrument panel. I hadn't been alone with her for a long time. She hadn't talked much on the flight to Rome or driving to meet Ada.

Why has she been so distant lately? There was no console in this big sedan. She could have sat close to me, but she had chosen not to. I was really becoming concerned. We had been so close in Thailand. What happened? Had she tired of me already? Maybe she decided my kind of life wasn't for her. Perhaps it's too dangerous, too full of unknown twists and turns. I didn't know what to think, but I had to know. I knew I really loved Ann. I wasn't about to lose her. I couldn't let her live her life with someone else.

I hadn't seen another car or even a farm house for at least a half hour. At the next wide spot at the side of the road, I slowed down and pulled off onto a wide gravel area and stopped, turning off the engine and the headlights. The wind was just as strong as it had been fifty miles back in the foothills where Ada and Roberto lived.

I thought about Ada's sad life with Bruno, the pain she suffered from his drinking and abuse, and the loneliness she must have felt when he was at sea. Thankfully, she found Roberto and even though they didn't have many material things, they shared a loving relationship much like my parents had, much like the life I hoped Ann and I could have.

As I looked up, like an omen the clouds parted. The moon highlighted the landscape. I could see the road winding down through a wide canyon and a bridge at the bottom. A few trees dotted the landscape with verdant clumps of brush sprinkled between. It was peaceful and beautiful. I half expected to see a wolf or even a deer from the hills nearby, but none appeared.

Ann opened her eyes and sat up. "Where are we?"

"I'm just taking a break."

"Oh, nice," she said.

"It's really beautiful out here in the moonlight."

"Yes, it is."

We sat in silence taking in the countryside, feeling the subtle sway of the car from the wind. An occasional tumbleweed bounced across the roadway in front of us, creating a miniscule whirlwind as it struck the ground and then moved on. Many questions filled my mind, but I didn't know how or what to say.

"I need to ask you something, Matt," Ann finally said softly. She was staring straight at the windshield.

"Okay," I said, turning to look at her. "What would you like to ask me?"

Her face was partly hidden in shadow. I was surprised when I saw a tear fall. Embarrassed, she quickly wiped it away with her handkerchief. "I want you to tell me the truth." Her voice was trembling.

"About what?"

"What happened in that mine? What happened when you and Stephanie were together in that mine?" She turned and looked at me. "I'm sorry. I know it's none of my business. I also know you both thought you were going to die. I'm sorry I have to ask you, Matt, but I just can't get the thought of you and Stephanie together in that mine out of my mind. Please tell me."

I didn't know quite how to start, so I didn't reply for a minute. Finally I said, "I think Stephanie must have told you several days ago. In fact, that's about when you started avoiding me. I'm sorry it happened, Ann. We really couldn't help it. We had to use most of our clothes to keep the gas from coming in. When the gas stopped, our clothes were soaking wet, and it was very cold. We had to hold onto each other to keep warm enough to work our way out of there."

"Stephanie told me all of that, Matt. She also told me you seemed to somehow know that you would find a way out. She said you felt confident that you two would not die in that mine."

"Well . . ." I started to say.

"Why did you make love to her, Matt? If you were sure you were not going to die in that mine, why did you make love to Stephanie?"

I looked at her in total surprise. "I've never made love to Stephanie, Ann, not in the mine, not ever." I was angry that Stephanie had lied to Ann. Raising my voice, I said, "I did kiss her. In fact, I kissed her passionately. I'm not saying I wasn't tempted because I was, but I didn't make love to her. I swear I didn't. Luckily, we managed to escape. Why? What did Stephanie tell you? Did she tell you we made love?"

"Well, now that I think about it, no, she didn't. She just kind of let me believe something happened. I guess it was just me assuming and imagining things. All this time I've been thinking the worst about both of you, and at the same time, trying to understand."

Ann didn't say a word for a few minutes, and neither did I.

Suddenly she turned and buried her head on my chest, gripping my shirt and pulling me close as she sobbed uncontrollably. Minutes later, she dried her eyes and then softly kissed me.

"Are you okay?" I asked.

"Yes," she said. "I'm more than okay now, Matt."

I held her tight. "I love you, Matt," she whispered.

"I love you too, Ann," I replied as I kissed her.

* * * * *

The sun was starting to rise over the rolling hills. Not one car had passed by during the night. The world had been ours alone as we talked about what happened and where we had been since the night we first met.

"Maybe we better go, Matt. It must still be a long way to Rome."

"You're right. We better get on the road. But before we go, something has been nagging at me. It's probably nothing, but I have to know. Can you please hand me Bruno's shoebox? It's on the floor by your feet."

Ann handed me the box. I turned on the dome light. I started taking everything out and handing it to her. She laid each piece on the seat.

"What are you looking for?" she asked.

"There's something strange about this box. I wonder if it could have a false bottom or something?"

"What?" Ann said, surprised.

"Bruno had to have written the latitude and longitude down somewhere. What better place than the box with all his mementos. The bottom of the box looks a little different. Either the box manufacturers in Italy make their shoeboxes this way to give them more strength, or someone has modified this one. Look inside! The edges of the bottom are folded down and have been glued tight to the sidewall of the box. There is no glue showing. It looks professionally made, but I've never seen a shoebox made like this. Hand me that old pocketknife please."

It was hard to open the blade and the knife was dull, but I carefully sliced through the bottom.

"Look at this!" I said surprised. "There is about a quarter-inch space, and then the blade hits the real bottom."

Ann watched in the dim light as I sliced a large square piece out of the false bottom. There it was . . . written on the original bottom of the box . . .

32° 15 ' East 34° 12' North

CHAPTER TWENTY-SEVEN

Jerusalem

Dr. Levi carefully closed the door to his office. "We can't be too careful," he said as he seated himself behind his desk facing Ann and myself. "That's why I had you wait until tonight after our employees had gone home. When you called requesting we meet, you insinuated you might have some good news. Am I correct?"

"Yes," I said with a big grin. "We believe we know the location of the sunken Italian cargo ship."

Dr. Levi looked at me in surprise. "Is this really true?" he said searching our faces for confirmation. "You mean the sailor's widow knew where the ship sank?"

"No, but her first husband, Bruno, had an old shoebox where he kept a few miscellaneous papers and memorabilia. He had told his wife to take good care of it the last time he went to sea. Luckily, it didn't go down with his next ship."

"Go on. What else did his wife tell you?"

"Well, apparently Bruno was friends with one of the ship's radio operators. They were together in the radio room that night when the ship hit a mine and started sinking. The radio operator tried desperately to send out an SOS and give the ship's position, but the engine room was flooded and had no power. They never got out even one distress call. The ship sank quickly.

"Bruno described the events of that fateful evening to his wife, Ada. All the sailors abandoned the ship. The oil slick was ablaze and burned many of the men. He and the radio operator and a few of the others swam away from the flames, but then the sharks moved in. He wrote that he heard screams for hours as the shark frenzy continued.

His friend, the radio operator, was right next to him when he was bitten in half, but Bruno's life was spared. Miraculously, a raft floated close by and a surge of adrenaline allowed him to climb on board. He drifted for almost a week until an Italian patrol boat rescued him. He didn't realize he was the only survivor until he got back to his home base.

"When he was questioned by high-ranking Italian officers regarding the incident, he failed to mention he knew the ship's position when it sank. He told his wife and later recanted that he had memorized the latitude and longitude while trying to help his friend send out the distress signal.

"He wrote in his notebook that the war would soon be over. Little did he know in 1940," I added. "Once when he was drunk, he told Ada another sailor on the ship told him the trucks down in the hold were full of gold and precious gems. He told her he was going to dive down and get the treasure himself after the war if it wasn't too deep. Later he told Ada to forget what he said about the treasure, that he was drunk and only wanted to impress her.

"Ann and I discovered last night Bruno had glued a false bottom in the old shoebox. Written on the original bottom was a latitude and longitude position."

"So," Dr. Levi said, "if the Italian navy didn't look for or find the wreck, it must still be down there."

"That's what we are hoping for," I said.

"Have you determined where that latitude and longitude is?"

"We have. It's in the Mediterranean about one hundred miles northwest of the port city of Acre, Israel."

"How deep is the water?"

"It is deep in most places, but the bottom varies in that area," I replied. "It could be fairly shallow, less than two hundred feet, if it's up on one of the plateaus, or it could be in a very deep canyon."

"What do you plan to do next, Dr Lane?"

"It's all up to you. We are guests in your country."

"Yes, so you are," he replied in deep thought. "I have the authority to give you permission to search for and retrieve artifacts and treasure in our country, but everything found in Israel belongs to Israel and must remain here."

"I'm well aware of that, but the treasure, if it is still on the wreck, is in international waters. We could dive on the wreck and perhaps claim a portion of the treasure for ourselves."

"Yes, that's true. That's why I asked the question."

"If we had intended to do that, I would never have told you we found the location of the ship. If we find the treasure, it belongs to Israel, and it will be returned to Israel. But if we should find the Ark of the Covenant, we have one stipulation."

"And what is that?" Dr. Levi asked.

"The Ark of the Covenant must never be hidden away for only a select few to see. It absolutely has to be on display for the whole world to observe."

"Wonderful, wonderful!" Dr. Levi replied. "I was hoping you would feel that way. Yes, we would want everyone to be able to see it. We certainly would agree to that in writing if you like. This is so exciting, Dr. Lane. This is wonderful news. I only wish my country could help you search for this ship, but as you know, Israel is in a very serious financial crisis. Our department's budget has been cut and then cut again. No one really believes any treasure exists. Most don't believe it ever existed. There will be no appropriations to search for a treasure. My department won't be able to give you any help with financing or even professional divers."

"I understand that," I said, "but there might still be one way you could help us."

"What is that?" Dr Levi asked. "We will help in any way we can."

"Officer Zivah told me you were an officer in the Israeli navy before you retired and became head of the Department of Antiquities."

"Yes . . . yes, I was."

"How long were you in the navy?"

"I retired after twenty-five years of service," he said proudly.

"Is it possible that you have enough influence to get a naval vessel we could use for our dive boat? A naval ship would keep curiosity seekers away. The wreck is in international waters. The less anyone knows about what we are doing out there, the better. We don't need any competition diving for that treasure."

Dr. Levi thought for a minute. Then his face lit up with a smile. "Yes, I believe I could get you a vessel for that purpose."

"Great," I replied. "And if our dive is successful, we will be needing some of the equipment your navy uses all the time."

"Yes . . . yes, I see what you mean. Perhaps I can provide more help than I thought, and if you locate the treasure, I'll see if I can get enough equipment to help you bring it up. It may not be too high tech, but I have something in mind that might work. I think we can cooperate in our joint endeavor and make this work."

The search was on again!

CHAPTER TWENTY-EIGHT

We were all very concerned. According to our GPS we had arrived at the last known position of the Italian navy cargo ship, "Brenero." She tragically sank right here some eighty years ago. The depth of the Mediterranean in this area varied from 150 feet to more than 2,000 feet.

It was getting dark when we dropped our anchor at the 180-foot depth. The wreck could be anywhere after all these years. It had to be in this area, but if it found its final resting place in a deep canyon, the treasure on those trucks may never be recovered.

The sea was calm. The moon came up bright and clear, lighting up the dark ocean all around us. It was a breath-taking sight, but it was also a little unnerving, especially for the women. We were one small boat one hundred miles from the nearest land. We couldn't even see a light from a distant ship or another boat – complete isolation from the rest of the world!

We sat on the aft deck chairs eating the soup and grilled cheese sandwiches Ann and Stephanie had prepared in the small galley. Somehow they had smuggled a cherry pie onboard and were beaming with self-satisfaction at their ingenuity as they served us.

I turned off the extra lights to conserve our batteries. We sat in silence, each absorbed in thought. A large splash broke the surface of the water near us. Ann scooted her chair closer to me and grabbed my hand. Jim wrapped a blanket around Stephanie and assured her it was just a little fish checking us out. We were excited but also apprehensive about what we might encounter on our dive tomorrow.

"Well, we'd better get some sleep. Tomorrow will be a big day. Ann and Stephanie, you can take the bunks below. Jim and I will make do here on the deck."

After saying good night, Stephanie went below, and Jim rolled out his sleeping bag. I went up to the bow to make sure the anchor rope was tight. Ann followed me.

"Matt, you will be careful tomorrow, won't you?"

I assured her Jim and I wouldn't take any unnecessary risks. Kissing her on the check, I pulled her close to me. I'll never forget that feeling of holding her tight to my chest in the moonlight on the bow of that boat in that big ocean.

The next morning we awoke to a slight breeze. The mild swells tossed the small dive boat just enough to make you grab onto the table or a door jamb from time to time, but it could have been worse.

With our boat right over the area designated by the coordinates, we were hoping luck was still with us. We were over a plateau. We knew the wreck would probably not be found directly below us. We would have to work the grid we had charted. We just hoped the currents on the ocean floor had not moved it too far from where it sank.

We started our first dive. I went down, Jim following close behind me. There was less and less sunlight as we continued to descend.

Finally we reached a sandy bottom. My depth gauge read 178 feet. This was deeper than we had ever dived before. We stood on the sand face-to-face with no way to communicate except sign language.

Jim pointed to a large shark swimming past, its dead eyes revealing nothing of its intent. We felt like we were in a giant aquarium with clusters of coral growing amid the rocks. Visibility was about thirty yards. I looked at my compass, taking note of the rock formations close to us and turned until the needle pointed to magnetic north. Starting to swim, we angled up about fifty feet above the sandy bottom. We saw nothing but fan coral waving slowly back and forth, a large school of grouper, another shark, and sand and rocks. When we had gone about one thousand yards, I turned right and we swam east.

About five hundred yards into the third leg of the search pattern, looming up at us like a ghost in the blue light, was the encrusted stern of a ship. It was so covered in crustaceans we could only read BRE---- RO. That was close enough to BRENERO for us. We already had our Italian cargo ship. Unbelievable! We couldn't believe our luck in finding it so quickly and that it wasn't any deeper.

That old derelict was in one piece, resting peacefully on the white, sandy ocean floor. It was a little askew, but luckily mostly upright. What an incredible sight!

Upon further examination, we saw that the portholes in the crew's quarters were intact, the glass not broken. Strips of peeling paint on the majestic steel mast supporting the lookout tower waved with the current. Schools of fish were oblivious to our presence as they swarmed around the wreckage. Even a white-tipped shark cruising the ocean floor paid no attention to us.

With our excitement, I realized we were using more oxygen than I had anticipated. I looked at my watch. Our oxygen mix at this depth would soon be depleted. Getting Jim's attention, I pointed straight ahead, past the ship, and then up. He nodded in agreement.

We swam the length of the ship about twenty feet off the bottom and parallel with the starboard side. We could not see a hole in this side, but the sandy bottom disappeared. The first hundred feet of the bow was protruding over a ledge. We swam to the edge and looked straight down into a dark ominous canyon. We had no idea how deep it might be.

Slowly we started our ascent. We would be back in the morning.

* * * * *

Dr. Levi had been unable to obtain a navy boat for our exploratory dive. Instead I had rented the only available boat in the area. It was a small vessel equipped for scuba diving and excursions for the thrill-seeking tourist, a bare-bones solution for our needs. We would have no protection provided by the Israeli navy here.

As Jim and I were suiting up for our second dive, Jim was his usual jovial self. "I think I saw this in a movie, Matt. The ship was resting in about one hundred and eighty feet of water, but it was right on the edge of a cliff that dropped off to twelve thousand feet."

"What a coincidence," I replied, grinning at him.

"In the movie, the bow is protruding out over the edge of a cliff and when the divers . . . that's you and me, Matt . . . are inside, it slides over the edge taking the hapless divers to Davy Jones' locker."

We continued to get our dive gear on.

"I saw that movie. You're right. The situation down there is just about like the movie. And since we know how that movie ended, I just won't go out into the bow, unless you're standing on the stern. That way it will be balanced. It won't slide over into the abyss. It will be a piece of cake."

"A piece of cake? I think I remember you saying that back in Thailand. Yes, you did say that. I had just arrived in Bangkok. You took me out to dive down in the river to that submerged aircraft. You said it would be a piece of cake."

"No, I didn't. You didn't hear me right. I said I was going to need you for crocodile bait."

Jim stopped putting on his tanks and stared at me. "Oh, so that's what you said!"

"Yes, that's what I said. Maybe you need to buy some hearing aids. Listen carefully now. This time I need you to keep the sharks away from me. This time I need you for shark bait."

"My hearing is excellent. You just said you want to face those sharks alone, and you don't want to be late. Right?"

"No, that's not quite what I said. Now I know you need hearing aids. By the way, my friend," I said as I was putting on my flippers, "I can understand you're getting a little too old for this kind of work, needing hearing aids and all. You don't have to dive on this wreck if you don't want to. I'm going because I have got to know what's in that cargo hold."

"Are you kidding? Of course I have to go. I can't let you go down by yourself. Besides, who is going to save you when the teetering vessel slides into the abyss? Without me, the movie may not have a happy ending."

"You guys better be joking," Stephanie said, clearly not appreciating their cynical humor.

"Of course we're just teasing," I said. "That canyon in front of the ship probably isn't much more than two thousand feet deep."

Laughing, and all suited up now, Jim and I flipped over the side of the boat.

Stephanie turned to Ann. "Seriously, Ann, please tell me they were just kidding about the abyss and the sharks."

"When Matt described it to me last night, he didn't think there was much danger of the ship sliding over the edge. They weren't serious about that, at least I hope they weren't," Ann said. "However, there is no doubt that what they are doing is very dangerous. What worries me most is the sharks in these waters. Many of them are oceanic white tips. They have killed more humans than any other species."

"You've got to be kidding me." Stephanie exclaimed." Now I'm even more worried. When did Matt tell you all that last night?" Stephanie asked. "I thought after we had dinner, everyone went to bed."

"Matt and I sat up on the bow for a while and talked. He told me then."

"Oh, I see," Stephanie said, trying to hide her jealousy.

* * * * *

We didn't follow the anchor rope down. I wanted to see which direction the current would move us. When we reached the proper depth, we did not see the bottom. We were out over the canyon. The current had moved us on our descent. Using the compass, we started swimming north and soon spotted the bow. The eerie looking vessel was upright on the bottom, but the bow was indeed protruding over the deep canyon, and the entire ship was angled down at the bow ten to fifteen degrees. I studied it from the side. I suppose it was possible the whole ship could slide and plunge bow first into the canyon, but it had been down there a long time, and it hadn't gone over yet. If we didn't treat it too roughly, it probably wouldn't.

The glass was broken out on the bridge. Rust and crustaceans were devouring the entire vessel. The 'Brenero' was six-hundred feet long, and it was definitely tilted to the port side. If those ten trucks were in the cargo hold, I hoped they had been chained solid to the deck and not crushed against each other.

We wouldn't have a lot of time on the wreck at this depth. Even using nitrox in our tanks, we had to allow plenty of time to ascend.

Jim followed me as I swam over the bridge. The ship's wheel was still intact, a hint of brass still visible under a coating of barnacles. The cargo doors just in front of the bridge were smaller than the very large double doors covering the main cargo hold amid ship. We could never open these massive doors. We had to find another way in. Hoping the bottom had not been completely blown out, we moved over the old derelict to the port side.

The first things we saw were several large wooden crates splintered open sitting in the sand. Behind the crates partially covered by the sandy bottom was a large gaping hole. This would lead to the smaller cargo hold in front of the bridge.

Pieces of tank track made of steel laid in broken crates on the sand and were so covered in rust, they were almost unrecognizable. There was barely enough room between the sandy floor and the top of the jagged hole to squeeze through. The space was dark and foreboding. Even with our powerful lights, visibility was down to six or eight feet. Suddenly, a school of fish swirled past us.

Our lights revealed more of the same type crates, most of them cracked open with their contents spilled out on the deck . . . batteries and more steel track, all spare parts for tanks. We swam past several corroded engines and more tank parts. No door leading to the main cargo hold here.

Disappointed, we came back out and swam up to the bridge. In a passageway behind the bridge, we went down through an open hatch to the deck below. Here we found a passageway with several doors.

Nervously, Jim followed me. We both knew we could easily become trapped by debris, tangled in electrical wiring, struck by falling cargo, or trapped in a compartment if a hatch swung shut.

We proceeded cautiously, parting the hanging electrical wires as we went. We searched all three compartments in that passageway, hoping to find a watertight vault. If the Ark of the Covenant was not in a watertight vault, the saltwater would have ruined all the wood. Nothing would be left but the gold and the tablets of stone.

The doors were all open because of the list to port. Two bunk-bed frames, two lockers, and a steel desk in each room told us we were in the officers' quarters. Peeling paint, shredded mattress material, and old blanket cloth were lying on the rusted deck. The rooms were empty. These sailors had all gotten off the ship only to be burned, drowned, or killed by sharks . . . *The poor devils!*

We stopped and looked at our watches. We would have to leave soon.

We found another steel stairwell and followed it, passing through three decks, working our way toward the bottom of the ship. Our progress was stopped by a closed heavy steel door with two steel dogs in the locked position. It took both of us to get the big door open. The movement of the door stirred up the silt, and our lights couldn't penetrate through it for a few seconds.

Finally I was able to step through the door. Two eyes glowered at me only three feet from my face . . . an oceanic white-tipped shark, a killer! Startled, I sprang backward colliding with Jim causing both of us to collapse on the deck. Abruptly a six-foot shadow passed over us as the shark moved toward the other end of the area. The danger had passed for the moment.

Warily, we crossed the threshold. I recognized the equipment. This was the main engine room. Shining our lights around, we spotted the complete skeletal remains of a sailor who probably worked in this room. He was lying under the catwalk down by the base of the engine. Remnants of his blue work clothes were still attached to the white bones. He was probably killed when the mine blew a hole in the hull. Otherwise he might have gotten out. Maybe he was lucky after all, I thought.

Our air supply was down to just a few more minutes. Exiting the engine room, we continued searching for an inside door to the main cargo hold. Swimming around pipes and more electrical cables, we spotted a door with an old rusty padlock. Jim quickly opened it by striking the padlock with the head of a fire ax, the wooden handle long ago rotted away. Again, it took both of us to shove the corroded door open. We had to wait and let more precious minutes tick by while the silt in the water settled.

The area was immense. We shined our lights up hoping to see the doors above that would assure us that we were in the main hold, but there was too much silt floating in the water. After securing the door so it would not close and trap us inside, we moved forward. We had not gone ten feet before the cab of a World War II army truck emerged in the silt-filled light. We maneuvered to the back of the truck. There were more trucks . . . five of them in a row, one parked behind the other, and five more lined up beside them. They were all chained to the deck. The windshields and windows were not broken, just covered with silt. The beds were covered with shredded tarps hanging from metal framework. Two trucks, side-by-side in front, were empty except for benches in the back, probably used to transport the sailors. Each of the other eight trucks were loaded with plywood crates. Gold coins were spilling out onto the bed in one of the trucks. Jim and I high-fived each other!

It was an eerie sight, all those trucks parked in the bottom of that old ship! They had been down here almost eighty years. Yet except for the flat tires, they looked like they were waiting to be started and driven away!

The visibility was a little better now. We elevated ourselves a few feet above the top of the ten trucks and shined our bright lights back on them. That scene will forever be locked in my memory. We had found the treasure. Would the Ark be in one of those crates? Our air supply was dangerously low, and we had to allow time for our safety stops in our ascension. We had to surface.

Back on the dive boat, we were all talking at once about what Jim and I had discovered.

Finally Ann looked at me and said, "Okay mister! You know me . . . I have to see it."

I started to argue with her, but she was adamant.

"I'm a certified scuba diver . . . maybe not as experienced as you and Jim, but I can dive, and I want to see it with my own eyes. I am going down there whether you like it or not!"

I knew it was no use trying to talk her out of it. If I made her mad, she might just go down by herself without telling anyone. At 180 feet, that could be deadly.

At 8 a.m. the next morning, Ann and I were in Brenero's cargo hold. She was as excited as Jim and I had been, and we brought a few gold coins back up to the surface.

Stephanie had never been scuba diving, so she could not go. She seemed satisfied just looking at the pictures we took.

CHAPTER TWENTY-NINE

Everyone was leaning close, listening intently to the conversation between me and Dr. Levi on the radio. A storm just off the coast was causing a lot of static.

"I'm sorry, Dr. Lane. I was hoping with my military connections, I could send you out better salvage equipment. Our navy has a wonderful vessel, but it is being used on another project. Our government is not convinced that you have found anything of significant value, and they don't want to get involved in a recovery operation at this point. What I was able to procure is on its way. It's an old barge with a derrick crane mounted on it. It's quite large and has a capable engine, but only to move it around the harbor for dredging. It was never built to travel one hundred miles out into the open sea."

"I take it that it doesn't belong to the Israeli navy," I said wistfully, hoping for some protection.

"I'm afraid not, and it's not the navy grey color we wanted. I'm afraid it is black with a red cabin and crane. The owner and captain is a friend of mine. He and his deckhand have rigged the crane with a longer cable and are anxious to get started. If the storm here passes quickly, they'll be on their way.

"I am able to deliver something I'm sure you will appreciate. It will be much more comfortable. It is a naval yacht, rather old, but nice, and it has a scuba-diving platform on the aft deck. This ship will give you some of the naval presence you asked for. It's the usual navy grey color and flies our Israeli flag. With the number painted on both sides of the bow as well as other markings, it is easily identified as a naval ship. It doesn't have a deck gun, but the three sailors I've sent to guard the vessel are all well armed."

"Thank you. That's great," I added with a sigh of relief. The crew nodded in agreement and clapped in approval. "We will all feel a lot safer as well as more comfortable."

"Dr. Lane, I've also taken the liberty of sending Officer Zivah out to you. She will be on the yacht. She knows her artifacts and can be very helpful to you. She is very anxious to come out and help in any way she can."

"Good idea. She can also witness that we don't pillage the wreck and abscond with the funds, so to speak," I said laughing.

"I trust you completely, Dr. Lane. I know you would not do that."

Jim's face lit up when he heard this, and he winked at me. Joanne was cute as a button, very intelligent and very knowledgeable about artifacts from this part of the world. I knew Jim had taken her to dinner at least once before we boarded our dive boat and came out to sea, and she was on the dock to wish us well and see us off when we left port.

I waited for a few seconds for the static to clear. "I'm grateful for what you have been able to procure," I said. "But the trucks in that wreck are all Italian built Alfa Romeo - 800's. They are each three-ton trucks, and the beds are packed with crates. At the one-hundred-eighty-foot depth we are working at, it will take Jim and me a long time to put everything in the crane bucket." I paused for a few seconds. "I don't want to leave this site unattended, but if I came ashore briefly, would I be able to lease a private salvage vessel myself, one that is equipped with a manned submersible?"

"I know you have the means to do that, Dr. Lane, and I appreciate your offer. I've already researched that. There are no available salvage vessels operating in this part of the world. It would be months before one could be brought to the site."

"That won't work," I replied after the static cleared. "In a few days, I'm afraid the word will be out. With the treasure in international waters and only down one hundred eighty feet, we could end up in a gun battle out here."

Just then the static became so bad I couldn't hear much. A garbled message came through.

"Sorry . . . couldn't . . . vessel . . . wanted you . . . have, but . . . you . . . like surprise package . . . good use of it. . . . Only . . . for . . . few days. . . . luck." Then the line went dead.

I stayed on the upper deck. Everyone else went below.

Dr. Levi was exhausting all his resources to help us retrieve the treasure before anyone else discovered our operation. I had a very uneasy feeling. We were exceptionally vulnerable here.

Yesterday I had asked Dr. Levi to find out if the bodies of Jack, Drake, and Tiny had ever been located. His reply was unnerving. The bodies had not yet been found, although the police felt sure that all three men had died in the desert. They were convinced their bodies were carried off by wild dogs, and they were searching the rocks in the foothills for the remains.

I had my reservations about that theory. I confided to Jim what I had learned. We considered telling the girls, but they were coping with our sparse accommodations and even laughing at our jokes. We decided to tell them about Jack later.

The rain and lightning that had caused the communications problem never affected us. The sea was fairly smooth and we all had a great afternoon swimming and sunbathing. When we swam, one of us always stayed on board to be the shark lookout. We knew there were quite a few in this area so we didn't venture very far from the dive platform.

The sunset was spectacular. A shining red ball slowly disappeared into the sea, all the while reflecting brilliantly on the water. We hadn't seen land or another vessel since we arrived.

We spent the evening on the rear deck of the small boat. As we were having dessert, someone brought up the subject of the next life.

During that conversation, Stephanie said, "Well, I hope when I die I get to see my mom and dad again."

"Oh, so do I," Ann chimed in, "and my grandmother Jelena and even her mom and dad."

Then I added, "If I get to live a long time like the ripe old age of one hundred and eight, I hope I won't have to stay looking old forever. I mean maybe everyone starts growing young again. I think I'd like to go back to when I was twenty-five. I was in pretty good shape at twenty-five."

"I think you're in great shape now," Ann said smiling and squeezing my hand. Then she added, "I hope everything in heaven is beautiful – lots of lawn and flowers and no person, animal, or any living thing has to kill to eat. We may still want to enjoy a wonderful meal, but maybe they have plants that when cooked taste like a great steak or chicken, but animals don't have to be slaughtered. And I hope the lion can actually lay down with the lamb, and sharks like to eat seaweed."

She got applause for that one.

"Hey, I've got a great idea for heaven assuming I actually get there," Jim chuckled. "I don't think we should have to work up there, you know like mowing the lawn, cooking, cleaning, making the bed. Maybe they have robots to do all the hard, boring stuff."

"For your sake, I hope you're right," I added. "You wouldn't know how to do any of those things."

Everyone laughed at that, even Jim.

"I hope we don't get bored up there. I mean eternity is a long time," Stephanie said.

"Oh, I think God will keep everyone busy," I remarked. "I hope we are assigned a real exciting job like taking the robots Jim talked about and having them round up some dinosaurs to be placed on a new exciting planet like the earth once was."

Everyone thought that would be fun especially since all the dinosaurs would only eat vegetation. No meat eaters should be allowed in heaven, we all agreed.

* * * * *

Jim and the girls were having breakfast in the small galley. I had eaten early and was up on the top deck with binoculars searching the horizon. Jim came up and handed me a cup of coffee.

"See anything yet?"

"Not yet."

"It's really peaceful out here this morning, isn't it?"

"It's beautiful," I replied.

"So what do you think this surprise is, Matt?"

"I just don't know. It's going to take forever to retrieve all that treasure, and in the meantime, we're sitting ducks out here."

"Do you think the Ark could be in one of those trucks, Matt?"

""If the actual Ark of the Covenant was on board my vessel, I would have had it taken to the most secure place on the ship," I replied. "It's too bad the ship yard that built the 'Brenero' was bombed during the war and the blueprints destroyed. Our sunken vessel may or may not have a water-tight vault."

"Well, we have searched just about every place a vault big enough to hold the Ark could be," Jim said.

"I know, but I still keep hoping we will find one. Some old freighters were equipped with walk-in, water-tight vaults to store anything that could be damaged by water. There are still some areas we haven't explored like the steel bulkhead behind the trucks. After we remove the crates, we will be able to see back there. If it is in one of those trucks, it won't be in very good condition. We should know soon."

Weather conditions were perfect this morning. The sapphire blue water was calm with only a slight breeze sending an intermittent ripple across the water. Threads of gold shimmered on the surface as the sun broached the horizon.

About 9 a.m. we spotted the barge in the distance. Following close behind was the yacht painted battleship gray, a most welcomed sight. The captain had slowed it to a crawl of about eight knots to accompany the cumbersome floating platform safely to its destination. Peering through our binoculars, we watched the two vessels plow through the water leaving a 'V' as the water rolled in their wake.

The barge appeared to be about eighty feet wide and probably about one hundred feet long with the flat steel deck rising eight to ten feet above the waterline. Mounted on the black diamond-plate deck was a crane tower. I could see the glass windshield in the operator's cab twenty feet up on the tower. The arm of the crane had been partially dismantled, its large pulleys and cables anchored to the deck. Behind the ruby-red tower stood a rectangular building. Steep stairs on the side led up to the bridge where we spotted a heavy-set man dwarfing the man at the controls. The only railing on the barge was a loosely attached, sagging rope between removable steel posts around the entire periphery.

Then we noticed an atypical object secured to the deck under the crane tower – a bright yellow, bullet-shaped cylinder with a bulging glass-eye shape on one end from which protruded a claw. Could it be?

As it inched closer . . . "Yes!" I exclaimed.

It was a manned submersible, and Jim, with a big grin, gave me a thumbs-up. It was small, only meant for two people, but it was the answer to our operation. Dr. Levi had delivered!

Jim now had the binoculars trained on the yacht. I watched him as the serious look on his face turned to a smile. Handing the binoculars to me, he said, "Look who's standing at the bow."

I knew before I put the binoculars to my eyes who it would be. Joanne Zivah's curly blonde hair was blowing slightly in the breeze. She wore a crisp short-sleeved white shirt tucked into her tan shorts and stylish tan and white tennis shoes. She was smiling and waving as the yacht approached our little dive boat. We all waved back enthusiastically, especially Jim. He gave her a big hug the minute she stepped on board.

Then Ann, Stephanie, and I welcomed her. We were all happy to see Officer Zivah join our team.

Within two hours, we had the barge anchored directly over the wreck, and the starboard side of the yacht tightly snubbed up to the barge, cushioned against the large roughed-up tires which hung from steel cleats.

My hand disappeared in a bear-like clasp as Captain Jeb Berkowitz, owner-operator of the barge, introduced himself and his deckhand, Jacob Gentz. His shiny dome and reddish-brown beard framed a smile that matched his five-foot-ten stout stature.

"Dr. Levi has explained this is a major recovery mission," Captain Jeb told us as he hitched up his tan coveralls over a plaid flannel shirt. "Jacob here has been with me for fifteen years now and can out-work ten men," he said giving Jacob a friendly wallop on the back that sent him forward a step.

Jacob's small wiry frame was accented by oversized jeans and a gray sweatshirt, but his shy grin acknowledged the Captain's accolades.

Mincing no words, Captain Jeb declared, "Let's do it." We were impressed as both seasoned sailors sprang into action and started to rig the crane arm.

We turned our attention to the Israeli navy yacht, the IN Dolphin, a small floating hotel. The one-hundred-foot vessel was commanded by a young Israeli navy segen. That rank I knew was equal to a lieutenant junior grade in the U.S. navy, and his first officer, a segen mishne, was equal to a navy ensign. A cook, cook's helper, and a cabin steward completed the crew of five. After bringing our dive boat alongside the yacht, the crew transferred our gear to our individual staterooms. It wasn't an imposition for us to transition from a cramped "dorm" room to a "five star Marriott."

The dive boat we used to discover the wreck was sent back to port, and a gangway was installed between the yacht and the barge.

As we gathered in the lounge, we were introduced to the three young sailors who would guard the vessel twenty-four hours a day. They would rotate their shifts, patrolling the barge, walking the outer deck of the Dolphin, and standing guard through the night. Should anyone approach, they were to alert me immediately.

Exquisite walnut paneling and mirrors behind an elaborately carved teak bar amplified the size of the opulent lounge. Lush velvet upholstery and a large hand- woven maroon carpet completed the decor.

Chatter filled the room as we got acquainted with the personnel who had just arrived. I could tell by the laughter that we had a congenial group to work with. The room was filled with anticipation.

By 1 p.m., the submersible was rigged and ready to be set in the water. All we needed was the pilot, who had not yet arrived. I would operate the submersible's mechanical arm.

With limited time, the navy had temporarily installed the communication's cable and monitor that came with the small sub in a space behind the bridge on the barge. From there, Jim would be able to view our underwater operation and communicate with us in our small submarine. Jim would monitor this equipment and be in command of the salvage operation.

High above from the crane tower, Captain Jeb would position the cable hook . . . up, down, back, forward . . . as Jim directed via a two-way, hands-free radio. Precise coordination would be key to our success.

The small helicopter seemed to appear out of nowhere. Hovering over the bow of the Dolphin, the submersible pilot was lowered to the deck on a cable. After brief introductions, an overview of the project, and some lunch, the pilot and I were on our way down to the wreck. From the seat next to the pilot, I practiced manipulating the mechanical arm. The pilot, Paul, was friendly and very qualified. He took it slow and easy during our descent. Upon my direction, he rotated the craft 150° at the 160-foot level. There, in the bright lights of the submersible, the dark metal hulk lay resting on the light-colored sand. The view through the clear Plexiglas-bubble in front of us was astounding. Large fish and a few sharks swam away from the bright light.

In a few minutes, we were hovering over the two main cargo doors and were ready to begin the tedious task. Each long door had a port and starboard steel component. Four panels had to be opened to retrieve the treasure. On my second try with the mechanical arm, I managed to snag the cable from the barge and attach the hook to the first cargo door.

The pilot notified Jim upside that the lift could begin. Slowly and cautiously, the cable from the deck crane tightened. The old steel door hadn't been moved in eighty years. We held our breath as Captain Jeb applied more pulling power on the cable, fearing it may snap. In an instant, a loud pop and an avalanche of silt flooded the area. As the particles settled, we saw the door was open about a meter. With more pulling, the first door continued its upward pivot until it was fully open. Repeating the process, soon all four cargo doors were wide open. Now we could maneuver the submersible to the trucks below. We descended into the yawning abyss, down to where the bizarre columns of barnacled vehicles waited.

Everyone topside, with the exception of the sailor on watch and Captain Jeb in the crane tower, was in the room with Jim watching the monitor.

The disturbed silt was like swirling snow in headlights while driving in a blizzard. When the silt dissipated and settled, Paul maneuvered the sub around the trucks. Now and then a glint of gold showed between the open seams and cracks in the wooden crates. We grinned at each other as we listened to the gasps and cheers coming from Jim's control room.

Captain Jeb scrambled down the ladder from the crane cab and raced up the stairs. Staring at the monitor, he exclaimed, "Well, I'll be darned!"

Paul was careful to not tangle or damage our umbilical cable that conveyed the audio and video signal to the control room.

Jacob operated the big spool of cable mounted on the deck of the barge, releasing more as needed. He would wind the cable back on the spool when it was time to resurface. The sailors not on watch pitched in where help was needed.

What an amazing sight for all of us to witness!

I hoped bringing all that treasure up to the barge would go well.

That night Jim and I helped Jeb and Jacob cut and weld legs to the bottom of an angle iron frame and expanded metal container that was on the barge.

The next morning Jim, watching his monitor, gave instructions to Captain Jeb who was operating the crane, as he skillfully set the bucket between the rear bed of one truck and the front bumper of the truck behind it. Using the mechanical arm, we placed a cable around the first crate. With Jim giving instructions to Captain Jeb, the crane pulled the crate backward onto the waiting bucket, which was then hoisted to the deck of the barge. Again and again we repeated this operation. If the old crates disintegrated, and some did, the contents fell to the floor of the expanded metal box we had rigged. The steel mesh on the bottom of the box allowed the water to pass through but caught the smallest coins. It was slow, tedious work, but the system was working.

Every bit of the treasure would be brought to the surface. If need be, Jim and I could dive back down and pick up what was left behind after the submersible left.

Once on deck, the three girls and the ship's crew removed the crating and began stacking the treasure on the deck of the barge, dividing it into groups.

There were carved busts of ancient Israeli kings and leaders, ceremonial swords and at least fifty gold shields. We felt sure these had once belonged to King Solomon's personal body guards.

The treasure was extensive. Much of the immediate value was in the many chests of ancient gold and silver coins, probably from the church coffers. There were beautiful pieces of pottery with bands of delicately carved silver and gold around them and gold and silver jewelry boxes filled with precious gemstones. The treasure was worth millions just in the value of the gold, silver, and gemstones, but we still had not found the Ark of the Covenant.

After the fourth day of salvage, we were in the lounge discussing all that had transpired in the last few days. The crew was in good spirits, complimenting each other on how they had overcome the handicaps and a job well done.

"It was disappointing that we didn't find a water-tight vault," I commented. "I've looked at all the rest of the crates. I don't believe the Ark was ever put on those trucks."

"Maybe it's for the best," Jim said. "The Ark frame was made of wood. It was plated with pure gold inside and outside. The salt water would have warped the wood. We would have only found twisted, thin, hammered sheets of gold. The beautiful golden cherubim would be sagging from a broken, twisted frame. Of course, the stone tablets would have survived, and that is the main treasure."

A hush enveloped the lounge.

"Well, even if we didn't find the Ark of the Covenant, it still is an adventure I'll never forget," Ann commented.

"I just hope the people of Israel will recognize and appreciate what this treasure means not just to them, but to everyone who believes in the Bible. This treasure dates back to Old Testament times, and they didn't even know it existed," Stephanie added.

"I still can't help but wonder . . ." I said in deep thought.

"Wonder what, Matt?" Ann asked.

"I keep thinking about the inscription on the wall in the cave, 'If ye seek treasure, look up toward God's heaven.'"

"It was just a statement," Ann said, "like Jim said when we first read it. It was meant to tell whoever found the treasure that it was just gold and silver and items made by man. The real reward in life will be found when we die and, hopefully, go to heaven."

"I suppose you're right. That's probably what it means. But what the map led us to was just a temporary hiding place for the treasure. It was too far from Jerusalem to be a permanent vault," I insisted. "I believe the treasure was to be stored there as a last resort. If they were ever invaded by an enemy, they could temporarily move it out of the city. So why," I added, "would they plaster some walls and carve the inscription if it was only to be used as a temporary hiding place? It's not a place where anyone would normally carve a profound religious statement."

No one spoke. Realizing I had unintentionally put a damper on the party, I proposed a toast to the zealous squad thanking them for their long hours of laborious work.

"Oh well," I whispered to Ann, "I'm glad we found the treasure, but disappointed that we still haven't found the real treasure, the Ark of the Covenant."

"Maybe it will be in the last truck you unload, Matt. And if it isn't, we'll keep looking. Someday we will find it." She squeezed my hand.

We had a lot of treasure still in the trucks and our allotted time with the submersible was almost up. I was concerned. Rumors had spread of a strange activity in the area. I was also aware that we had enjoyed great weather, but if a bad storm came up, that old barge could go down.

"I'm going up to check the weather," I said.

"I'll go with you," both Ann and Stephanie said simultaneously.

Jim, sensing the tension, said, "Let's all go."

The moon was just a sliver, but the stars were brilliant. The night air was warm. The guard met us at the gangway. I reminded him again that Jim and I were to be alerted if any vessel even remotely looked like they might be heading toward us. We were not in the shipping lanes so we did not expect anyone. The three armed sailors had each brought two weapons and plenty of ammunition. Jim and I could not own weapons in Israel, but we were far out to sea. If we needed a weapon, we knew where to find them, and we knew how to use them.

CHAPTER THIRTY

It was late afternoon. All the trucks had been emptied. Heavy clouds were rolling in, and the wind was whistling across the deck. The submersible, the pilot, and the three armed sailors had been picked up a few hours ago. To take their place a sixty-five foot Coast Guard cutter with a skipper, first mate, three armed men, and a machine gun mounted on the deck was tied securely to the other side of the barge, opposite the Dolphin. They would accompany our two vessels all the way back to port. Jim and I were feeling better about our security.

We prepared for our final dive. Almost all of the treasure had been catalogued and moved to the yacht. A few boxes of gold coins being cleaned, dried, and stored in plastic tubs were still on the deck of the barge. The yacht, with all the treasure, was sitting precariously low in the water, and we couldn't risk adding any more weight, particularly if the seas became rough.

"We'll be back soon," I told Ann. We are going to search one last area. It's the only place we haven't looked. If the Ark is on that wreck, we have to find it before we leave here. This will be our last chance."

"It's almost dark, Matt. Why don't you wait till morning?"

"It's very dark inside the ship anyway. If we don't find it on this dive, when we get back up, we'll head for port tonight. We'll hurry."

Jim and I began the descent. The sun was just sinking below the horizon, with rain clouds all around. Jacob flipped on the high-powered crane lights. One bright light was positioned to shine directly on the cable down in the water, while lights on the crane arm brightened the deck of the barge making it easy for the girls to see the encrusted gold coins, break them apart, and stack them in the plastic tubs.

Taking a break, Ann and Stephanie walked over to the front of the barge. Standing at the edge behind the safety rope, they stared down into the bright beam of light surrounding the cable from the boom above.

"I just wish they would finish their search and get back on board. I'm worried that they'll have an accident down on that wreck," Stephanie said.

"I was hoping they wouldn't go back down," Ann added, "but Matt just had to have one final search for the Ark. He still can't believe it's not on the wreck. You know Matt . . . he has to be positive."

It had just gotten dark when the skipper of the cutter stepped onto the barge and ran over to Captain Zeb where he and Jacob were helping Ann, Stephanie, and Joanne with the last of the coins.

"We just received a Mayday. Someone is in trouble! It looks like a small boat . . . maybe a fishing boat. We have a small bleep on our radar. They are actually not far from us, and we are the only vessel in the area. By law we have to respond. We'll be back as soon as we can. If the boat is sinking, we may have some extra passengers with us when we return."

"Well, use your radio. Let us know if we can be of any assistance," Zeb told him.

The big engines on the cutter roared to life. The search lights came on as the cutter disappeared into the night while the remaining group returned to cleaning the last of the coins. All five were concerned for the safety of those on the boat in distress. It wasn't long before they heard the cutter returning.

"It sounds like they are already coming back," Jacob said, stopping what he was doing. "That's strange. I wonder why they didn't use the radio . . . tell us what was happening."

As the cutter approached, Captain Zeb told Jacob they needed to go help them tie up and put the gangway in place.

The cutter's first mate was at the wheel. He skillfully brought her alongside the barge again. Captain Jeb and Jacob secured it fore and aft and repositioned the aluminum gangway.

Everyone had stopped working and gathered around the cutter to see if they could help. The first mate and one seaman were the only ones on deck. The first mate shut off the engines. The door to the room below the cockpit opened. The young skipper stumbled up the steps and out on deck, a somber look on his face. Close behind and surrounding him was a group of men.

As they stepped out of the dark into the lighted deck of the barge, Ann and Stephanie gasped and retreated back several steps.

"No! No! This can't be happening!" Stephanie uttered.

Joanne grabbed Ann as she appeared faint and on the verge of collapse.

Jack, Drake, Tiny, and two Asian men dressed in black jumped aboard the barge, each pointing their automatic weapons at the crew.

Suddenly Jack fired several rounds from his gun in the air as he stepped from the cutter gangway to the barge. He bellowed out orders. "Okay, listen up! Get your hands in the air. Now! Right now!"

His actions and facial expressions alluded to a distinct possibility he was high on drugs and had also been drinking. Ann and Stephanie knew that was when he was most dangerous and vicious.

"Just what I expected," Jack said to his four men, slurring his words but still very much in charge. "Matt and Jim are not here. Tiny, you check the bridge on this barge. Drake, you take Gan and Benz. Check the yacht. Look everywhere. Find them and bring them to me along with any weapons you come across. Whatever treasure they brought up besides these measly gold coins must already be on the yacht. Locate it and bring me the keys to the yacht's ignition. Drake, leave Gan and Benz on board. Have one of them stay at the back of the boat while the other patrols the perimeter. Tell him to watch the water. Is this everyone?" Jack yelled.

"This is everyone," Ann snapped as she stepped forward.

"Well, look who's here," Jack said looking across at Ann. "It's great to see you again, sweetheart."

"I'm not your sweetheart."

"Well, you were for a while," Jack said with a grin. "Where are Matt and Jim?"

"They went ashore this morning," Ann said.

"Don't lie to me, Ann. They didn't go ashore. They are either hiding like cowards, or they are down at the wreck. Either way, they'll soon be fish food. We'll find them, or we'll surprise them when they come up. I'm going to kill Matthew Lane myself this time. Seems I can't trust anyone else to get the job done."

"They're not cowards!" Ann retorted.

Abruptly, Jack's face changed expression. He had just seen Stephanie. Machine gun in his left hand, he grinned as he ambled over to her. "Hello, cousin. I've got to know one thing. How in the hell did you and Lane get out of the mine?"

Stephanie was in shock, shaking so hard she couldn't speak.

"I've got to admit I was really surprised when I found out the two of you were not only still alive, but you were in Israel telling your whole sad story to the police."

Then he turned to Ann. "Sorry, Ann. Things didn't go quite as I planned. Unfortunately, we had a little mishap in the canyon."

"You're high on drugs again, aren't you, Jack?" Ann said in disgust. "Without drugs and booze, you probably couldn't get out of bed."

Jack's face twisted from a grin to hatred. Fist clenched, he started toward Ann. Aware of his intentions from her experiences with Jack, Stephanie stepped in his path, "How did you ever find us out here?"

He forgot about Ann for the moment. Assuming a pompous air, he said, "I told you before, I have friends in high places. I even have friends in the Israeli Antiquities' Department. We just had to do a little detective work, twist a few arms, and grease some palms."

"He also kills people!" the Coast Guard skipper shouted. "He murdered my gunner's mate . . . shot him in cold blood!" The angry skipper continued his imprudent discourse. "They filled their boat partially full of water and pretended it was sinking. When we came to help, they pulled out machine guns and took us by surprise."

"I told all of you not to give us any trouble, and no one would get hurt. But no, he had to try to be a hero, and you're pressing your luck now," Jack snarled in response.

Captain Jeb grabbed the skipper's arm, pulling him back and urging him to shut up.

"Now, Stephanie," Jack said, turning back to her, "tell me where Matt and Jim are. Are they still diving on the wreck? "

She didn't answer.

"A ship with the submersible attached to the deck sailed past our little fishing boat a few hours ago. I figured the treasure was probably all up from the bottom by now, and it was time for us to come and claim it." His fiendish laugh would have chilled even the bravest of men.

Just then Drake came down the gangplank. In front of him, with hands in the air, was the five-man crew of the Dolphin. "We didn't find Matt or Jim, boss. We searched the entire yacht. There's no one else on board."

"What about the reason we're here? Is it on the yacht?"

"Oh yes," Drake grinned, showcasing crooked, brown-stained teeth. "They have treasure stacked neatly all over the open decks and in most of the cabins. Let's get what they are sorting over there and get out of here."

"What about the Ark of the Covenant?"

"The what?"

"The Ark of the Covenant, you idiot! Did you see anything that might resemble a box covered in gold?"

"I don't think so," Drake answered with a hint of trepidation in his voice. "We didn't see anything like that. We don't need it anyway. I mean, there is so much in every available space."

"You have no idea what the Ark of the Covenant is worth, do you?" Jack said in contempt.

Without warning, Jack's temper raged as he grabbed Stephanie by the hair and twisted her arm behind her back. "Where are Matt and Jim?" She screamed in pain. Before she could answer, Jack said, "Wait a minute. The crane bucket is still down at the wreck. I'll bet they are making one last dive. They are, aren't they? They waited until now to bring up the Ark. That's what they are doing down there, isn't it? They went back down to bring up the frosting on the cake, didn't they? The Ark of the Covenant! How long have they been down?"

"They were just starting down as you pulled up," Ann lied, hoping to buy some time.

Tiny came back. "They're not anywhere on this barge, Jack. And they're not on the yacht."

"Okay, we'll just follow our plan. Grab those gold coins and put them in the plastic tubs."

While Jack was busy watching Drake and Tiny gather some of the gold coins, Stephanie quietly moved under the light at the front of the barge. She stared down into the bright spot in the water around the cable.

"All right, Stephanie," Jack yelled at her, raising his pistol. "Move back over here. I don't want you warning them when they surface."

Ann was between Jack and Stephanie. She looked at Stephanie inquisitively. She saw several gold coins in Stephanie's hand as she slowly released them into the water next to the cable, right in the beam of the light.

Jack rushed over, grabbed Stephanie by the arm, spun her around, backhanded her, and pushed her away from the edge. "I said get away from there," he yelled. "I don't want you warning them."

There was nothing more anyone could do. Stephanie knew Jack had not seen her release the coins.

"Tiny, you and Drake carry these tubs. Put them with the rest of the treasures. Then, Tiny, you come back to this barge and hide behind the bridge. It's dark back there. I saw some iron bars welded to the back of this barge. It's a ladder to a dinghy they usually tow. That ladder and the dive platform are the only way they can come back on board. Watch that area. Keep an eye on the front where the light is shining, Drake."

Drake and Tiny lugged the heavy plastic tubs one at a time and put them on the yacht.

"Drake, you stay on that side of this group, and I'll stay on this side. Everyone move back from the edge of the barge. The first one to warn them will be the first to feed the sharks. I understand there are a lot of them in this area."

"The treasure is all on the yacht, Jack. We have what we came for. Let's kill them, and get out of here!"

Jack glared at Drake. "I'm so glad you're not in charge. You are so stupid. We're not shooting anyone else unless we have to. I want everything to look like an accident. If any body parts are not eaten when they drown, I don't want anyone to find a bullet lodged in a pelvic bone. They would probably trace it back to us. Everyone thinks we're dead. Let's keep it that way. Besides, I'm waiting for Matt and Jim. They have to surface soon."

Jack paced back and forth as he waited. No one said a word.

After several minutes with nothing happening Jack finally said, "I guess we waited long enough. As much as I'd like to get the Ark and feed Matthew Lane to the sharks, we'd better stay on schedule. The shock of seeing that cutter and this huge barge crane coming down at them with all these people trying to avoid the sharks will have to do. It will be a fitting end to Mr. Lane and his buddy and for that matter, all of you. Jack threw his head back in rancorous laughter. "And no one can prove it wasn't an accident. Drake, go get Tiny. Open the scuttle valves. We're going to have a party! . . . A swimming party!"

CHAPTER THIRTY-ONE

The Ark of the Covenant was not on the old freighter. It hadn't taken long to search the last deck. It just wasn't there.

We were on the last leg of our ascent. The dark water was changing to light blue as we followed the cable up toward the spotlight. Jim was just below me.

Suddenly he grabbed my fin. I paused to look down at him. He held up a gold coin. Why would Jim take time now to show me a coin he found on the wreck? Puzzled, I continued the ascent. Something bounced off my head. It was a gold coin. Looking up, I saw three more coins coming down. Something was wrong.

I signaled Jim to follow me. We swam away from the cable and surfaced in the dark under the bow of the Coast Guard cutter.

"What's going on, partner?" Jim whispered, pulling his face mask off.

"I don't know, but I don't like it. Stay here. I'm going out and take a look."

I came up way out in front of the barge. It was pitch black out there, but the lights on the crane arm lit up the barge. The cutter was tied to the barge on my left with the bow facing me, and the Dolphin was on my right, the bow also facing me. The gangplanks were still in place leading from both ships to the deck of the barge. Everything was just like we had left it. However, it seemed strange that everyone was standing together in a group in the middle of the barge, even the Dolphin crew.

A bulky man broke from the group and walked toward me, stopping close to the cable. As he bent down peering into the water, light reflected across the machine gun he was carrying. He straightened up. At first, I saw the brown ponytail. Then I saw his face. I was stunned as I identified our nemesis, Drake! He was waiting for Jim and me to surface.

How did he get out here, and who's with him? My question was soon answered as Jack appeared under the crane spotlight. I knew Tiny had to be there and probably more henchmen. This meant trouble with a capital "T"!

I swam back and told Jim. He was just as dumbfounded as I was when I relayed what and whom I saw up top.

"What's our next move, brother? How are we going to get these creeps off our boats and rescue the crew without any weapons?" Jim whispered.

"I don't know," I replied. "We can't board the cutter from here. Our only access is the dive platform at the back of the yacht or the ladder up from the dinghy station."

"Jack's bound to have someone guarding the yacht with all that treasure onboard. In fact, I'm surprised they haven't already headed for port. What are they waiting for?" Jim asked.

"They're waiting for us, Jim. Jack's got the gold, but he also wants revenge. He wants us dead. Besides, dead men tell no tales!"

"Maybe we can overpower one of Jack's men and get a gun."

"We'll play it by ear," I said as I put my mask back on. We swam under the barge toward the dive platform on the back of the yacht.

The deck of the barge was eight to ten feet above the water line. When Jim and I came out from under it, we could barely see the steps leading down to the platform where we always entered the water at the stern of the yacht. The deck of the barge was lit up with the crane light. The side of the yacht above the barge was visible in the light, but the dive platform and the steps leading up to the next level were in the dark shadow of the barge.

We inched our way through the murky water toward the back of the yacht. Someone wearing a black trench coat was standing on the dive platform, a machine gun cradled across his left arm. As he stared into the water below his feet, we retreated to the darkness around the corner of the barge. Quickly I outlined the only plan I could think of to get past this guy. It was risky at best.

The guard tensed when he heard bubbles from Jim's oxygen tank on the far side of the dive platform. I had turned my oxygen off. Holding my breath, I swam underwater alongside the barge. I positioned myself in the shadow between the barge and the dive platform just below the surface. He had his gun aimed at the water, sure we were coming up. He was ready for us! Moving to the edge of the platform, the guard was anxiously watching the bubbles Jim was releasing below. All his attention was focused on those bubbles now getting closer to the surface.

The guard never saw me swim under water to just below his legs. Water lapping at the back of the platform masked any sounds from my movement. I surfaced, breathed deeply, looped the man's legs with my right arm in one swift action and pulled hard. His feet went out from under him. Down he went, sliding into the water, his weapon clattering onto the rubber mat embedded in the fiberglass landing. The hired killer didn't have time to utter a sound. He was no match for the power of my fins and my oxygen tank, which I had turned back on. Holding his legs, I pulled him straight down. Struggling and fighting with every ounce of his strength, the man kicked his legs trying to free them. At the same time he was clawing the water trying to reach the surface. He hadn't had time to take a breath when his head went under. He was totally panicked. Finally, he stopped struggling.

I knew what I had done would probably haunt me for the rest of my life. I was not a killer. I had killed before, but it was always to save my own life or the life of someone I loved. I had no choice. If we didn't get a weapon, a lot of innocent people were going to die, including Ann, Stephanie, and Joanne.

Jim surfaced and cautiously made his way up the steps to the deck above, picking up the weapon as he went. He stopped at the open area where we usually put on our dive gear and discarded his tank. It was total darkness. Jim heard something, someone moving just a few feet in front of him. He couldn't see anyone, but he sensed someone was there. As he crouched down, his head bumped into a life ring mounted on the bulkhead.

"Is that you, Gan?" a voice in front of him said as his flashlight exposed Jim's hiding place.

If Jim didn't shoot now, the man with the flashlight would. He raised the gun toward the light.

In a split second, a flash of silver whizzed past his ear. The flashlight fell to the deck followed by the man who had been holding it. It took Jim an instant to realize the knife had been thrown from someone behind him. Wheeling around, he saw me in the subdued light from the flashlight lying on the deck. "Nice throw, partner," he whispered.

We knelt and made sure the man was dead. It was another man dressed all in black.

Quickly we explored the yacht for more people, but found none. Now we each had a weapon, two of Jack's men were dead, and we had control of the yacht.

Jim stopped in the galley, grabbed a meat saw, and headed toward the bow. Quietly under the cover of the bow enclosure, Jim cut the rope holding the bow to the barge. Then he moved aft and cut the rope at the stern.

Surprised to find there was no one guarding the area, I climbed up the welded ladder to the deck of the barge behind the bridge. I could hear Jack talking to Drake and Tiny, but I couldn't see them or hear what they were saying. Quickly I crossed the open deck and slipped in the back door. Grabbing a dish towel from the small kitchen, I wiped the water from the gun. Glancing at my watch, I headed up the inside ship's ladder to the bridge. From there, I'd be able to see what was going on.

Down where the bow of the yacht curved away from the barge, Jim waited. He was sitting in a truck tire hanging from the deck of the barge. He had one arm looped around the top of the tire, his shoulder against the smooth fiberglass of the yacht and his other arm against the cold black steel of the barge. He watched the illuminated dial on his dive watch. Counting down the last twenty seconds, he began pushing the yacht away from the barge. It didn't budge an inch, but he knew if he just kept steady pressure and wasn't fighting a wind or current, the yacht would slowly move away from the barge.

In a few minutes, the narrow space widened. He could now use his legs to push. The strong breeze he felt before he entered the water was in his favor. The breeze would help move the yacht. Within two minutes, the distance between the two crafts was five feet and increasing. All hell was about to break loose!

* * * * *

"Did you get the scuttle valves open?" Jack yelled.

"They're wide open and water is pouring in," Drake hollered back. "The cutter will sink before the barge. The engines are already flooded."

"I'm not too sure," Tiny said. "The barge has two big valves and it's filling fast. With this tall crane, it will probably roll over before the cutter goes down."

"This is going to be fun to watch," Drake said grinning from ear to ear.

"We'll stay here for a few minutes to make sure they both go down. Maybe by then, Matt and Jim will join us," Jack chuckled. "But when this barge starts to feel unstable, we'll watch from the yacht."

"I'm all for that," Drake shouted back at Jack.

Meanwhile, Jack continued to bark orders. "Take another look behind the bridge, Tiny. They have got to be coming up soon. Stay back so they don't see you. Drake, go make sure Gan is awake back at the dive platform on the yacht. They should have surfaced by now. I'm no diver, but I know they can't stay down this long on a deep dive."

After checking the scuttle valves one more time, Drake started walking toward the yacht. Just then the gangway between the yacht and the barge fell into the water. He yelled, "Jack, the yacht! . . . It's loose! . . . It's drifting away from the barge!"

Furious, Jack started running toward the yacht. "Tiny, guard these people! Gan . . . Benz . . . what's going on?" No one answered. The space between the barge and the yacht grew wider and wider. "Jump . . . jump, Drake."

"You jump, Jack! I can't make it. It's too far out. I can't jump."

"Run back to the stern, Drake. It's still close, only six or seven feet away. You can jump to the stairs on the dive platform. The cutter and the barge are sinking!" he yelled. "If you don't bring back that yacht, we're all going to drown!"

Drake lumbered behind Jack who was frantically scrambling to the back of the barge watching the expanse increase by the second. Drake was scared. He didn't think he could jump that far, and he knew he wasn't a good swimmer.

"I can't, Jack."

"Yes, you can!" Jack screamed as he pulled out the steel rods holding the rope railing, throwing them down on the deck. "Just run and jump! Do it now and you can make it. Jump, Drake, jump!" Turning, Jack waved his pistol in Drake's direction.

Each second the space between the two vessels widened, and the light from the barge lit up the water. Having no choice, Drake moved back about fifteen feet, hesitated, and then ran as fast as he could to the edge of the barge and vaulted into space. He stuck his big hands out to catch the rail on the side that enclosed the rear platform. Missing the chrome railing by inches, his face hit the edge of the fiberglass. His nose sprayed blood down the side of the vessel as he plummeted into the sea. Dazed, he surfaced coughing and sputtering as he flailed his arms in panic.

Jack unleashed a barrage of profanity and commands. "Swim to the platform, you idiot! Swim around the corner to the platform . . . damn it! You've got to get on that boat!" Jack was now pleading with Drake. "It's close. Just a few more strokes and you're there!"

Drake's fingers touched the platform just as something cold brushed against his side. He turned and saw the fin flash across the moonlit water. He froze with fear. That fear changed to panic as the shark turned to make the deadly run.

Jack saw it too. The shark was swimming right toward Drake. "Pull yourself up, Drake. You can do it!"

Exhausted, Drake tried repeatedly to get his right foot on the first step under the water to no avail. He let out a bloodcurdling scream as the shark bit into his leg and pulled him under. Briefly he surfaced again yelling, "Help me, Jack!"

His bloody body skimmed the surface as Drake passed Jack before disappearing into the sea.

Above the din of the pandemonium, Tiny heard the cries for help from Drake. Still aiming his gun at the crew, he rushed to the edge of the barge. His only friend needed him. Stunned at the blood and carnage in the water below, he lowered his gun. That was a fatal mistake.

With Tiny in shock, Captain Jeb moved closer and hurled his sixteen-inch crescent wrench as hard as he could at Tiny, hitting him on the side of his head. Tiny stumbled and fell into the water bleeding. With the shark population already drawn to the smell of Drake's blood, Tiny didn't stand a chance. The turbulent water turned crimson.

Jack was just turning to Tiny for help to retrieve the yacht when he saw the silver wrench spin over and over in the air, striking Tiny. He watched as Tiny stared up at him, moving his mouth trying to say something. But no words were audible as he was dragged down the last time, meeting the same fate as Drake . . . best friends together forever in eternity!

Jack seemed to be in shock. It had all happened so quickly. Out of his army of five, he was the only one left. The yacht with the treasure was now twenty feet from the barge. The cutter was about to go under, and the barge they were standing on was listing heavy to port. The cable going down to the bucket on the ship wreck below was banging against the steel hull, and the light at the end of the giant crane arm was aiming at an odd angle. Everyone had their legs spread out bracing themselves on the tilting steel deck.

Jack's head was spinning. He grabbed Stephanie with his machine pistol pointed at her. Ann stepped in front of Stephanie. Jack hit Ann with his forearm and knocked her down. Like a madman, he grabbed Stephanie by her hair and jerked her head back. "This is all your fault, you rotten bitch. You've been a curse to me since the day you were born!"

Jack got behind her and put the gun to her head. Turning toward the crew, he lashed out, "Okay, who's going to close the scuttle valves? If someone doesn't close them, we are all going to die. But I guarantee she'll be the first, and Ann will be second."

Jack was now with his back to the bridge. Everyone was facing him.

"Don't shoot," Captain Jeb acquiesced as he moved toward the building below the bridge. "Jacob and I will close the valves."

The wind was picking up and now a strong gale was moving the yacht further away. Without warning, the stressed steel in the old barge let out a groan, and she listed even more. It wouldn't take much to make the big flat barge stand on its edge, dumping everyone on it into the shark-infested sea. Everyone started to back up toward the starboard side to help offset the list.

Jack was facing them with Stephanie still in his grasp. His back was to me as I crept across the twenty feet of open deck between the bridge building and Jack. I was three feet away when Jack heard me. Removing the pistol from Stephanie's forehead, he started to turn, aim, and fire. I blocked the side of Jack's arm with my forearm, and the shot went wild. I punched him in the face and then wrestled the gun from his hand. When the gun clattered to the steel deck, I elbowed Jack in the stomach. Turning toward me, he threw a couple of punches that glanced off my arm. I hit him hard in the ribs. My feet were bare, but I spun and kicked him on the side of his head. After some quick brutal blows to his body and face, he went down. His nose was bleeding. I grabbed the gun and shoved it under his chin. I was ready to pull the trigger, but I didn't.

"I should kill you for all you have done, Jack," I shouted at him. I remember thinking I hoped the day would never come when I would wish I had pulled that trigger.

Cautioning everyone to remain on the high starboard side of the barge, Jeb and Jacob raced to close the scuttle valves and start the bilge pumps. The skipper of the Coast Guard cutter and his men rushed to do the same. The three-inch hawsers securing the cutter to the barge had snapped when the barge listed to the port side. We could only watch as it slipped under the surface and slowly disappeared. The body of the sailor Jack had murdered was in the closed quarters of the vessel as it went straight to the bottom of the sea.

When Jim could not push the yacht any more, the breeze continued to move the vessel away from the barge. When the gang plank fell, Jim was already on board. He hotwired the ignition and brought it back to the side of the barge.

I retrieved the keys to the yacht from Jack's pocket. Jim duct-taped Jack to a chair. When he started screaming obscenities at everyone, Jim also taped his mouth shut.

In the morning, two more Coast Guard cutters were tied to the barge, which again was stable and level in the water. Jim and I made one more dive. We put the body of the gunner's mate in the bucket, and Captain Jeb reverently raised it to the surface.

Word of the treasure we had found and retrieved was broadcast all over the world. When we sailed into the harbor at Acre, Israel, thousands of people and TV cameras were there to greet us. The treasure was returned to Israel.

I was proud of what we had accomplished, and I felt sure that some of the items we brought up were actually a part of the original treasure of King Solomon, the richest and the wisest of all the kings in the Bible.

CHAPTER THIRTY-TWO

We returned to the house just outside the walled city in Jerusalem. The next two weeks were frantic. To the people of Israel, we were heroes, interviewed again and again by reporters from around the world.

The treasure was immense. There were crowns and jewelry ancient kings had worn, some with a name engraved on the piece. Everything had to be cleaned and the inscriptions deciphered. Everyone was anxious to see if any object could be identified as belonging to a biblical name. There were goblets of gold encrusted with jewels, ceremonial swords, and gold-handled knives. We had inventoried fifty ornate chests made of brass and covered in jewels and gold leaf. Ten were brimming with a collection of gemstones and forty were loaded to capacity with gold coins.

Everyone wondered if the gold ceremonial shields were the ones Solomon had made for his army, the shields described in the Bible in the first Book of Kings and in second Chronicles.

There were marble busts with faint etchings. Maybe they could be identified as a prominent king or prophet from ancient history. Every piece would have to be cleaned by experts and be properly cataloged before the treasure could be displayed. Due to the extensive media coverage, the entire civilized world watched in fascination as cameras panned the colorful treasure that had been salvaged from the old ship on the ocean floor.

My dad, Senator Lane, and my grandmother, Estelle Lane, were in the audience when everyone involved, including Professor Kempson, was formally recognized and thanked by the Prime Minister. The government even offered to fly Ada and Roberto from Italy to Israel for the ceremony, but they declined, preferring the simplicity of their quiet life. Captain Jeb received generous compensation for damages to his barge.

The next night, dad and Estelle hosted a black-tie reception at the private estate of an old friend of theirs. They invited many dignitaries, including Dr. Levi and all who had been at the ocean site. Guests included Captain Jeb, his deckhand Jacob, and Officer Joanne Zivah, the skipper and crew and security team from the Dolphin, the skipper and his crew from the Coast Guard cutter, and Paul, the submersible operator.

Estelle was renowned in Washington circles as the consummate hostess. For many years, my grandmother had assisted my father, planning and executing the many receptions and soirees required by his position.

Tonight Estelle, as she preferred to be called, stood tall and stately next to the Senator, charming each dignitary, her smile making each feel special and welcome. No one would guess she was in her seventies.

Estelle had chosen a long black gown with a sweetheart neckline overlaid with chiffon that extended down her well-toned arms. Simple pearls complemented her creamy complexion and flaxen hair. Glamour and elegance exuded from this lady – my grandmother!

All the men, except those in the military who had their uniforms on, wore tuxedos. Even Captain Jeb and Jacob cut a polished appearance and appeared to enjoy their notoriety.

Estelle proposed a somber toast to the Coast Guard gunner's mate whom Jack had murdered and asked for a moment of silence in his behalf. We all were saddened to have lost him during our harrowing experience.

After a beautiful dinner, Estelle made it a point to visit with both Ann and Stephanie. She managed to meet and converse with each girl separately without it seeming like an interview.

I love and respect my very wise grandmother. She started with nothing. She was from a very poor family. She worked hard and started her own business. She was twenty-eight years old and her fashion-design business was really starting to grow when she met my grandfather. He was working for his father in the timber and land-developing business. Life for her got easier after they were married, but she never forgot what it was like to be really poor. They only had one son, my father, the senator. They went through some rough times in the timber and land business over the years, but they were frugal, wise investors and eventually became quite wealthy. My grandfather died a couple of years ago after a long battle with cancer.

Instead of dwelling on the loss of the love of her life, Estelle turned her attention, time, and money to many worthwhile charities. She tries to give a hand up to the deserving poor. She is an inspiration to everyone who knows her.

My father, Senator Clifford Lane, is a distinguished looking man. He's handsome and charming, kind of the Sean Connery type, with a full head of hair now graying at the temples.

He had met Ann at other functions and family gatherings back in Washington and greeted her with a big hug.

He shook hands as I introduced Stephanie and after a little coaxing, engaged her in telling him and others who were with the senator's group how she happened to be involved in the search. She told about her uncle who had found the map years ago in Israel, and a little of how her parents were killed by stampeding elephants when she was a little girl.

I was embarrassed as I heard her praise me for helping her find her father's legal papers in an old metal box in the cave in the Thailand jungle, which led to finding the map in the wreckage of her uncle's plane. She didn't speak at all about Jack or any of the other bad things that happened.

Everyone was captivated by the beauty and charisma of both women and by Stephanie's story.

As the guests were saying their goodbyes, Estelle whispered in my ear, "Come see me soon, Matthew. We need to talk."

"Oh, oh," I said to myself. When my grandmother Estelle talks, I listen. It's always been that way.

* * * * *

The sun was going down, and I had just arrived at the apartment Estelle had rented for the month in Israel. It was a beautiful evening. The butler escorted me to the second floor balcony where Estelle was waiting. She invited me to join her at the railing where we looked over the brilliant rose garden below.

I gave her a big hug and a kiss. She held me close and then looked directly in my eyes.

"Thank you for coming, Matthew," she said smiling sweetly. "My, you're a handsome devil! You resemble your father all right, but you look almost exactly like your grandfather looked at your age . . . God rest his soul . . . except for your eyes. Your eyes are remarkable, Matthew. I've never seen eyes like yours. Your mother had vivid blue eyes, and your father has green eyes, but your eyes are blue green, a very striking blue green. No wonder you can attract such beautiful women."

Before I could reply, Estelle continued. "Take Ann Tyler. She is drop-dead gorgeous, a wonderful human being. I saw that when I met her last year. And Stephanie, she could top most Hollywood movie stars with her beauty. Both women are intelligent and poised. How are you going to decide which one to keep?" She turned and waited for me to answer.

Taken aback, I shifted my stance and smiled at her, pulling her to my side, and giving her another hug.

Then I said as I put my arm around her slim waist and walked her to the settee, "First, thank you for the compliments. It makes me feel good coming from a charming lady like you, that you see me as handsome. And second, yes, both women are smart and beautiful. But how do you know I would have a chance to keep either one of them?"

"Don't kid me, Matthew. I spoke to both of them apart from each other. We didn't even talk about you, but those girls are in love with you, Matt. I'm serious, and I'm worried about it. I think you have a real problem. Besides wanting to see you, that's the main reason I wanted to talk to you. I would not want to see either of those girls hurt, or you for that matter. From what I observed, both are very jealous of your attention. I think they care for each other too, but one of them is going to get hurt. I just want to make sure that you are aware of the problem."

"I appreciate your concern, Estelle. I know things can't go on the way they are. I've been so busy, I pushed it to the back of my mind. I love Ann. I fell in love with her on Mount Ararat, and I'm still in love with her. I will admit Stephanie is intriguing. If I hadn't met Ann first, I'm sure I'd have fallen for Stephanie. But I did meet Ann first, and I am in love with her."

Estelle studied my face for a few seconds. "You haven't convinced me, Matthew. Are you sure you're not just trying to convince yourself?"

"I'll work it out, Estelle." I paused. "I think I might even ask Ann to marry me."

"Really?"

"Yes, I think so."

"You can't just think so, Matt. When you ask a girl to marry you, you need to be positive, no regrets, no changing your mind. Maybe you'd better not do anything yet, not until you're really positive."

"You're probably right, Estelle. You're probably right."

"Of course I'm right. I'm your grandmother," she laughed. "Coffee or tea, Matthew?"

"Coffee, please, with cream, no sugar."

Estelle poured coffee for me and tea for herself.

"Now that you have found Noah's Ark and the lost Israelite treasure, are you going to continue searching for the Ark of the Covenant?"

"Yes, I am. We need to find that artifact now, more than ever. There are more people than ever before who don't believe in God. They don't worry about what might happen in the next life if they kill someone. Some place very little value on human life, even to the point of trying to kill anyone who is not of their religion. This has to stop. No one is safe in an environment like that. Many of our elected leaders have become greedy and are not really serving the people who elected them. Those are the things that drive me, Estelle. I've been concerned about all these things since I was a teenager. I'm sure you must be tired of hearing it."

"Not at all, Matthew. I'm proud that you are upholding the standards your father and grandfather have always stood for. They felt it was the responsibility of each and every one of us to live by the law of the land and the Commandments God gave us."

"I keep hoping if we can find the Ark of the Covenant and people can actually see it, their belief in the Bible may deepen. Maybe that discovery will change some minds. Maybe there will be fewer killings, less bombs and a safer world. Maybe someone with a gun in hand will think about it and won't pull the trigger. I have to keep searching for the Ark, Estelle. I have to."

When I left Estelle, it was late . . . too late to shop for an engagement ring. But soon . . . very soon!

CHAPTER THIRTY-THREE

Jerusalem

It had been raining all evening. At 10 p.m., I excused myself. We were all exhausted from the barrage of world figures wanting to meet us and countless reporters wanting exclusive personal interviews.

In my room, I opened the box and gazed at the ring I had purchased from a jewelry shop in the ancient walled city of Jerusalem. I laid down, deep in thought. I didn't want to rush the proposal or make it a public spectacle. Everything had to be perfect, just the two of us alone.

Ann had no idea I was going to ask her to marry me. She might even turn me down. We really had not had a chance to talk privately since we got back on dry land. I was concerned Ann might have seen Stephanie enter my room late at night on the yacht. The two times Stephanie did come to my room after others had gone to bed, we had talked about the book she was writing. If Ann did see Stephanie, I hoped she didn't get the wrong impression.

My thoughts drifted to Stephanie, every man's dream. She always volunteered to help, even if it meant digging in the dirt alongside me. Her desire to learn about archaeology and Jim's and my many expeditions was insatiable. She told me she loved me when we were in the mine, and the way she acted when we were alone led me to believe her feelings hadn't changed. I never told Ann what Stephanie said to me in the mine. Some things are best left unsaid.

Estelle was right. When Stephanie finds out I have asked Ann to marry me, she was going to be hurt. I cared too much for Stephanie to hurt her. It would be best to wait for a while before I ask Ann to marry me.

Another sleepless night. I watched the seconds – minutes – pass away on the illuminated face of the clock on the nightstand.

Soon I was deep in thought about the Ark of the Covenant. It was an obsession that overshadowed my every waking moment. It was like a song in my head that played over and over again. I had to see my quest for the Ark through to the end before I could move on with my life!

There has to be another room in that cave. The treasure that ancient Israel would have protected above anything else was the Ark of the Covenant.

I had no doubt that Professor Kempson was right in his research. That special hiding place for ancient Israel, with an army to watch over it, was built by Solomon. He had it built specifically to save the Ark of the Covenant from ever falling into the hands of another nation. The place that held the Ark of the Covenant would have been sealed and camouflaged. The city's treasure of gold, jewelry, and artifacts may have been brought in later, perhaps in a rush as the invaders were at their gates. I think the Ark of the Covenant was concealed in that cavern long before the rest of the treasure was hidden there. . . . But where?

Finally, I nodded off into a fitful sleep.

*****

Strike the stone!
Strike the stone!
Strike the stone!

I bolted to an upright position in bed. I was drenched in sweat. I stared at the clock. The green digital numbers indicated 11:34. I was wide awake as I swung my legs over the edge of the bed.

I knew what I was going to do. I had to do this and I had to do it alone . . . just me.

I made the bed and left a note on my pillow . . . *Can't sleep . . . Going to the cavern.* Putting the bag containing bottled water, an apple, and a hastily made sandwich on the passenger seat beside me, I turned the ignition key. Without turning on the headlights until I had backed away from the house, I headed south out of Jerusalem.

I drove alone down the highway and then the dirt road across the desert in the rain to the rim of the plateau. Finally my headlights lit up the area where the trail started down. I paused, thinking this is crazy. I should never be going down the side of this mountain alone, especially at night. It's not an old road . . . it's an ancient trail. No one has ever driven a vehicle down here except me a few weeks ago. It was dangerous then when the trail was dry and it was daylight. It's been raining all day so the trail will be slick. If I slide off and roll this Hummer to the bottom of the canyon, no one may even find the wreck or know I died out here. All this to save a few hours' driving time. Yet I felt a compulsive urge to go forward, imprudent as it may seem.

I put the Hummer in gear and moved closer to the edge on my right side. I couldn't see where the trail started down. Rain pelted me as I got out of the car. Straining as I peered into the dark and through the rain, I struggled to find the large boulder that marked where the trail began its perilous descent to the valley floor. It was almost impossible to get my bearings with the deluge of torrential rain, but at long last I discovered where I thought my front wheels had to be.

Wiping the rain from my eyes, I got back in the car. Taking a deep breath and putting the transmission in low gear four-wheel drive, I turned the wheels slightly to the right and started forward. All I could see in front of me now was black with sheets of rain coming down in the headlights.

Did I really have the Hummer in the right place? Was my right front tire going to be on solid ground? I held my breath, feeling as though I was suspended in mid-air. It seemed like forever before both front wheels dropped down on rock. Then the sheer rock wall appeared on my left.

With my mirror folded in, only a four inch space separated me from the wall. If I moved over, I risked plummeting off the edge of the narrow trail into the abyss below. My palms perspired as I gripped the steering wheel and maneuvered down – down the trail, often sliding in the wet gravel. In front of me was only a narrow steep rocky trail. I couldn't see anything but black space on the right side, and I knew it was a long way down.

After a tense terrifying ride, I arrived on the canyon floor. I hit the brakes and just sat there. When my hands quit shaking and I stopped chastising myself for doing such a crazy thing, I proceeded toward the canyon wall.

Finally my headlights were shining on the plywood door covering the entrance to the cavern. The clock on the dash read 2:45 a.m. I was half expecting a guard, but no one was there. Only yellow crime scene tape and keep-out signs on the makeshift plywood barrier separated me from the cavern. Thankfully the closure stone was still in its natural open position. Three large galvanized hinges and a hasp for a padlock had been bolted to the rock face, securing the plywood across the opening.

Standing in the headlights, I knocked the padlock and hasp off the plywood with one blow from a sledgehammer. The sand was wet, but it had stopped raining.

Turning off the Hummer engine, the headlights soon clicked off. Taking the ladder which I had borrowed from the garage off the luggage rack, I walked toward the entrance. The moon came out from a clearing in the clouds and lit up the entire canyon. I paused and took in the beautiful sight. Off in the distance, wild dogs or jackals were howling. All other night sounds were gone, and it was so quiet I could hear myself breathing. The air was fresh from the rain. Stepping across the threshold, I entered the cavern.

With the flashlight standing vertical on the shelf, I once again looked at the Hebrew words so carefully chiseled into the surface of the stone so many centuries before. The professor had translated them into English. "If ye seek real treasure, look up toward God's heaven."

It seemed like a long time had passed since we discovered this. Could it really have only been a few weeks ago? With one foot on the ladder and the other on the ledge at the base of the alcove, I said, "Okay, let's just see what we can find up toward God's heaven. Let's see if it's up behind this wall."

I picked a spot just above the alcove, not wanting to damage the ancient letters. After asking God for some help, I swung the heavy sledge as hard as I could. The hammer sprang back . . . Nothing. The plaster splintered, but the rock was solid. Gritting my teeth, I swung the heavy hammer again striking the same place. Again the hammer ricocheted back. I hit it again as hard as I could. This time a crack formed in the plaster. A rectangular shape appeared about a foot wide and eight inches high. Solid rock would not do that!

Anxious, I struck the same spot again. The rectangular section moved back a quarter inch. The third, fourth, and fifth blows knocked the piece completely out. I heard the rock fall on the other side. It didn't fall very far. A black hole appeared above the alcove.

"I knew it!" I hollered out loud. "I knew it!" I scrambled up another rung on the ladder and shined my light through the opening. To my surprise, I saw a dust- covered stone floor. The beam of light suggested some steps in the distance. Minutes later, I had a hole big enough to crawl through.

I hadn't brought the others with me because I didn't want to involve them in any criminal activity such as defacing ancient artifacts. Of course, Joanne would never have allowed me to strike the ancient plaster with a sledgehammer. But now, I wish they were all here to share this with me.

Excited, I crawled through the hole and dropped down about six feet to the stone floor. Exercising a degree of caution, I stood up, finding myself in an eight- foot-wide corridor. Twenty feet out, there was a staircase ascending upward. Fascinated, I played my light on the plastered walls and ceiling, which revealed faded ancient hieroglyphs similar to those in the Egyptian tombs in the Valley of the Kings south of Cairo.

I moved through the stone corridor to the steps ahead of me and started up. The air was very musty. Fifty steps later, I reached the top. The pitch-black area absorbed most of the beam of light from my flashlight. The corridor continued another twenty feet.

A solid stone wall ended the corridor, but a doorway had been chiseled into the stone on the far right side. This was an unbelievable experience. I was anxious to see what I might encounter, but fearful at the same time. Would the Ark of the Covenant actually be here or would it be just another disappointment?

Cautiously, I approached the entrance. Something flashed in my light as I entered. On my right was a solid wall running parallel with my line of sight, and twenty feet in front of me was another solid stone wall. My flashlight was no match for this pitch-black space. In the corner standing on the floor in front of me was a gold-covered vase.

I wasn't prepared for what was on my left. Turning my beam, the whole space brightened with reflected light. It was a long room with a gold-covered table where bowls and dishes, a pitcher and a candleholder had been placed a long time ago. Everything was made of gold, a little dusty, but still bright. The objects were very ornate and adorned with bronze and silver trim. Gold and onyx articles were everywhere I shined my light. Everything was neatly placed.

There was a path in the center. All the beautifully hand-crafted gold, silver, and bronze pieces were on the floor. In front of me was a veil. It stretched twenty feet wall to wall. Supporting the veil were four gold-covered pillars with bronze and silver trim. The veil itself was a fine smooth linen with blue, purple and scarlet colors with cherubim designs. The linen was sagging and tearing at the top, but still hanging from the silver hooks with a bronze base. Mesmerized, I approached it. Afraid to touch the old fabric, I paused and took a deep breath.

There was a slight opening in the center. Cautiously, I pushed my hand through and peered into the room. Chiseled stone formed the walls and ceiling. The large area was empty except for something covered with a colorful cloth in the center of the room. The shape was intriguing. Standing next to it and shining my light on the very top, my heart started palpitating. It looked like fragile fabric. I looked closer. There was a slight tear in the fabric and something made of smooth gold was underneath, maybe the tops of wings! Being ever so careful, I touched the cloth. Nothing happened.

My mouth felt dry. I wiped my sweaty palms on my pants. The strange shape was wide to my right and left, about three feet across in front of me and maybe four feet high.

I put my flashlight on the stone floor with the bright beam shooting straight up to the ceiling high above. The reflection illuminated the room a little more. Kneeling, I reached down to the floor and reverently gathered some of the material in each hand. Slowly I rose and began to lift it up. The first thing I remember seeing was a gold-covered pole running horizontally down low. At that point, I was really excited. Is this really happening? Suddenly gravity took over and the covering fell to the floor.

A thrill went through my whole body as I gazed in amazement at the greatest biblical artifact of all time – The Ark of the Covenant! I couldn't stop staring at it. It looked very much like the artists had imagined and drawn over the centuries. I felt strange. I was trembling. The only light in the room came from my flashlight. It was unfathomable. I was alone in the middle of the night in a remote desert canyon looking at the greatest artifact of all time. This hadn't been seen by man for centuries.

The lid, also known as the mercy seat, was divided into two panels. Finally I started to reach out to touch the amazing box but pulled my hand back, remembering the stories of what happened to some of the people who had touched it before.

I uttered a prayer. *"Father in heaven, please let me proceed and touch the sacred Ark of the Covenant or let me know that I should not."*

Then I slowly reached out again. I lightly brushed the wing of one of the cherubim with the back of my hand. Nothing happened. Cautiously I brushed it again. I was still unharmed. Carefully, I laid my open palm on the gold wing. The electrical shock I half expected didn't happen. I started to lift one half of the heavy lid upward. It wasn't stuck, but the hinges creaked a little. I continued to lift until the lid was vertical. The weight of the wings acted as a counterbalance. The lid came to a stop when it reached the vertical position.

Though anxious, I dismissed the urgent desire to look inside. Instead, I used the same procedure to lift the other half of the gold-plated lid to the vertical position. I tried to swallow but my mouth was too dry. My heart was beating so hard I thought I could hear it in the hollow rock chamber.

With the flashlight in my right hand, I shined the light down into the box. Within eight inches of my hand was another colored cloth. It was lying flat and smooth, covering something. The cloth was like the veil material. I peeled the cloth back. There, side-by-side, were two slabs of stone. They looked very old. My head was spinning. They were each rectangular with a slight curve on the top, about eighteen inches wide and twenty-four inches in length. They were two or three inches thick. There were lines of ancient writing on them. The surrounding surface was smooth. I didn't recognize the characters, but they were cut deeply enough in the stone to easily be deciphered. Again afraid a jolt of electricity might strike me if I touched the stone, I slowly and very cautiously brushed the edge of one of them, then quickly moved my hand away. No shock. The stone felt cold.

 I stood mesmerized and gazed at the now open gold-covered box with the two tablets lying on a cloth. I couldn't see if the tablets Moses threw down and broke were under this set or not. I didn't want to remove them . . . at least not now. I felt so very privileged, even chosen, to be here to see this, to take this all in. I stood and gazed upon it for a long time, not wanting this special moment to end.

 Finally, I started to examine everything, the gold covering the acacia wood, the gold-covered poles in their rings so the Ark could be carried, the beautiful veil, and the gold-covered pillars that supported the veil. The round carrying poles were a little warped, and the gold plate covering them had a few split seams. The veil sagged, but didn't fall apart when I touched it. It wasn't in tatters as I would have imagined it to be.

 I looked around with my flashlight at everything in the area. I came back to the Ark. Suddenly I felt a cool breeze. The veil moved a little, startling me. I stopped dead in my tracks. How could there be a breeze in here? Maybe the air is moving through the hole I made. The breeze grew stronger, moving the veil of the holy of holies. A little dust fell from it. Now I was apprehensive. The strong breeze was not natural. I was too scared to move, almost afraid to breathe. Minutes passed. The breeze continued. The air was no longer stale. It smelled fresh. Then the breeze slowly died down. As it did, the most surprising thing I could ever imagine happened. The Ark started to glow. A light was emitting from within the open box, becoming brighter and brighter.

I felt myself trembling as I stared at the glowing wood box covered in gold. The light was intense now and lit up the whole area. It was as if I were in a trance.

A voice . . . I heard a voice! A soft gentle male voice! Where was it coming from? There was no one else in the brightly lit space!

The calming voice spoke distinctly. "Do not be afraid, Matthew. I am but a messenger. You have also been chosen to be a messenger, Matthew. This is the message you are assigned to deliver for all on earth to witness. On the first day of the next season of this current year, a sign will appear. The sign will remain for eight seasons, and then it will be taken up. The sign and the recording of this sign will affirm and strengthen the faith of all who are willing to see, hear, and believe, for the next one hundred generations of mankind. The message you deliver, Matthew, will prepare the way for the sign. The appearance and the taking away of the sign are to be witnessed and recorded for all on earth to see."

There was a pause. I stood paralyzed, my rapid heartbeat resonating against my chest.

Then he said, "The sign will appear in the land west of Mount Sinai at a latitude of 28°17'36" North, and a longitude of 33° 08'12" East."

I waited for him to speak again, but he did not. Somehow I had the feeling I shouldn't question anything I was told or even speak. The breeze didn't come back, and the light from inside the Ark of the Covenant slowly dimmed until I was left standing alone in the almost dark room.

I realized my flashlight was still on. "Are you there?" I felt compelled to ask. No one replied.

I had been surprisingly calm while the voice was speaking to me, but now I was shaking. My knees were so weak I had to sit down. Did this really happen, or did I just imagine it?

I hadn't written anything down . . . the dates, when the sign is to appear, the latitude, longitude. I began to panic. . . . I would not remember what was said to me. The sign was to appear west of Mt. Sinai. Then I realized I did remember all he said. I remembered every word. I couldn't forget it if I tried.

How can I do this? If I announce this to the world, no one will believe me. Even I wouldn't believe someone telling such a story. But wait . . . I'm not just someone. I just found the Ark of the Covenant!

* * * * *

"Wake up. Wake up, Matt!"

It was Jim. I could hear him, but I was struggling to open my eyes.

"Is he going to be all right?" That was Stephanie's worried voice.

"Here, Jim. Put this damp cloth on his head," I heard Ann say.

Where was I anyway? I just couldn't wake up. Something was wrong with me.

"Let's get him to a doctor," Stephanie pleaded.

Finally, I blinked and began to focus. Three concerned faces were staring at me from the dark. They were all holding flashlights . . . Jim, Stephanie, and Ann. But what was that behind Jim? Then I remembered. It hadn't been a dream. It was the Ark of the Covenant. But why did I feel so sleepy? I could hardly keep my eyes open.

As they helped me sit up, I was bombarded with questions.

"What time is it?" I finally asked.

"It's noon."

"Noon?"

"Yes, it's noon, Matt. Are you okay?" Ann asked, taking my hand.

"You found it, buddy," Jim said. "You actually found it. I can't believe it!"

"How long have you three been here?"

"We just arrived," Jim said. "We've had a hard time waking you up. It's like you were unconscious. When did you discover this?"

"I think about four this morning."

"Four a.m.? What have you been doing since then, Matt?"

I didn't answer. Closing my eyes, vivid flashbacks replayed last night's mystical experience.

Jim gently shook my arm. "Have you tried to touch it yet?"

I stood up, and they followed me as I staggered over to the Ark.

"Yes, I touched it last night."

"Did it shock you, Matt? Maybe it shocked you, and that's why we found you unconscious."

"No, it didn't shock me. I'm the one who opened it up. The top was closed when I found it. But something did happen. You probably won't believe me, but I'll tell you later. Right now, I want to show you the stone tablets."

You could hear a pin drop when I shined my light down into the box.

CHAPTER THIRTY-FOUR

We were having dinner in a restaurant in Jerusalem.

"It's pretty hard to believe, Matt," Jim said. "Are you positive it really happened? If you are positive and you really believe it happened, then I believe you, but remember how hard it was for you to wake up? I think maybe you were unconscious from breathing that bad air from the cave. I mean you had just opened a room full of air that had to be about twenty-six-hundred years old. It probably didn't contain enough oxygen or had too much carbon dioxide. It's amazing you didn't die."

"Yes, Matt, that would explain it," Ann said.

"I thought about that," I said. "But remember, I told you about the breeze. I could smell the damp outside air in that breeze. I think whoever spoke to me created that breeze to keep me alive. I was so fascinated and anxious to find the Ark of the Covenant, I didn't take the precautions I should have before I entered."

"That's right," Ann said. "You didn't clear out the bad air. You breathed it into your lungs and hallucinated. You imagined the light and the voice. Your body was starved for clean air. You obviously imagined the clean cool fresh air you were breathing before you entered. Like Jim said, I'm surprised you didn't die."

"But I'm so glad you didn't," Stephanie interjected, smiling at me.

"I'm sure you guys are right," I said as I picked up my coffee cup. "That's what it had to have been, but guess where I plan to be in about six weeks?"

"Six weeks?" Ann said. Then she caught on and frowned. "Well, I'm guessing you want to spend the first day of spring in the desert west of Mount Sinai," she said coldly.

We all laughed.

* * * * *

Weeks passed. Anchormen on television were interviewing people arguing over who should own the Ark of the Covenant.

I had always believed that finding and showing the Ark of the Covenant to the world would help stop the violence, but the world situation had not changed much. Even seeing the Ark of the Covenant and the stone tablets on television every day hadn't put much of a dent in the crime and violence. It hadn't stopped the murders that happened in the world every day.

TV cameras focused on the Ten Commandments actually cut in stone by the finger of God. The broken tablets were not found in the Ark of the Covenant. The Commandment, **thou shalt not kill**, was emphasized in places of worship all over the world, but things in general did not change as I hoped they would. Our discovery was now old news.

Humankind does need a sign, I thought, something impressive enough to finally wake the inhabitants of earth up before we annihilate ourselves.

Ann came up to me one evening before I was to go on stage as a special guest on a talk show. We were in the dressing room. I knew she wanted me to assure her again that I wouldn't tell the public about the messenger.

"Please don't do it, Matt. Please don't mess everything up for us. We can live normal lives again. Maybe there will finally be time for us . . . just the two of us."

"Ann, I have to do what I was instructed to do. I don't believe I was hallucinating. I really believe a voice told me to prepare for this sign. He wanted the first showing of the sign to be recorded."

"I can't believe what you are saying, Matt. You can't possibly believe that God is going to give us some kind of a sign. Believe me, Matt, it's just not going to happen. If you insist on telling people that, you're going to look like an idiot!" Ann was really agitated. "Tell me this, Matt. Do you think God will cancel if you don't bring a big enough crowd?"

"I don't know, but maybe I was chosen because I'm capable of bringing a big crowd."

"You're talking about science fiction, Matt – pure science fiction, just like the movies! No one is going to believe you. If you let the media know that you believe God's going to show us a sign in the desert by Mount Sinai on the first day of spring, you'd better be there with your camera to take a picture of it because you will be the only one crazy enough to go out there. You're going to be the laughing stock of the world!"

Ann stormed out in tears.

I had told three more people. I was hoping someone would understand and believe me.

Dad and Estelle were amazed at my story, but it was soon apparent neither believed it could have happened. They both warned me that I could be ruining my career if I mentioned it to the media.

The last person I shared my experience with was Professor Kempson. The professor tried to understand and suggested I might have been delirious from fatigue. He strongly urged me to take a sabbatical from work and go on an extended holiday.

They did their best to convince me to put it out of my mind and to forget the whole experience. I had a hard time doing that.

* * * * *

I was the first guest on the live late-night television show in New York. I had done this same program before on other talk shows. My father, Estelle, and Professor Kempson were the only people I had told of my experience beside Jim, Ann, and Stephanie. What if it was real? What if I hadn't been hallucinating? Time was running out. It would soon be spring.

With prompting from the host and the audience, I gave a brief synopsis of everything related to our finding the treasure on that sunken ship, the men who tried to steal the treasure from us, and ended with how I found the Ark of the Covenant. The studio showed photos of everything as I explained it. Everyone already knew the stories from the news, the personal interviews, and the tabloids, but they still wanted me to tell the story.

I continued, "The Israeli government promised the treasure and the Ark of the Covenant with the stone tablets would soon be on permanent display for everyone to enjoy without charge. I'm hoping it will inspire people to really try to live the Ten Commandments."

After the standing ovation the audience gave me, my heart started to race, and my palms got sweaty. It was hot under these bright lights. I knew I had to do this. I couldn't wait any longer. It was now or never. I had never been so nervous in front of an audience. I felt like someone else was speaking as I heard my shaky voice say, "I will probably lose all my credibility when I tell you a little more of my story, something I've never told the public before. My friends and colleagues, even my family, don't believe I should tell this part. They think I was hallucinating from bad air in the cave when I discovered the Ark of the Covenant. Maybe they are right, but I'm going to tell you what I experienced, and let you be the judge."

The audience grew very quiet in anticipation. The host didn't know what to do. Backstage in the dressing room three people watching the monitor gasped.

"Oh, no," Jim and Ann said in unison. "I thought he said he wasn't going to tell the story."

"He had to," Stephanie blurted out. "He was told to spread the word."

"You're wrong, Stephanie," Ann said. "He didn't have to."

Jim didn't say anything. He was worried about my mental health. The crazy story was over the edge, but I was so adamant that it was true!

I told the story, everything the messenger told me to say. I ended by saying, "My friends were most likely right. I probably fell unconscious from the lack of proper oxygen in the cave and imagined the whole thing, but it seemed real at the time. I hope you will all be patient and will not tar and feather me, at least until after March twentieth." I laughed, but no one else did. "That's the first day of spring this year. I plan to be in the canyon west of Mount Sinai on that date. I'll let you know what happens if I'm invited back on the show. Thank you."

The audience was stunned! They sat in disbelief. The host nervously thanked me, and then quickly cut to commercial.

A producer on the show rushed over to me and said, "Matt, I'm having security take you to our limo. The police will escort you and your group to your hotel. That was one hell of a story, but let's take precautions. There are a lot of crazy people in New York. Thank you for being on the show. Someone will call you later tonight."

When we were in the limo, I told the driver, "Don't take us to the hotel where you picked us up. Take us to this address."

I handed him a piece of paper with a location written on it. I turned to Jim, Ann, and Stephanie.

"Sorry I had to do that. It was expected of me. All of our luggage is packed and waiting for us at the airport. We'll soon be on a private jet back to Israel."

Within thirty minutes, we were in the air.

The corporate jet I had chartered had four leather recliners equipped with seatbelts bolted to the floor around a coffee table. As soon as we were in the air, a flight attendant served coffee and drinks.

When the flight attendant moved to her small cubicle behind the cockpit door, Ann spoke for the first time. "Matt, how could you do such a thing? People will think you're crazy! You're going to ruin the wonderful image everyone in the world has of you, plus you put your life in danger."

"I had to, Ann. I don't believe I was hallucinating. And what if I'm right? I was asked by a messenger from another world to spread the news."

"The news of what, Matt? Have you really gone out of your mind? Because you would have to be either an idiot or mentally ill to believe God spoke to you or had someone speak to you? Do you really believe God is going to send us a sign? What kind of a sign, Matt?"

"I don't know what kind of a sign, but yes, I do, Ann. I believe God is going to send us some kind of a sign."

"Well, I'm sorry, I don't."

"Well Bro," Jim said with his dependable lighthearted grin, "you really know how to shake things up. I can't believe how they rushed you off that TV show tonight. No one was expecting the bomb you dropped on the whole world. I'll bet their ratings are skyrocketing. No one knew how to react. Too bad we can't pick up the TV broadcast in the plane, but I'm sure the world will be buzzing tomorrow."

"I think you two are forgetting one important thing," Stephanie said.

"And what might that be, Stephanie?" Ann said dryly.

"What will they say about Dr. Matthew Lane when the sign appears?"

I looked over at Stephanie and gave her a big smile. "Thanks, Stephanie. Now it's two against two."

Jim chuckled, but Ann just glared.

"God, I hope you're right, Stephanie," Ann said. "I hope the sign somehow appears, but I, for one, am not going to waste my time camping out at Mount Sinai."

* * * * *

The phone had not stopped ringing. I took it off the hook. We all silenced our cell phones. All of us, including Joanne and Hanna, our housekeeper, watched as I flipped through the cable channels.

"I guess you're right, Jim," I said. "My news did shake things up a bit."

"A bit?" Ann said sarcastically. "Every news channel on the planet is talking about you."

I changed to another channel, one of those talk shows. The host was speaking. "I think he's really lost it. I heard they had to sneak out of New York last night. He was getting death threats."

I flipped to another channel. "Famous archaeologist, Dr. Matthew Lane, dropped a bomb in New York City last night. He claimed God spoke to him."

"I didn't say God spoke to me!" I yelled at the TV.

I changed to another news channel. A woman sitting on a couch with two other people was speaking. "I feel sorry for him. He was such a great man. He found Noah's Ark just last year and the lost treasure of Israel and the Ark of the Covenant. And now this. Maybe it was just too much for him."

"I'm afraid he has really backed himself into a corner," a man on an overstuffed chair in the group said. "What's he going to say when there is no sign, and, believe me, there won't be a sign. Think of it. He is just like the people who claim the world is coming to an end. Well, it hasn't yet. It's not going to, and there will be no sign. Mark my word."

The camera turned to another woman on the couch. "Well, it's been over two-thousand years since Jesus Christ lived and died for us. With all the greed, corruption and murder, slaughtering of innocent children, the violence is unbelievable. I would love to see a sign that God is still out there, still in control. I'll be praying that he is right. I'll be praying that a sign does appear."

I turned the TV off. "Well, at least that last lady has the right attitude," I said.

"You've created a terrible situation, Matt," Ann said. "I'm really worried. Some of those phone calls were people who were really angry. One was demanding I let him speak to the devil, Dr. Matthew Lane. Some people on TV said you had lost your senses. One said you had been down in one of your caves too long, and everyone around him laughed. On another station someone said you were the victim of a joke. They said a man in Jerusalem has admitted he followed you into the cave and hid behind a curtain. He whispered all those things to you, and you were dumb enough to believe it. It was all a joke. This has really gotten out of hand, Matt."

Just then a brick was thrown through the front window, the glass shattering all around the TV. We were all startled. Ann and Stephanie ran to another window trying to see who would do such a thing. Jim and I rushed to the front door but only saw a man running down the street and disappearing into a crowd of people.

Had I done the right thing? I wished I really knew. If I was just hallucinating, I've really blown it.

* * * * *

We had to move. We weren't safe here. The new place I leased was a beautiful estate, complete with a stable and swimming pool. It was several miles from Jerusalem. I brought Hanna, the housekeeper, to the new place. Officer Joanne Zivah came to visit often. She especially wanted to spend time with Jim. We all stayed close to the estate. We used the pool extensively and did a lot of horseback riding together.

No one wanted to watch TV. I had to know if the news had finally shifted away from me so I turned it on every evening. My crazy prediction was still a hot topic. As the 20th of March approached, the news media continued to scoff at the very thought of a sign from God that was supposedly going to somehow appear near Mount Sinai in Egypt. The late-night talk shows had a field day making jokes about Dr. Matthew Lane.

I worried about the safety of Jim and the girls. I continued to hide the location where we were living, adding more fodder for the talk shows.

"Dr. Matthew Lane! Where is he? Someone said he was taken up in a spaceship." Everyone laughed at the joke. "Will he somehow appear on March 20th at Mount Sinai in a robe, with snow white hair and a long white beard like Moses?"

It seemed no one was taking this seriously.

I knew Stephanie was worried about me. She wanted to believe me, but it was just too hard to accept. She surprised me by saying she was excited about the possibility of going to Mount Sinai. I knew she was hoping Ann would stay angry and refuse to go.

Ann was still upset and embarrassed because of what I had done, but she really didn't want to stay by herself in Israel and let Stephanie be alone with me. Soon she was selecting the clothes she would take.

Jim, of course, wouldn't miss the show. Even if a sign from God did not appear, he would still be there with me. Jim was the best friend anyone could ever have. He would be the first to make light of the entire incident to help take the heat off me.

The first day of spring on the Egyptian calendar, was fast approaching.

CHAPTER THIRTY-FIVE

The dusty road was just two tracks in the desert. The large van I had rented was not built for this rocky terrain, but I managed to dodge most of the big rocks. I tried to rent a motor home for this trip, but motor homes in Egypt were few and far between. Besides, I might have gotten it stuck in the sandy valley. In this remote, desolate area, the only animals we had seen since we left the paved road were sheep, goats, and camels. After hours of traveling on a jarring, washboard road, the rugged walls of Mount Sinai loomed in front of us. The land on our left had been mostly dry rolling hills, but was now flat and with a lot more vegetation.

"Surprisingly, this road has been recently traveled," I said. "There are a lot of tire tracks in the dirt."

"The sheepherders probably moved their camp today," Ann said sarcastically.

I ignored her remark, not wanting to start an argument.

Jim was watching our position on the GPS. We were getting close. There was a hill in front of us. When we reached the top, the whole valley below opened up. The land mostly flat, sloped gradually down a couple of miles to the base of the mountain. To our amazement, we were looking at a sea of tents set up around the base of Mount Sinai.

Slowly we drove closer. People were busy setting up their camps, pitching tents, and building campfires. There were lots of kids playing together. The dusty desert road ended here.

I stopped the van about a quarter mile from the large camping area. We got out to take in the welcomed sight. It was a little after 4 p.m.

"Guess we're not the only people here, Matt," Stephanie said, grinning as she gave me a big high-five.

Ann didn't say anything.

"Look at all those tents. There must be several hundred people camping out here," Jim said.

"How are we going to find the tents you had set up for us, Matt?" Stephanie asked.

"Someone is supposed to be watching for this van."

About fifteen minutes later, a young Egyptian man drove up to our van. "Dr. Lane, I presume? Please follow me."

Our small complex had been set up a short distance from the main camp. There were two latrine tents, one for the girls and one for Jim and me. Each was equipped with a portable toilet, a portable sink, plenty of towels and a mirror. One tent even had a battery-operated pump shower . . . all the comforts of home. Within an hour we were eating dinner. We had a cook and a maid, and we each had our own sleeping quarters.

We opted not to venture far from our tent complex. Instead we just sat around the fire and talked about what tomorrow would bring. Ann was sullen and excused herself, going to bed early.

I was exhausted from our long trip here, but I couldn't sleep as time slowly crept by. At 12:01 a.m., March 20th, we were all standing at the entrance of our tents looking down the canyon for a sign. All we could see was the glow of campfires, a sky full of beautiful stars, and the outline of Mount Sinai. Stephanie made a pot of herbal tea, explaining it would help us relax. By 1:30 a.m. we were all back in bed.

I woke up about 5:30, just as the sun was rising. Our cook was scrambling eggs and making pancakes. The maid was setting out an assortment of cheese, fruit, and breads. I wasn't hungry, but grabbed a cup of coffee while Jim was shaving. After breakfast, I started washing the dishes. The cook and the maid were nowhere in sight, and the girls were gathering their cameras and whatever they needed for the day.

Jim grabbed a dish towel and started drying them."I'm not sure the only man who has conversed with God in thousands of years really has to do the dishes."

"You're right. I don't think I should have to either, but that's just the kind of humble guy I am." We laughed.

Just then the cook and the maid came into the tent and insisted they finish with the kitchen detail.

About 8:30, the four of us casually walked down into the camp, not knowing what to expect. A path led through several camping sites. In many areas, the tents had been pitched in a circle, with the opening facing a large space where children were playing and small fires were burning. We assumed these were family groups. The women, mostly Egyptian, were cooking in front of the tents. There were folding tables containing bags of groceries and coolers. No one paid much attention to four young Caucasian people ambling through the camping areas. As we wandered through the camp, we encountered people from several other countries. Some were from India; some were Asian. One group was from the UK. Since they were speaking English, we almost approached them but didn't know how we would be received if they recognized me. Everyone seemed friendly, giving us a nod or a wave, but we hadn't seen one person from the US.

I knew people didn't camp out here in this barren deserted area. This was not a campground. These people were all here because of me. *Had a voice really spoken to me? Had I dreamed it?* Dear God, I prayed to myself as we walked. I prayed I was not hallucinating and that a sign will soon appear. As I said the prayer to myself, I felt a warm feeling come over me – a comfortable feeling, a feeling that seem to restore my confidence.

Someone shouted my name, "Dr. Lane, Dr. Lane."

I turned to see a middle-aged Egyptian man coming toward me. He introduced himself. "It is my great honor to meet you, Dr. Lane. I recognize you from television."

Soon a large crowd was around us. We were taken to a big open tent for shade. The people asked us if we would sit with them for a while. Countless people shook our hands and offered every kind of food and drink imaginable. As word spread through the camp, more and more people came to see us.

Out of the blue, an old man wielding a broom ran at me. He pummeled me on the head and shoulders yelling, "Do not mock Allah. Do not mock Allah with your lies!"

Several men grabbed him and put him in the back of a van and drove him away.

Everyone felt bad and apologized. Ann urged me to return to our camp, but I waved it off, smiled at the people, said, "It's okay," and sat back down.

Hearing about the incident, a group of reporters found us. They suggested we move to their camp. They said we would be safer there. We agreed. I knew they wanted to interview us, and they especially wanted to film me at the end of the day. A satellite would relay their stories to TV stations all over the world. They knew Dr. Lane's prediction that God was going to come and talk to us was not going to happen. But success or failure, both make good news!

I thanked the people for their hospitality. Then we were loaded on golf carts and taken to a camp in the canyon that was right at the base of the mountain. The area had been set up to broadcast the special event. There were tractor-trailer rigs, generators, lights, TV cameras, and microphones. We were brought to a semi- trailer with one long side panel let down to a horizontal position and rigged as a stage with comfortable seats for interviews. Surprisingly, everyone we met – the Egyptians in their camp, the reporters and crew in charge of the broadcasting equipment, even the truck drivers – had treated us with kindness and respect . . . that is, with the exception of the one broom-wielding man.

All four of us talked freely to the reporters about everything from Noah's Ark, to the sunken treasure, to the Ark of the Covenant, cameras recording everything we said.

Finally, I was asked to explain to the world how I felt about my prediction, and how I was holding up under the pressure as the hours of the day continued to slip away.

I simply said, "I have complete faith in the messenger. I do not believe I was hallucinating."

Then, with the cameras still on me, I tried to explain that a sign from God wasn't really all that unusual. "It only seems unusual and unlikely because it doesn't happened very often, and it hasn't happened for a long time. God has always made his presence known, but usually only every couple of thousand years. It was only two thousand years ago that his son Jesus Christ was born. Think about the virgin birth, the star that was totally out of place guiding the shepherds and wise men to Bethlehem. Remember when Jesus was baptized. God spoke from the heavens and said, 'This is my beloved son, with whom I am well pleased.' The people that were there and heard that must've been dumbfounded. That incident alone was probably talked about for years. And then all the miracles Jesus performed healing the sick, making the blind see, raising the dead, feeding the five thousand people, walking on water. Jesus did all these things because God gave him the power to do it. Just a few hundred years before that, God brought the plagues to Egypt and parted the Red Sea. God has always communicated with man. What about Adam and Eve? What about Noah? What about Abraham? What about the miracle that happened in Mexico City in 1531, now called Our Lady of Guadalupe? What about the reports of modern-day miracles like the story of Bernadette in Lourdes, France, in 1858? . . . Or the three shepherd children from Fatima, Portugal, in 1917? There have been many unexplained miracles in modern day. What about these? I don't think God wants us to forget he still exists. Whenever man gets in trouble, God somehow renews our faith in him.

"This sign is to help us out of the trouble the world is in now. The world really needs this sign. We need it now! This sign, whatever it might be, is supposed to help people believe in him for two or three thousand more years. After that, God may send man another sign."

I realized I was just digging myself a deeper hole. I sounded like a religious fanatic. I didn't think anyone onstage was really listening to me anyway. The cameras were rolling. Everyone onstage was watching me, but no one was really listening. No one really cared. They knew nothing spectacular was going to happen out here in the desert. They were being paid to help me make an even bigger fool of myself, and that's probably what I just did.

I quickly summed up my feelings, thanked the reporters for covering the event, and left the stage.

Then I thought, "Well I guess I've done what I was chosen to do. The sign will be recorded if there really is one. I just hope that God now does his part."

It was 8 p.m. The girls went back to our camp to rest, but Jim stayed. We were given more food than we could eat. As the evening wore on and it began to grow dark, everyone became a little quieter. Still, nothing had happened.

It was late. The entire camp had grown quiet. No more dogs barked. All the children and most of the adults had gone to bed.

Sitting around a campfire away from the stage with Jim and a group of reporters, I glanced nervously at my watch. It was 11 p.m. I didn't know what to think. In one hour, the appointed day, the day I told everyone a sign would appear, would be over. How could I have been so wrong? How could I have believed such a thing? The stars were bright above. The night insects were making their usual sounds. The air was still, not even a slight breeze. It had been a long day.

I probably should get up and say, "I'm sorry. I guess I was wrong," excuse myself, and go to bed. Tomorrow I would have to face the humiliation, the disgrace. I had embarrassed everyone, not only myself but my grandmother, my father, Jim, Ann, Stephanie . . . everyone who believed in me. It was 11:30. Nothing changed. One by one, the reporters we had been sitting with bid us good night and walked to their campers and tents. All those men could have kidded me and joked about our modern calendar being wrong, but no one did. They were all too polite, too respectful. They knew the pressure the four of us had to be feeling, and they respected that.

At 12:01 a.m. we could hear and see the reporters standing on the portable stage in front of the cameras reporting to the whole world the sign did not appear. Soon everyone was gone.

A sad and disappointed Stephanie hugged me. Knowing I needed to be alone, she asked Jim to take her back to camp. Disgusted and embarrassed, Ann had left a long time ago.

I walked over to the rock wall of Mount Sinai. Using the light in my cell phone as a flashlight, I saw a sloping natural cleft in the rock. I climbed up, sat down, and leaned against the rock wall. The weather had been nice all day, but now it was getting cold. The wind was coming up, and I could see lightning far down the canyon. I was all alone, twenty feet up from the desert floor below. I had never felt so low in my life! How could I ever have believed such a thing? I was a rational man. I knew better. God doesn't show us signs except, of course, when he spoke to Adam and Eve and Noah and Abraham and

Moses and so many of the prophets and the voice from the heavens when Jesus Christ was baptized.

It was supposed to happen on the first day of spring. The entire day had come and gone. Nothing happened. The thunderstorm was getting more intense and now moving closer to us.

I was tired. I had been sitting here a long time, almost in a trance. I watched again as a long exaggerated flash of lightning lit up the area. It was 12:40 a.m. Feeling totally defeated, I leaned back against the stone wall and closed my eyes.

Soon it was all coming back to me. Everything was happening so fast. Fleeting glimpses of a dense jungle, a feeling of almost drowning, a sunken airplane, a cavern, an old ship sitting on a seabed . . .

Suddenly I was wide awake. It was raining a little, but the ledge I was lying on was shielded from most of the rain. The thunderstorm had not diminished. I looked at my watch. It was 1:30 a.m.

I thought about the dream I had just experienced and realized it was everything that caused me to be here, everything that made me believe God was going to show us a sign.

Then I remembered that the first day of spring had come and gone with no major event, as it always had and as it always will. What a fool I had been! I knew I should get up and go back to our camp, but I just didn't want to face anyone yet.

I must have fallen asleep again.

CHAPTER THIRTY-SIX

"Dr. Lane! Dr. Lane!"

Someone was gently shaking me.

"Dr. Lane, we have good news for you. Dr. Lane, spring hasn't actually started yet!"

"What?" I said, popping my eyes open.

Two young men were on the ledge beside me. A light rain was falling, and I was shivering from the wet and cold.

"Yes, Dr. Lane, it's true," the other one said, his black hair wet with rain. "We have been calculating the exact time when the seasons change ever since your announcement, and according to our calculations, spring won't officially start here until 2:40 a.m. today, March 21."

"Are you serious?" I tried to absorb what they were telling me.

"Yes, yes, Dr. Lane, we are very serious." I knew from the accent that these young men were from India.

"What time is it?" I asked.

"It's only 2:10 a.m.," they said. "Spring won't actually start in this part of the world for half an hour."

I was so excited I hugged them both. I didn't question their data or calculations. I just knew there was still a chance it would happen!

I asked them to go and find where the TV reporters were sleeping. "They will be in some of those trailers down below us," I said. "Please wake them up and tell them what you just told me. Who knows, you two may become famous."

I jogged in the light rain to our camp for a rain slicker and to tell everyone that spring was still a half hour away.

At exactly 2:40 a.m., an extremely bright flash of lightning hit the top of the mountain, illuminating the entire mountain and desert floor. The sound was deafening even though it was a long way off. Streaks of lightning spread across the horizon as we heard the bolts hit, and we even felt the percussion. The intense light from above kept the entire area ablaze, exposing dark black clouds high above. The continuous thunder was reverberating down the valley. Crowds of people gathered outside their tents as parents tried to calm the crying children. They were frightened and beginning to panic, as this was no ordinary thunderstorm!

The four of us left the tent complex and ran out away from the mountain into the desert. When we turned to face the mountain, we saw throngs of people had left the shelter and safety of their tents and had followed us. I slipped my arm around Ann and pulled her close. Stephanie was hovering beside me, and Jim was standing next to her. The girls were both trembling not from the rain, but fear. Fear had consumed everyone as we began to witness an incredible sight.

To my surprise and relief, one camera man was already filming the fascinating, yet terrifying scene. He had filmed everything from the very first lightning bolt. Soon the rest of the cameramen and news teams were jockeying for the best angle and aiming their cameras at the mountain.

The barrage continued. The lightning originated from a great height and followed a vertical path down, targeting the apex of the mountain over a mile back from the rock face. The arcs somehow formed a gigantic circle on one section of rock. Again and again rocks exploded as the strikes continued. The powerful electrical arcs from each lightning strike were blinding. All that electricity was still originating from the one massive, dense black cloud high above. Our eyes were glued to the spectacle. The onslaught continued for more than three hours. Finally the lightning slowly subsided. The cameras had filmed everything, and we had witnessed it all.

It had stopped raining. Smoke was filling the air, stinging our eyes and burning our nostrils.

"The smoke smells different . . . strange!" a reporter said. "The heavy night air is bringing it down from the top of the mountain. Look, you can see it in the flashlight beam."

We all concentrated our lights in the direction he was pointing and saw the gray rays drift down the mountain and eventually dissipate over the valley. Close by, the sparse areas of short grass with raindrops still attached, glistened like diamonds under the beam of each flashlight. Gradually, one by one, most of the flashlights were turned off.

None of us knew what to expect. What we had witnessed was uncanny. It was a phenomenon. I had never seen anything like it before and doubted anyone else had. It was still too dark to see as we gazed out toward the mountain, but there was a bright red glow where the lightening had been concentrated.

Stephanie slipped her hand in mine. "I'm scared, Matt. Shouldn't it be getting light by now? I think it's almost six a.m."

To stave off the chill, a few campfires were now burning. A group of people behind us were singing in a language I didn't recognize. It sounded like a hymn.

The light drizzle finally stopped. It was quiet. Once in a while, a small child would speak to their mother or ask a question. Most people just whispered. Finally the sky started getting lighter. We could now more easily see the outline of the top of the mountain. There were no stars. The black cloud was still high above the mountain. It was the most bizarre sight I think I've ever seen.

Someone yelled, "Look . . . look at that!"

Above the rocky outline of the mountaintop where the electric arc had been so intense, something strange appeared. A massive disc-shaped object, flat on the top and the bottom, but round like a wheel lying flat, started to slowly rise straight up out of the top of the mountain.

"It looks like a flying saucer!" someone yelled.

A cry went up from the opposite side of the crowd. "It's solid rock. It can't be a flying saucer!"

Slowly it rose straight up and then stopped in mid-air, perfectly still. From the black cloud, one continuous steady blue arc of electricity struck the massive piece of granite. This was unlike the lightning we had experienced just moments before. Millions of yellow sparks and chunks of rock fell back into the cavity from where the quarried piece had risen. We were mesmerized for another two hours as the flame continued to cut and shape the disk. A ray of sunlight reflected off the object. Smoke was blowing away from it. It was too far away and too high to estimate its size, but we knew it was enormous.

As quick as the arc had started, it halted, retracting up into the black cloud. Silence now blanketed the area. Slowly, still smoking, the object commenced moving high above the mountain. It was inconceivable. We were riveted in place as the massive flat disk of solid granite moved toward us past the vermillion cliffs and out over the desert to a point almost directly over our heads. Several hundred people including the four of us stood looking straight up at it until we all realized it was getting larger. The wind began to blow. We all turned away shielding our faces from the blowing dirt and grass. The air below the object was being compressed as it began descending. It was coming straight down on top of where we stood. Panicked, we began to run.

I couldn't hear any sound coming from the massive object as it continued to drop at the exact same slow pace until it was about twenty to twenty-five feet above the desert floor. Then it simply stopped, and the wind stopped blowing. Everyone was dumbfounded at the sight.

"It must be two thousand feet in diameter," Jim said. "Just look at it . . . One solid round-shaped disk of solid granite!"

It resembled a flying saucer, but it was the same color as the mountain . . . tan, maybe a little darker from all the heat. Jim and I guessed it to be maybe a hundred feet thick. The outside perimeter surface was vertical from the top to a few feet down. At that point the side sloped in toward the center at about forty-five degrees. The sloping, smooth polished granite surface had been divided into panels with writing on each panel, like one might see on a granite memorial.

Jim and I approached the disk to get a better look. Ann and Stephanie followed at a distance, since the stone was still sizzling. No one else dared to venture closer. We could still feel the intense heat, but the breeze was cooling it rapidly.

The angle of the sloping surface made it easy to walk around the outside and look up at the inscription engraved on each panel. The bottom was flat, roughly cut, not polished. The only things polished were the readable forty-five degree sloping panels. We didn't know about the top yet.

The massive piece of quarried, shaped granite had never made a sound. No engines, no magnetic hum, nothing. It didn't move, it didn't spin, it seemed totally solid, but nothing was supporting it.

"It must weigh millions of tons, but nothing is holding it up," Jim said.

No one could believe it. Ann joined me as we walked nearer to try to read the writing on the panels.

"I can't read this!" Ann said.

I couldn't read it either. The characters were totally unfamiliar to me.

Ann started moving from panel to panel trying to make some sense of it. "Every panel is a little different . . . different characters, but I still don't recognize any of this writing."

Ann was proficient in several foreign languages, so we let her take the lead. She moved clockwise looking at each panel, trying to find something familiar. Cautiously, the crowd of people began to follow us.

"Wait!" she said excitedly. "I know these characters. I think this writing is Cantonese!" she exclaimed. "I recognize the characters, but I can't translate the language."

We continued walking clockwise around the perimeter, looking at the next panel, then the next, and the next.

"This is starting to look more like Chinese," Ann said.

Then it dawned on me. I was running now with Jim, Ann, and Stephanie in pursuit.

"I know what this is," I yelled as I ran glancing at every eighth or tenth panel. "Yes, yes! This is perfect. This is wonderful!"

"What?" Ann shouted. "What is it, Matt?"

"Every panel is a different language, and I know what message God sent."

We were about one quarter of the way around.

"There," I pointed as I came upon it. "There it is! This panel is in English. . . . 'I am the Lord thy God. Thou shalt have no other gods before me. Thou shalt not make unto thee any graven image' . . . It's the Ten Commandments! There's a panel for every written language on earth."

We were all hugging each other. We could hear people shouting and reading the panels in the language they understood. Many were on their knees, praying and thanking God. We were too! On my knees, with tears running down my cheeks, I thanked God for the sign!

The world news' cameras had filmed and broadcast everything live via modern satellite. I had accomplished my assignment as a messenger. The sign God sent had been witnessed and recorded.

CHAPTER THIRTY-SEVEN

It was one a.m. when we arrived back at our villa in Jerusalem. We were exhausted.

Most everyone slept a little later the following morning. We spent a few hours relaxing by the pool. Of course, what happened at Mount Sinai continued to dominate the conversation. We didn't answer the landline or our cell phones.

At six p.m. I turned on CNN. Almost all the news was focused on pictures and commentary about the miracle at Mount Sinai. Masses of news reporters with camera crews in tow were swarming the site. Yesterday I had been interviewed by countless news agencies from all over the world.

The TV station we were watching highlighted one particular segment. The reporter conducting the interview began by saying, "Many people feel they owe you an apology, Dr. Lane. We have received countless phone calls today asking us to convey their sincere apologies."

I looked directly into the camera. "There is no need for anyone to apologize. I'm sure I would have reacted the same way if the message had been delivered by someone else." I felt exonerated.

We had stayed one more night in the comfortable tent, close to God's marvelous sign. Hundreds stayed.

The Egyptian national police had arrived at the site. They cordoned off our area, allowing us some quiet time. It was peaceful and beautiful under the blanket of stars shining brightly above the suspended stone. It was still hard to believe it was real.

With Jim, Stephanie, and Joanne glued to the TV set, I slipped out to the patio. The sun was just setting, but it was still light outside. Ann was sitting all alone on the glider watching the horses in the pasture below. I walked up silently behind her. She was unaware of my presence, lost in deep thought. The description Ann had painted of her grandmother Jelena when she was a little girl, was sitting before me swinging in her ruffled gingham dress, her long auburn hair shining in the last glow of the sun cascading over her shoulders. Startled, she turned, looked and smiled.

"Hi," I said.

"Hi, Matt. I'm sorry. I didn't see you. How long have you been standing there?"

"Just a couple of minutes. I was wondering if you would like to go out to dinner? Just with me," I added.

She looked surprised. "I'd love to. Are you sure? What about the others?"

"They are all glued to the TV. Let's just sneak off."

"I'm all for it," she replied, hopping up.

We went out the side gate, giddy like a couple of school children playing hooky.

About three miles away, I parked at a quaint Italian restaurant. I had found this place several weeks ago. No one recognized us as we entered a vine-covered portal. We were the only ones in a side dining room with a warm fire flickering in the fireplace. We shared a bottle of wine with our pasta and veal dinner, a nice respite from the typical Israeli cuisine we had been eating lately.

After coffee and dessert, I said, "This place has a beautiful garden right out those doors, very much like where we first met . . . that restaurant in Washington D.C. Do you remember? You strolled right up to my table and introduced yourself. You were anxious to share something very important with me, but you didn't want anyone else to hear, so I took you out in the garden."

"Of course I remember. I'll never forget when we first met. The garden sounds nice. In fact, it sounds romantic."

It was romantic. There were a few tables along the pathways and flowers everywhere. I plucked a red hibiscus from a bush and Ann placed it in her hair. She was so beautiful, inside and out. No other customers were around. Soft lighting lit the path. The air was fresh, but the temperature was a little cool, so I held her coat as she slipped it on, just like I did when we first met.

Ann reached for my hand. We sat down at a table. She smiled. "Matt, I want to apologize again."

"You don't need to."

"I want to. I'm so sorry I doubted you. I should have known better. Everything you do just never ceases to amaze me. As hard as your story was to believe, I should have known by now to never doubt you. I can't believe I got so mad at you."

"Yeah, you did get pretty mad," I laughed, "but understandably so. I'm just so glad the sign really did appear. And what a message! Although not letting me know exactly when spring really started out there may have been the Lord's little joke just to make me sweat." We both laughed.

"It's all so exciting, Matt," she said, smiling at me. "I will never doubt you or get mad at you again. I promise. I can't believe I'm sitting here talking to the man who was actually chosen to deliver that astounding message. You're probably the most well-known and honored man on the earth, and here you are holding my hand. It's overwhelming."

"I don't think I'm so great, Ann. I've killed men . . . quite a lot of men. I had to actually drown one man. It was horrible. I'll never forget that."

"You aren't a killer, Matt. You only killed to protect others or when our lives were threatened. No, Matt, you were chosen to be the one to find the Ark of the Covenant and to be the one to alert the world that a miracle was about to happen, and it really happened. No one can doubt that sign is from the Creator of everything. I'm so glad I was there."

"I'm so glad you were a part of it, Ann. I love you. I know I've not said that enough, but I'm saying it now. I really do love you. You are everything to me."

"Oh Matt, I love you too. I haven't told you very many times either, but you know I do. I fell in love with you when we went to Russia and found the lost photographs of Noah's Ark."

I got down on one knee before her. Looking up into her warm brown eyes and taking her hand in mine, I said, "Will you marry me, Ann Tyler, for better or worse?"

Her mouth quivered as she softly replied. "Yes! Oh yes, Matt. I'd love to marry you. I'll marry you to have and hold forever!"

I slipped the ring on her finger and longingly kissed her again and again. I'll never forget the joy we felt holding each other that night in the garden.

* * * * *

It was after ten p.m. when I knocked softly on Stephanie's door.
"Who is it?"
"It's Matt, Stephanie."
"Just a second," I heard her say excitedly.

Stephanie opened the door with a smile. She had slipped on a light blue robe. Obviously, she was ready for bed, but still managed to look seductive in the soft light.

"Come in, Matt," she said. "Let's sit on the couch." Every bedroom in this house was very large, comfortable, and tastefully furnished.

"Can I get you anything?"
"No, Stephanie. I just need to talk to you."
"Where did you and Ann run off to?" she asked.
"I took her to dinner."
"Just the two of you?"
"Yes, just the two of us." I turned to face her. There was no easy way to say what I had to tell her. I paused for a few seconds. "I asked Ann to marry me tonight."

She didn't say anything. For a few seconds, she stared at me like she didn't want to believe what I just said.

"That's wonderful," she finally said, turning her face away and blinking back the tears. She tried hard not to cry, but she just couldn't. Suddenly she put her arms around my neck and her head on my shoulder and began to cry.

I just held her. I had a lump in my throat. I felt like the worst cad in the universe. Then drying her tears with her handkerchief, she looked at me. "You know I love you, Matt? I told you that in the mine. I love you more than anyone could ever love you – even Ann. I can be just like her, Matt," she said. "I bought some clothes and a purse just like Ann." She again put her arms around my neck and buried her face in my shoulder. Then she looked up at my face and pleaded, "Don't marry her, Matt. Please don't marry her. Give me a chance. Please, Matt, no one could ever love you like I love you."

I didn't say anything. I just pulled her close again and held her. Minutes went by.

"I guess I'm making a real fool of myself," she said. "I've always known you loved Ann. I hoped somehow you would change your mind. I hoped and prayed you would love me, Matt. I'm sorry. It was such a shock to hear you say you asked her to marry you. I just wasn't expecting that. I've done everything I could to make you pay attention to me, make you want me. I've even lied to Ann. I let her believe you made love to me in the mine. I told her the truth later, but I don't think she believed me. It was terrible of me to do that. I really like Ann."

"She told me, Stephanie," I said. "I'm sure Ann forgives you."

"I hope so," she said as she continued to dry her tears. "Ann's a wonderful girl, Matt," she said, sniffling. "I just wanted it to be me."

"I'm sorry, Stephanie. I've always loved Ann, but you're very special to me."

"I'm sure I'll get over it, but it's going to take a while," she said trying to smile. "Well, you'd better go. Ann will be wondering what you're doing so long in my room."

Stephanie walked me toward the door, but before she opened it, she said, "Can I ask a favor?"

"Sure, anything."

"Kiss me, Matt, like you kissed me in the mine! Just once more. You can tell Ann, or not tell Ann. I don't care."

Caught like a fly in a trap, caught between the love of two beautiful women, I felt suffocated. Truth be known, I still had mixed emotions, but I had made my decision. I kissed Stephanie one last time.

"I wish you everything that's good," I whispered. "If you ever need my help for any reason, just call me."

Slowly, I closed the door and left a part of my heart behind.

* * * * *

Everyone congratulated us. Even Stephanie tried to make her wishes for our happiness believable.

When Ann and Stephanie were alone, Stephanie asked if we had set a date. "Not yet," Ann replied, "but I'm sure our wedding will be soon. Will you come, Stephanie?"

"You know I can't, Ann. You know you're going to marry the man I love." Her voice was shaking and tears were filling her eyes. "I'm happy for you, Ann. I really am, but I love Matt, and I will always love him. I couldn't bear to see you two walk down the aisle together." She dried her tears and regained her composure. "I'm going home. A day or two after the big ceremony at Mount Sinai, I'll be leaving for Bangkok."

"I'm so sorry, Stephanie," Ann said, taking her hand.

Stephanie tried to smile. "Like I told Matt, I'm sure I'll get over it. It seems everyone gets over a broken heart. I think for some people it just hurts a lot more, and it hurts for a long time."

CHAPTER THIRTY-EIGHT

Jack Green was in a Tel Aviv jail cell. He was being held without bail awaiting his sentencing.

I knew something was wrong when I received a call from an Israeli police detective. "Jack Green escaped from custody early this morning," he said.

I was shocked. "How could that happen?" I asked in disbelief.

The detective probably sensed the anger in my voice. "I don't blame you for being upset, Dr. Lane. It should never have happened. Someone obviously underestimated this man."

"How did he get away?" I asked.

"Well, according to this report, about five this morning a guard found Jack on the floor of his cell. He was coughing up blood and had blood all over his clothing. He then fell into unconsciousness. Immediately he was transferred to a local hospital in an ambulance with a paramedic and a policeman.

"In one of the exam rooms at the hospital, he was somehow able to overpower the officer and the attending physician. He killed them both with a pair of scissors.

"A security camera shows him leaving the hospital in the doctor's clothes and white coat with a stethoscope around his neck at 6:03 a.m. during the shift change.

"A camera in the parking lot filmed him holding up his hand and then walking straight to the doctor's car. He simply pushed the red button on the key fob and followed the sound of the horn. I'm afraid he also has the doctor's wallet with his credit cards and whatever cash was in the wallet."

"Has he tried to buy gas or anything using the credit card?" I asked the official.

"Not at this point."

"Do you have any idea where he would be going?"

"I'm afraid we have no information on that, but I've been assured he will be back in custody in a matter of hours. Every police officer in the country is looking for him. I called you, Dr. Lane, because our files show your past history with Mr. Green. I understand he also has a cousin in this country, a Stephanie Green. We thought he might try to contact her."

I explained everything to the detective and expressed my concern that Jack would show up at the ceremony in Egypt, full of hate and revenge.

The detective felt sure that without a valid passport it would be almost impossible for him to cross the border into Egypt, and his passport was still in his file at the police station.

* * * * *

"I just don't understand why they didn't have more than one man guarding him," Ann said.

Stephanie was too distraught to even speak.

"Unbelievable!" Jim said.

I nodded in agreement with Jim. "Jack may have even bribed some guards. He always bragged that he owned people wherever he went."

In six weeks we would all be at the site of the 'sign' in Egypt for a special ceremony. World leaders and religious leaders from every nation were expected to attend.

We decided it would be safer to leave Israel for a while, hoping Jack would be apprehended while we were gone. Luckily, we were able to secure last-minute staterooms onboard a cruise ship leaving Tel Aviv within the week. The ship would sail in the Mediterranean for two weeks before docking in Barcelona. Jim arranged to rent a condo on the beach in Salou, about fifty miles from Barcelona, for another two weeks.

We were determined to have a good time, but no matter how much we laughed, relaxed on the beach, and enjoyed wonderful meals, just knowing Jack was out there somewhere spawned a feeling of fear and gloom that was hard to ignore.

When we returned to Jerusalem, Jack had still not been apprehended.

* * * * *

"Security will be impossible," Jim said.

"I know," I replied. "There is no way to secure this large open area. They have done the best they can with temporary fencing and metal detectors at the main entrance from the parking lot, and they have check points on the road, but anyone who really wants to shoot us, or our president or the president of Egypt or the premier of China or even the Pope, might still be able to get past security. They have hundreds of security guards plus choppers overhead, but the only real protection the dignitaries will have is the portable building with the bulletproof glass."

"You're right. It's the same kind of unit they use in D.C. when a president is inaugurated," Jim added.

"Do you speak before or after the president, Matt?" Ann asked.

"I think our president is actually going to introduce me," I said with a big grin. "How about that?"

* * * * *

It had been a wonderful ceremony. There had not been even one security incident. Many people had spoken, and leaders pledged world peace. I was introduced by the president of the United States and received a long standing ovation. Temporary bleachers were full of people from all over the world. The two track dirt road we had traveled on six weeks ago when the sign first appeared, was now four lanes, paved right up to a huge parking lot. A runway and temporary terminal had been built for small private aircraft to land and take off.

There was a wide, lighted concrete sidewalk around the entire perimeter under the engravings behind us. Four directories and easy to read lighted signs helped the thousands of visitors each day locate the Ten Commandments burned into the stone in their specific language.

There was, of course, no charge for anything except for refreshments, and that charge was modest.

When the sign was no longer with us, in a little less than two years, the area would be turned into a memorial.

Everyone marveled at the size of the suspended monument. Religious and political leaders from every nation were overwhelmed.

Our president said, "There is no doubt that this was quarried from the mountain. I saw from my helicopter where it came from. As far as man has advanced, this could never have been removed from that mountain in one piece, and there is no possible way we could make it defy gravity. It's stationary right here, just a few feet off the ground. Absolutely amazing!"

When all the world leaders had spoken and prayers had been said, security personnel were everywhere as the speakers prepared to leave. The private helicopter that had flown us out was standing by to take us back to Israel.

Jim was a few feet away in conversation with a security guard. They were laughing, probably celebrating that all had gone so well.

Stephanie, Ann, and I started making our way through the crowd, stopping many times to shake a hand or acknowledge a comment. How wonderful to be here, to experience the effect God's sign had on the world.

Instantaneously, the exuberant joy changed to terrified alarm as a woman directly behind us screamed, "He's got a gun!"

Everyone panicked and started running. We heard a loud rapid popping sound. I knew immediately it was shots being fired from an automatic weapon.

I put one arm around Ann and the other around Stephanie, and we started running away from the shooter. It seemed like everything was in slow motion.

We hadn't gotten far when Ann fell. At the same time Stephanie fell against me. I tried to break her fall, but she landed hard in the dirt. I had a horrible feeling as I realized both girls had been shot. I turned and there was Jack, wearing a security guard's uniform, coming right toward us with a machine gun. He was going to make sure we all died.

He was taking a new clip out of his pocket as he came. He was now only twenty feet away.

Filled with rage like I had never felt before, I charged directly at him. There was a row of folding chairs between us. Watching Jack's face as he hurried to insert the clip and raise his gun, I plowed through the chairs and hit him in the face as hard as I could with my right fist. He fell on his back still clutching the gun. I kicked the gun out of his hand, but not before he squeezed the trigger and shot me. I didn't know how bad I was hit. Most of the bullets had gone wild, and I was still on my feet. Jack got up and pulled a pistol from his holster. Before he could raise it to fire, Jim tackled Jack and pinned him to the ground. Blood was streaming from my left arm, and I had a lot of pain where a bullet grazed my ribs under my left arm.

Seeing Jim now had Jack face down in the dirt with his arms bent behind him and two security guards helping restrain Jack, I ran toward Ann and Stephanie. Paramedics from one of the three ambulances that were on the site in case of an emergency were hovering over both girls.

I saw that others had also been hit by Jack's spray of bullets. People were giving first aid to those who were hit. Blood was seeping through gauze and bandages.

Someone grabbed me and yelled, "I'll need some help over here. Dr. Lane is bleeding badly. Let's get a tourniquet on his arm."

I looked at my lifeless left arm. My white shirt was soaked in blood, and more was pumping out of my arm with each heartbeat. I started feeling weak. Ambulance sirens were the last sounds I heard as my legs buckled.

When I woke up, I was in an emergency room. My left arm was bandaged and immobilized in a sling. A nurse came over when she saw I was awake. I winced as I tried to sit up, now aware my ribs were taped and an IV had been inserted in my right arm.

"Well, Dr. Lane, that blood we gave you was just in time. How do you feel?"

"I feel weak and dizzy. How long have I been here?"

"Someone brought you in about two hours ago."

"Two hours?" I repeated. . . ."What about Ann and Stephanie . . . two girls that probably came in by ambulance . . . how are they?"

"I understand several women and two men were brought in, some by ambulance and some by car. Most were not hurt too badly, but two women are either in surgery or waiting for surgery. That's all I know, Dr. Lane. I'm sorry."

The nurse insisted that I lie back down and be still, but as soon as she walked out of the cubicle, pulling the curtain shut, I sat up, pulled the IV drip out of my arm using my teeth, and left the cubicle.

Pandemonium was everywhere in the corridors. There were doctors and nurses, and the area was full of anxious relatives of those who had been injured. No one paid attention to me. I still had my pants and shoes on and had pulled on a green scrub top I found hanging in a cubicle in my room.

In the sea of people, I spotted Jim. When he saw me, he rushed through the crowd to where I was.

"Where are you going, Bro? You should be lying down. You lost a lot of blood."

"I'm okay. Are you okay?"

"Yes, I'm fine," Jim said.

Have you heard anything about Ann and Stephanie?" I asked.

"I can't find out anything. I've asked, but I'm not a relative so they won't tell me. There is a nurse's station right down here. Maybe they'll talk to you."

The nurse recognized me. "Dr. Lane, you should be lying down."

"The two girls . . . Ann Tyler and Stephanie Green . . . they were brought in by ambulance. How are they?"

The nurse hesitated. Then she said, "One of them just came from surgery."

"Surgery? How bad was she hurt?"

"Someone else should be talking to you, Dr. Lane. Let me see if I can find a doctor."

"That will take too long," I said. "If you know anything about her condition, please tell me." I was beginning to panic.

"Well, I'm afraid it's very bad news. The girl who just left surgery may not make it. There was a lot of internal damage. I'm sorry."

"Oh no!" I felt my knees grow weak. "Which girl?"

"We have people trying to contact her family now."

"Which girl?" I asked again.

The nurse looked at the chart in front of her. "Stephanie Green. I'm sorry, Dr. Lane."

I couldn't speak.

"Is she still alive?" Jim asked.

"Yes, but she may not have much time. A doctor is with her."

"Can we see her?"

"Well, we were hoping someone from her family . . ."

"I'm the closest one to family that she has. Can we see her?" I said.

"Yes, go ahead, Dr. Lane . . . Just a minute. . . . I'm not sure which room she is in. It's been so confusing."

The nurse looked at another chart. "Okay, she is in either room 142 or 147. They are both down this corridor," she said pointing.

Stephanie may not make it. Oh God, the doctors have to be wrong!

Jim and I rushed to the first room, #142. There was no name on the door, but it was open. Stephanie was unconscious. She moaned like she was in pain. I reached for her hand. I couldn't believe Stephanie was going to die.

A nurse entered the room.

"How's she doing?" I said afraid to hear the reply.

"She's going to be just fine," she said with a big smile. "Her injuries were never life-threatening."

"That's wonderful," I said out loud, so relieved. "The nurse at the nurse's station said . . ." And then my words trailed off. A cold shiver went through me.

The thought hit Jim at the same time. We looked at each other.

"Ann," we both said at the same time.

"They had identical purses, Matt."

"I know. They must have gotten their purses mixed up when they were put in the ambulance."

Jim and I ran down the corridor to #147. I opened the door. The room was dark except for a dim light by the bed.

The doctor got up and met us.

"How is she?" I asked, praying he would smile and say she'd be fine.

"I'm sorry. I'm afraid she is very weak. Are you family?" he asked.

"Yes . . . yes, we are. She's my fianceé."

"We did everything we could. There was a lot of damage. She may not survive her injuries."

Jim and I were in shock.

The doctor moved away from the bed. "I'll be just outside if you need me."

I spoke to her as I moved close. "Ann." She didn't answer. She was just asleep. She would be fine. I knew she would. Ann can't die . . . She just can't!

"Oh my God," I said. "This is not happening!"

"Ann?" I said again.

She didn't reply.

I fell to my knees and started to cry.

Jim put his hand on my shoulder, choking back his own tears and unable to speak. Ann's eyes were closed, but we could see her chest rise and fall with her shallow breathing.

Jim said, "I'll give you some time alone with her."

Her hands were cold. She still had dried blood on her wrist. Only having the use of my right hand, I stroked her hair.

"Is that you, Matt?" Ann slowly opened her eyes.

"Yes, Ann, it's me." She was going to be all right. She had to live!

"Oh, I'm so glad." Tears welled up in her eyes. "I love you so much, Matt."

"And I love you, Ann." I bent over and kissed her.

"How's Stephanie?"

"She's going to be fine," I said, "and so are you." I was trying to convince both Ann and myself.

"Yes, I know I am. And I'm glad Stephanie is okay. . . . How long do you think they'll keep me here?" Her voice was labored and faint. I leaned closer to hear.

"Not long," I said choking back tears and trying to swallow the lump in my throat.

"Can you stay a while, Matt?" she whispered.

"I'll stay all night, Ann."

"Good. You can sleep right here beside me."

I laid my head on the pillow next to hers and clasped her hand.

"I've been thinking about our wedding," she said, her eyes closing. "It's going to be so beautiful."

Her voice trailed off as she stopped speaking. I stared at the sheet covering her chest. She was still breathing. Thank God! She had just fallen asleep. Our breath blended as if into a oneness, as together we struggled for life.

I saw Ann take a deep breath and slowly exhale and the room became silent. The sheet was not moving.

"Ann! Ann!" I cried out, but she didn't reply.

The monitor alarm screamed and the green neon line went flat. I ran to the door for help as the doctor and several nurses brushed by me.

A lifetime passed as the medical team employed every possible means to revive her. I held my breath and uttered a prayer.

The room became hauntingly still. Slowly the doctor turned to me and said, "I'm sorry. We did everything we could."

"No! No! She can't be gone! She was just talking to me," I cried.

The doctor and nursing staff left. I leaned over Ann and hugged her, my tears wetting her cheeks. I still couldn't believe she was gone. I just couldn't believe it. I held her until Jim appeared and gave me a brotherly hug. After a while Jim finally said, "We have to let her go, Matt."

* * * * *

I arrived an hour early for the viewing the night before the funeral to spend some private last moments with my beloved Ann. As I looked down at her beautiful face, I relived the memory of when I first saw Ann approach the table in that Italian restaurant in Washington D.C. Unknowingly, she had captured my heart from that moment on.

What a willing partner she had been as we trekked through Russia and Turkey in our quest for Noah's Ark.

Just recently, she and I had recalled our terrifying experience at the lake in Thailand, and how I held her in my arms that night in the jungle. We talked about how lucky we were to have survived bailing out of the airplane with one parachute. Now I am alone with those memories.

I bent over and touched her hand and the ring I had given her only weeks before. On that magical night Ann had accepted my marriage proposal with a resounding yes. I can still hear her excited laughter as we hugged each other. It was meant to be! . . . Now it would never be!

As I kissed her one last time, all the pain and blame and anguish fell on me. The tears came again, and I couldn't hold them back.

Ann's funeral was attended by hundreds. Flowers and condolences poured in from all over the world. She had no living relatives either in the United States or Russia, where she was born, but hundreds felt they had a connection with her. The crowd was so large many could not be seated in the Washington National Cathedral.

Stephanie had been shot in the leg, but she was able to attend the funeral. Jim and I and Stephanie were seated in the section reserved for the family as were my father, Estelle, Professor Kempson, Ira and Paula Jensen, Ann's roommate, and many of her friends.

The casket was open for viewing before the service. Ann looked beautiful in the bronze casket, but much too young to be there. It was so hard to watch her casket being closed.

I had an ache in my heart that I knew would never go away.

CHAPTER THIRTY-NINE

The air was cool and clean after last night's shower. Birds were singing. The trees were turning green.

Reading the inscription cut in the granite tombstone still brought tears to my eyes. It had been nearly two years since Ann died.

I sensed someone behind me.

"I'm sorry, I didn't intend to disturb you, Matt," Stephanie said.

Surprised, I stood up, turned, and put my arms around her. I hugged her to my chest.

"Oh, it's so great to see you. I'm glad you're here. Let me look at you."

She moved a step away and smiled.

"You're even more beautiful," I said, and I didn't lie. Her full, long, reddish hair framed her flawless complexion. There was now a certain look of maturity about her which only added to her beauty.

"I've worried about you, Matt. How's your arm?"

"It's okay now. Your leg?" I asked.

"All healed up," she replied. "Jim told me you had lost weight, so I expected that, but he didn't describe the dark circles under your eyes. He thinks you spend too much time here. It was not your fault, you know. You could not have prevented Ann's death."

"I know, Stephanie, but I can't help feeling guilty. She once told me she would follow me anywhere. Well, she did, and she died."

"I feel guilty too. After all, my cousin is the one who killed her and shot all those innocent people and you, but we have to go on living, Matt. Nothing can ever bring her back."

We slowly walked over the hill toward our cars.

"By the way," I said, "congratulations on being a best-selling author, and not just one book, but two books . . . and both bestsellers!"

"Thank you, but I had an unfair advantage over other authors who have to rely totally on their imagination to write a story. All I had to do to write the first one, 'The Lost Photographs,' was record the amazing story of how you three discovered Noah's Ark. Ann helped me write that book. Of course, I lived most of the second book, 'Burned In Stone.' I also had some professional help from talented editors at my publishing house, and the fact that people already knew my name took me a long way."

"I've read both books, Stephanie. You did a wonderful job with them. You may have had an advantage but it's not that easy writing a bestseller, and you've written two. I'm very proud of you."

"Thank you. I'm proud of both books. I'm glad I wrote them, and I'm especially glad that you like them.

"It's been almost eight seasons, Matt. Are you going? I mean, I'm sure you will be there. . . . May I go with you? Please. I won't be in the way. I promise."

"Yes, I'm going, Stephanie. Jim and I are going together. In fact, I have to speak again. We would love to have you with us."

* * * * *

The massive stone disk was a sight beyond imagination. The shape was similar to a flying saucer. Jim and I had not been far off in our initial estimate of its size. It was actually 2020 feet in diameter. That is wider than the length of almost seven football fields placed end to end, and it was 130 feet thick.

The ghostly phenomenon was suspended with no visible means of support. It stood perfectly still. It emitted no sound and had no vibration.

The flat bottom was twenty to twenty five feet above the uneven desert floor depending on where you were standing. There was a half-mile space between the outer perimeter of the disk and the tall granite walls of Mount Sinai. The color was a shade darker than the mountain itself. Scientists explained the extreme heat from the electric arc that cut it like a laser out of the top of the mountain, and then shaped and inscribed it, had darkened the color of the granite.

Hovering high above it in a helicopter, it was apparent that the top had not been shaped at all. It had been quarried from a rare area of the mountain that was relatively flat. It was solid granite. The rocks and boulders lying on the top were small, not at all like most of the top of Mount Sinai.

One remarkable characteristic that had been created by the presence of the massive stone was the lack of natural light under the center. Standing in the darkened space under the center of the stone and turning 360 degrees revealed a ribbon of daylight 1,000 feet from where you were. It was a strange sensation.

Attractive landscaping had been added to the grounds on the outside perimeter, but since very little vegetation would grow where the sun didn't shine, a much different landscape was designed for that area.

Eight elegant sidewalks made of exposed aggregate concrete with a slight "S" shape design, radiated out from a large center hub. Like slightly curved spokes in a wheel, they extended out to join the walkway around the perimeter. A multitude of comfortable benches were placed along these sidewalks and around the perimeter of the center hub. The sections between the walkways were covered in plants that didn't need much sunlight. Colored rocks and boulders with lighting that enhanced their natural beauty were in the spaces between. This lighting and the lighting spaced along the sidewalks were always lit. It was all very well designed and pleasing to the eye.

The "Sign" was open to the public every day, twenty-four hours a day, and the entire area seemed to always be full of polite, friendly people. There were a few who were afraid to venture very far beneath the stone. The fear of something that massive and heavy, suspended above them with no visible support, was a difficult sensation to overcome.

There was some talk of building a full-size replica of the sign. It would be constructed not far from the now-sacred place. It would be made of a light-weight carbon material, hollow inside. But with the number of columns needed to support its massive size, it would not have the same effect. I doubt that it will ever be built, but who knows.

The past two years have been magical for everyone. And it would never happen again, at least not in our life time, maybe not for 2,000 years. It was a life-changing experience for the millions of people who were lucky enough to come and see and feel the sensation of actually being there.

Jim and Stephanie and I spent a couple of hours at the site before the talks began. I had a lump in my throat just knowing how much Ann would have loved to be with us. Now she would never see it.

The political leaders and the religious leaders of the world had all spoken. Their words were both exciting and encouraging. I was the last speaker.

* * * * *

"Well, it has been eight seasons since we received the sign. I was told it would only remain for eight seasons. If God's seasons are the same as the four seasons we live by, soon the sign will be taken up. That is what the voice said to me.

"All the people of this planet have witnessed a miracle. Some refused to believe it at first. They thought it was a magic trick . . . that it was man-made. But I think everyone now realizes that it is real. Millions have come to see it for themselves. They have stood under it, trusting it would not fall and crush them."

The audience chuckled.

"Some have tried to deface it by throwing rocks at it. Some have tried to shoot bullets at it. The bullets and rocks were deflected before they even touched the stone. One man died trying to fly a jet fighter into it. That also was deflected away from it, and the plane crashed in the desert. Then there was the worker with a hydraulic crane installing light poles in the parking lot. He left his crew and drove the crane with the boom up straight toward the massive granite sign. The big machine would have easily struck the piece of granite suspended in the air. But what happened? The engine died and the brakes were mysteriously applied before it came within twenty feet of the sign. The engine would not restart, and the rig had to be towed away. I understand it is now running fine."

The audience applauded.

"But the most significant thing that has happened is evident to us all. There are no wars being fought, no wars being fought anywhere. That is amazing."

The audience cheered.

"It is astonishing what can happen when hate, dishonesty, corruption, and greed are no longer a part of our lives, and no longer part of any government.

"People of every religion are attending their churches and trying to keep the simple commandments we were given. The sign we have been privileged to witness is a simple sign. It is just the original Ten Commandments, the commandments that were etched in stone by God and given to the Israelites several thousand years ago. That was their sign!

"But this is our sign. This time the earth is much more populated, and the people of the world are much more educated.

"This time the sign has been given to us in every written language that is currently used on the earth today. And it was presented to us in a manner that we will not easily forget."

Everyone applauded.

When everyone quieted down, I continued. "The sign has been photographed and recorded on video and film probably millions of times. Soon it will be removed from our sight and somehow taken up, whatever that means. People, business leaders and political leaders of all the countries in the world have pledged to be more honest, more truthful. Those who have been prone to kill innocent people, like Al-Qaida and Isis and many more, have laid down their arms, swearing to keep the commandments, especially the commandment, "Thou Shalt Not Kill."

Again everyone stood and applauded.

"The Arab nations and Israel are embracing each other. They have adjusted their borders and settled their disputes. The Ayatollah and the people of Iran have stopped saying they will destroy Israel and death to America. Those who have put down their weapons have gone home to their families, are enjoying simple things like a good job with fair pay, picnics and camping and ball games with their children and their friends. Cities that were destroyed in the wars are starting to be rebuilt. Everyone is working who is physically and mentally able to work. Even the poorest countries are showing signs of an improved economy. Donations are pouring in from all over the world to help the poor in every country. The money donated all goes to the cause and not in some dictator's pocket.

"In my country, the United States of America, everything is much better. Our health-care system is starting to work because everyone involved is being honest. We now have a balanced budget, and we are paying off our debts. People are back to work. Our infrastructure in every state is being repaired, and more and more jobs are opening up. People aren't shooting each other like before. We still have people trying to wean themselves from drug addiction, but even that is getting much better. Since the sign appeared, the whole world is much safer and is a more enjoyable place to live. Most are kind and helpful to whomever they meet.

"I wonder, how long it will last? The memory of the sign we have been privileged to witness for two years will be passed down to a hundred generations of mankind. It is my sincere hope that all the people on earth now and in the future will remember and keep God's ten simple rules.

"Thank you all for coming. Bring your cameras tomorrow. It should be an interesting and exciting day."

* * * * *

Most of the thousands of people camped all over the hills and valleys in sight of "The Sign" didn't sleep at all from 12:01 a.m. on. No one wanted to miss it if the sign just suddenly vanished into thin air.

At dawn, thousands prayed, bands played, people sang songs, and everyone enjoyed great food from many different countries. No offensive music or speech was heard.

Just after lunch, a man and his wife tried to land a small helicopter on top of the sign. They were going to let the sign take them directly to

God in heaven. But an electric arc struck the craft and the man was forced to land nearby. Fortunately, the couple inside were not hurt.

At about four p.m., dark clouds began to form, and the wind came up. Canvas tents began to whip in the wind. Hundreds of news cameras were instantly trained on the sign. The sound of people talking began to quiet down.

The three of us stood on a boulder just a few yards away and watched. Stephanie took my hand.

The weather was strange and made rapid changes for a while. The sun was not visible. There were clouds all around us. The sweet smell of rain was in the air. We could see lightning and hear thunder in the distance, but it was not loud or intense. Just a cool slight breeze . . . now no dust . . . no rain . . . very quiet . . . thousands of people all with eyes and cameras glued to the massive granite monolith.

The Egyptian government had wisely ordered a no-fly zone within a twenty-mile radius of the sign except for those authorized to film the event. The dark clouds began to clear and soon a bright ray of sunshine illuminated the entire stone. Without a whisper of sound, at exactly five p.m., the massive sign from God began to rise slowly. It rose straight up. Soon it was several feet in the air . . . then a hundred . . . then two hundred. It had never made a sound. The clouds were gone. The sky was blue. Everyone for miles around could see it. The TV cameras continued to record, and the radio and TV stations announced every move it made. People all over the world were witnessing the miraculous event.

The sign continued straight up, slowly increasing in speed until it reached about twenty miles an hour. Before long, it was higher than normal aircraft could fly. We watched until we couldn't see it any longer.

When the crew on the international space station spotted it, they filmed its movements as it began to fly sideways in a flat horizontal plane. Leaving the drag of the earth's atmosphere, it could now move without breaking apart. Then, gaining speed rapidly, it headed into deep space. It was never picked up by the space telescopes. It was just never seen again.

* * * * *

The large round crater that remained where the sign was removed from the solid granite has now been fenced off and is being studied by scientists. Free tours are available for anyone who can climb up to the top of the mountain. The original stone tablets that God gave to Moses and the Ark of the Covenant that contained the stone tablets will soon be displayed for all to see in a special museum in the Old City of Jerusalem.

Noah's Ark is now on display in a massive facility at the base of Mount Ararat.

Both ancient biblical artifacts are expected to have record numbers of visitors this year. The admission is very minimal.

* * * * *

I had taken Stephanie to the airport in Tel Aviv, Israel. It was raining outside. Stephanie's flight to New York was leaving soon. Jim and I wouldn't fly out to Washington D.C. until tomorrow. We said goodbye in a quiet area.

"I love you, Matt. I always will. When the time is right for you, just let me know. I will go anywhere just to be by your side, and I'll stay with you as long as you want me."

Before I could reply, she kissed me and ran to catch her plane.

CHAPTER FORTY

Ann was still in my thoughts and in my dreams. It was hard to believe she had been gone two and a half years. I still had a difficult time accepting her death. I would never forget her and all we had been through together. I miss her so much.

Jack is still in an Israeli prison. He was convicted of murder in the death of the Israeli Coast Guard sailor and was sentenced to life. I wish he had been sent to Thailand where the prisons are not as comfortable. I know Jack all too well. Unless he is dead, Jack could still somehow become free again.

My good friend and boss, Ira Jensen, thought searching for the exact place where Moses led the Israelites across the Red Sea would be a good project for me. He was right. After weeks of diligent research and looking in all the wrong places, we found exactly where the Israelites crossed the Red Sea to escape the Egyptian army.

Some believe this story from the Bible is more fairytale than truth, just as they regarded Noah's Ark and The Ark of the Covenant. With the hundreds of chariot parts, bronze armor, bones of horses and men we have found in this one area by vacuuming the deep silt from the seabed, there is no doubt in my mind that the story is true. We found the exact place where it happened. Many of the chariot parts that were buried in the deepest mud are in very good shape. I can't wait to see them cleaned and on display.

Jim and I have been working together, and I am beginning to feel like myself again. Reporters fly out every week to see what artifacts we have brought up from the ancient seabed. Everything is filmed, sorted, and cataloged here on the salvage ship. We then put the items in crates and ship them to the museum in Cairo.

Because of this discovery, Jim and I and the great team on this vessel are all over the news. Headlines read,

Richard Ira Carroll

"Another unbelievable archaeological treasure has been found by Dr. Matthew Lane and his team of archaeologists."

* * * * *

Jim is still dating Joanne, flying off to meet her every time we leave the ship for a break. Many times he has coaxed me to come along on a double date with a girl I've never met, but I still have someone else on my mind.

We returned to the salvage vessel a couple of days ago.

I was in the galley having lunch when I heard a helicopter approaching.

"Jim, are we expecting anyone?"

"I'm not sure," Jim replied.

"Jack couldn't possibly have escaped from prison again, could he? . . . I'm going up to check," I said as I reached for my pistol.

Quickly making my way up a series of ship's ladders, I stepped out on the main deck. The day was cool but pleasant, with a slight breeze.

A helicopter was preparing to land on the bow. I squinted as I stared into the sun at the chopper setting down. The door opened.

Out stepped someone dressed in a khaki jumpsuit, Marine ball cap and wearing aviator sunglasses. Reaching behind the cockpit, he pulled out a duffle bag. My hand tightened on the pistol grip.

Jim came out of the hatch and stood next to me.

Turning, I shouted over the noise of the chopper, "It looks like he's planning to stay a while."

Looking back, I saw the individual advancing in our direction. Then the downwash wind from the rotors caught the brim of his cap and blew it into the sea. Long reddish-auburn tresses fell down around her shoulders. I was stunned as she removed the sun glasses from those beautiful green eyes. She stopped ten feet in front of me.

"Hello, Matt. . . . Jim thought it was time we got reacquainted."

A big smile lit up her face as Stephanie ran into my open arms. I held her close to me, knowing I could never let her go.

ABOUT THE AUTHOR

Richard Ira Carroll

Born: Pierce, Colorado
Richard Carroll, a retired air conditioning contractor, has always had an active imagination and a thirst for understanding the how and why. His creativity is unending, having invented and patented the first trailer to be pulled behind a motorcycle. The second patent he received was for a double load truck bed. In his work, he was always implementing new methods to facilitate and improve the end product.

As a teenager, Richard enlisted in the US Navy and had sailed on an aircraft carrier on the seas of the Far East and back to San Diego before he turned eighteen. In 1977- 1980, Richard worked in Saudi Arabia, traveling through many countries on his trips back and forth to Arizona.

Richard has three children, and the family has since grown to include sixteen grandchildren, and fourteen great-grandchildren. Richard's first novel, "The Lost Photographs", was written with the thought that it would be appropriate reading and exciting for all ages, including his grandchildren.

Mr. Carroll and his wife, Yvonne, divide their time between the desert of Mesa, Arizona, and the cool pines of Show Low, Arizona.

Since they retired, they have traveled extensively visiting many countries of the world and every wonderful state in the USA. They once spent six weeks on a successful dig for gem stones in the Outback of Australia. All these travels provided inspiration for his first novel, "The Lost Photographs", and this sequel, "Burned in Stone".

Like Richard's characters in his novels, he finds life an adventure to be experienced and lived to the fullest.

Visit Mr. Carroll's website at RichardIraCarroll.com to learn more. Both novels are now available through Amazon and ebook Kindle Direct Publishing.

www.ingramcontent.com/pod-product-compliance
Lightning Source LLC
Chambersburg PA
CBHW070047080526
44586CB00013B/946